King Arthur's Country

King Arthur's Country

One Land, Two Kings and Two Centuries that Changed Britain Forever

Stuart Laycock and Christopher Gidlow

Pen & Sword
MILITARY
AN IMPRINT OF PEN & SWORD BOOKS LTD.
YORKSHIRE – PHILADELPHIA

First published in Great Britain in 2024 by
Pen & Sword Military
An imprint of
Pen & Sword Books Ltd
Yorkshire – Philadelphia

ISBN 978-1-39905-359-4

A CIP catalogue record for this book is available from the British Library.

Printed and bound in the UK by CPI Group (UK) Ltd,
Croydon, CR0 4YY.

Pen & Sword Books Limited incorporates the imprints of After the Battle, Atlas, Archaeology, Aviation, Discovery, Family History, Fiction, History, Maritime, Military, Military Classics, Politics, Select, Transport, True Crime, Air World, Frontline Publishing, Leo Cooper, Remember When, Seaforth Publishing, The Praetorian Press, Wharncliffe Local History, Wharncliffe Transport, Wharncliffe True Crime and White Owl.

For a complete list of Pen & Sword titles please contact

PEN & SWORD BOOKS LIMITED
George House, Units 12 & 13, Beevor Street, Off Pontefract Road,
Barnsley, South Yorkshire, S71 1HN, England
E-mail: enquiries@pen-and-sword.co.uk
Website: www.pen-and-sword.co.uk
or
PEN AND SWORD BOOKS
1950 Lawrence Road, Havertown, PA 19083, USA
E-mail: uspen-and-sword@casematepublishers.com
Website: www.penandswordbooks.com

Contents

Introduction

England today is a rich, complex mix of identities, cultures and heritages. However, in the fifth century that could have changed. In the decades after Roman Britain collapsed, the cultures of the Angles and the Saxons, with significant degrees of homogeneity, spread rapidly westwards across much of eastern, southern and central England.

Then it stopped. Or was stopped. For the area where the Anglo-Saxon expansion stopped is characterized by a network of military and economic links across the island, originally formed during the Roman period. Perhaps significantly, this includes parts of Britain traditionally associated with King Arthur, said to have lived and fought in the late fifth or early sixth centuries.

In the seventh century, the multi-ethnic and multicultural kingdom of Mercia, in alliance with British kingdoms in Wales, became the first imperial kingdom in England, spreading across England under the mysterious King Penda, and dominating the earlier Anglo-Saxon kingdoms with its wealth and military power. The region that gave birth to Mercia is also a region that was the most likely base for the elusive figure of King Arthur.

The true story of what happened in those key years in this island's history has become largely lost. Much of what we know is only in historical fragments, or faintly discernible through Arthurian myth and legend.

In this book, we will use historical and archaeological evidence, including new research, to explore those historical fragments, myths and legends, and investigate how Dark Age power was projected right across the island

Figure 1. Some of the places mentioned in this book.

and altered the course of history. We will attempt to locate lost Arthurian battlefields and understand what may have happened there.

This is the story of one region, two kings and 200 years that helped make England and Britain, and English and British identity what they are today.

'Whoso pulleth out this sword of this stone and anvil, is rightwise king born of all England.'

King Arthur is one of the most famous of all the medieval kings of England. However, you will not find his name in any list of medieval English kings. Or in the lists of kings of any of the other British kingdoms, before or after the Norman Conquest. How could such a significant figure simply disappear?

The thirteenth-century writer Jacques de Longuyon came up with the idea of 'The Worthies of the World' – the top nine knights, selected from across time and cultures. Arthur was the first of the Christian worthies, along with Charlemagne, the first Holy Roman Emperor, and Godefroy of Bouillon, one of the heroic leaders of the First Crusade. There were also three Jewish worthies: Joshua, who led the Israelites in the conquest of the Holy Land; King David, the multi-talented psalm writer and giant killer; and Judas Maccabeus, leader of the Jewish resistance to the Greeks. The three pagan worthies were Hector, from the Trojan War, Alexander the Great and Julius Caesar. This idea proved incredibly inspirational in art and literature. The Worthies were all shown as medieval knights, dressed in medieval armour, jousting, living in castles and motivated by the same code of chivalry. Romances about them had the same mixture of high fashion, courtly love, and magical phenomena. What happened to alter this was the Renaissance and the growing understanding of the ancient world. We now no longer imagine the heroes and rulers of the Bronze and Iron Ages as knights in armour. But we still group Arthur alongside the other medieval Christian knights, despite his time being nearer to that of Julius Caesar than to Godefroy of Bouillon. Indeed, Arthur was as far distant in time from Jacques de Longuyon and the medieval romance writers as they are from us.

Any search for the historical King Arthur raises a set of expectations of the characters, names and episodes involved. He is inexorably linked to the Round Table, Camelot, the Holy Grail and the Sword in the Stone. It is almost impossible to think of him without his supporting cast of Lancelot and Guinevere, Merlin, and the Knights of the Round Table. The question is inevitably raised: were they historical too?

The nearest thing we have to an authorized account of the legends is *Le*

Morte d'Arthur. This was published in the summer of 1485. William Caxton, the first printer in England and a shrewd businessman, presented his book as a response to public pressure. He specifically references the Nine Worthies of the World, having previously published books based on classical works and on Charlemagne and Godefroy de Bouillon. His readers, he says, are keen that he should now turn his attention to Arthur, who 'ought most to be remembered among us Englishmen before all other Christian kings'.

Although Caxton was an accomplished translator, he chose to edit an English work written by Sir Thomas Malory in 1469–70. Malory was a prisoner in the lawless times of the Wars of the Roses. He describes his source as 'the French book' but draws his comprehensive story from a variety of sources. One is an English poem called *Le Morte d'Arthur*. Written at the height of the Hundred Years' War with France, it tells of the heroic exploits of Arthur and his knights fighting in France and even taking on the Roman Emperor. It is written in the English patriotic alliterative style, making a clean break with previous French versions and, incidentally, accounting for adversaries such as the Lord of Libya, Sultan of Syria and the Giants of Genoa. Another Arthurian poem of the same period, *Sir Gawain and the Green Knight*, also uses the alliterative style, for the same reason.

Most of Malory's sources, however, are indeed French. A large chunk is drawn from the mid-thirteenth-century *Prose Tristan* (Tristram, as Malory calls its hero). The characters may have been real figures from sixth-century Cornwall and Brittany, and the French prose romance is effectively a crossover, bringing them fully into the continuity of the Arthurian legends. As is usual with such crossovers, various encounters allow the characters of the Tristan tale to measure up against the established Arthurians to allow readers to judge who is the greatest, most chivalrous, and most romantic.

The biggest source of the *Le Morte d'Arthur*, though, is what we now call the Lancelot-Grail Cycle. Starting with material about Merlin the Magician, then proceeding to the introduction of Sir Lancelot of the Lake and his son Sir Galahad, the cycle of French prose romances includes prequels, sequels and spinoffs in its extended Arthurian universe. These prose romances were written at various times in the early thirteenth century. It is to them that we owe the abiding image of a King Arthur ruling from Camelot, surrounded by the Knights of the Round Table. Sir Lancelot, the adulterous lover of Arthur's wife, Queen Guinevere, is the first among them, but his sins prevent him from completing the ultimate quest for the Holy Grail, leading to the fall of Arthur.

These prose romances were an innovation of the thirteenth century. Previously, fictional material, romances, had been presented as long poems, some originally composed for oral recitation. Prose had been the medium for history. But let us be clear, despite their frequent protestations of following ancient texts faithfully, the authors were writing fiction. They had no compunction at all about changing or adding details, no matter how crucial to the plot. Thus, an original serving plate for fish, a grail, carrying something to a mysterious personage off scene, could become a magic stone or a holy cup used by Jesus. The knight questing to discover the answer to the grail mystery, Sir Perceval, could be swapped for a more famous character, Sir Gawain, or replaced by a completely fabricated character, Sir Galahad, complete with retrospectively revised backstory. Arthur's famous sword might be pulled from an anvil in one version and then presented to him by a water fairy in another. Trying to find the Arthurian 'truth' amongst such untrammelled whimsey and invention is a doomed exercise.

Prose romances did build on earlier verse romances, principally those by Robert de Boron and the late twelfth-century genius, Chretien de Troyes. It is Chretien who popularized the genre of tales linked to individual knights, Sir Perceval, Sir Yvain and most influentially Sir Lancelot, loosely connected by their being members of the court of the famous King Arthur. Arthur had become so famous that even Chretien's audience in Champagne and Flanders were expected to have heard of him. This international fame was largely due to a blockbusting 'history' book written in the 1130s.

Geoffrey of Monmouth's *History of the Kings of Britain* exists in a huge number of manuscripts, fifty from the twelfth century alone, testifying to its popularity and influence. Geoffrey tells the story of Britain from about 1000 BC to the seventh century AD, but his centrepiece, over 20 per cent of the book, is focused on King Arthur. Geoffrey anchors Arthur in time, an early sixth-century figure who fights his last battle in 542 AD. He presents him as the leader of the Britons fighting and defeating the invading Saxons before leading his men to overseas conquests. Geoffrey's source for the battles on the continent is not known. The suspicion is that these are aimed at the interests of his intended royal and noble audiences, who hailed from Normandy, Anjou and Brittany as well as holding lands in England. Geoffrey very occasionally claims his source is an ancient book in the British (that is the Welsh) language, but for various reasons, not least Geoffrey's verbatim quotes from known Latin works, this is unlikely to be the case. Suffice it to say that no such work earlier than Geoffrey's exists. However, we do know the source of Geoffrey's account of Arthur the war leader against the Saxons. It is a work, written in the ninth century, called the *Historia Brittonum*, the History of the Britons. As this work is the earliest known source presenting Arthur as a historical figure, we will be devoting a lot more attention to it in this book.

Before we look at the earliest sources, it's worth pausing to consider what exactly is meant by 'King Arthur's Country' in its broader context.

Yes, there are particular parts of Britain with which Arthur and, later, Penda can be connected, however, Caxton and Malory had no doubt, as the opening quotation shows, that Arthur was English and his country England. Malory takes great pains to anchor the legends in his contemporary England. Arthur's capital, Camelot, was Winchester, the sword in the stone outside a great church in London, possibly St. Paul's, Arthur's last battle was fought on Salisbury Plain, and Lancelot's castle was at either Alnwick or Bamburgh. The earlier romances, however, were aware that this was an anachronism. They called Arthur's kingdom Logres, the Welsh name for England (Lloegr), one of several kingdoms which made up Britain.

Exactly how a large part of Britain, the eastern lowlands, came to be an 'England' distinct from Britain as a whole is something we shall be covering at length. It was a source of linguistic confusion in the past as it can often be now. The end of the Roman period left the whole island called 'Britain' and all its inhabitants south of the Roman frontier 'Britons'. For official purposes, the Britons spoke and wrote in Latin, the language of the Western Roman Empire and its Christian Church, but privately, especially in the West, their language was British, what we would now call a Celtic language. No one at the time recognized its affinity with the other Celtic languages spoken in the British Isles, Irish and Pictish, nor used the word 'Celts' for those different peoples.

The conventional history of the transition comes from a book called *The*

Ecclesiastical History of the English People, written by a monk called Bede in the eighth century. As the title indicates, this tells the story of how Bede's people, the Angles, or the English, became part of the Christian Church. The Angles, according to Bede, were one of a group of fierce Germanic peoples, along with the Saxons and the Jutes, who took over lowland Britain from the mid-fifth century onwards. Jutes and Saxons settled in the South, Angles to the North. Bede gives the Angles primacy in what he views as God's plan to bring Christianity once more to the island, even though they are not the first to be converted. The missionary expedition had been inspired, according to a tradition Bede passed on, when the pope had seen some very beautiful young slaves for sale in Rome. He asked where they had come from and was told they were from Britain, and that their people were called the Angles. 'They have the faces of Angels!' the Pope exclaimed, and so began his mission to bring these angelic-looking people to God.

The power of Bede's narrative, giving a special place in God's plan for the island to the Angles, meant that when the lands of the Angles later came under the rule of the West Saxons, those kings called their united subjects the Anglo-Saxons and later just the Angles or English and the whole of their country England. That route was not however followed by the Britons nor by the Irish or the Picts. From the sixth century, the natives of the British Isles had not made any distinction between the Germanic invaders and called all of them Saxons, as they still do today.

The name of Britain and the description British for its language and people fell out of use at around that time. The Britons, especially those in the largest western peninsula, called themselves the Cymry or Fellow Citizens. The English, however, called them Welsh or foreigners, and their country Wales.

If we are to understand how Arthur fits into the chaos of Britain in the years following the end of Roman control, and what this figure meant for the centuries after that, we are going to have to start by taking a detailed look at the history and archaeology of the period.

In researching this book, we have consulted numerous ancient and modern sources. Of the modern sources, we would particularly like to acknowledge and thank, in no particular order: John Conyard, Elizabeth Usher and Comitatus, The English Place Name Society, Rivet & Smith's *The Place Names of Roman*

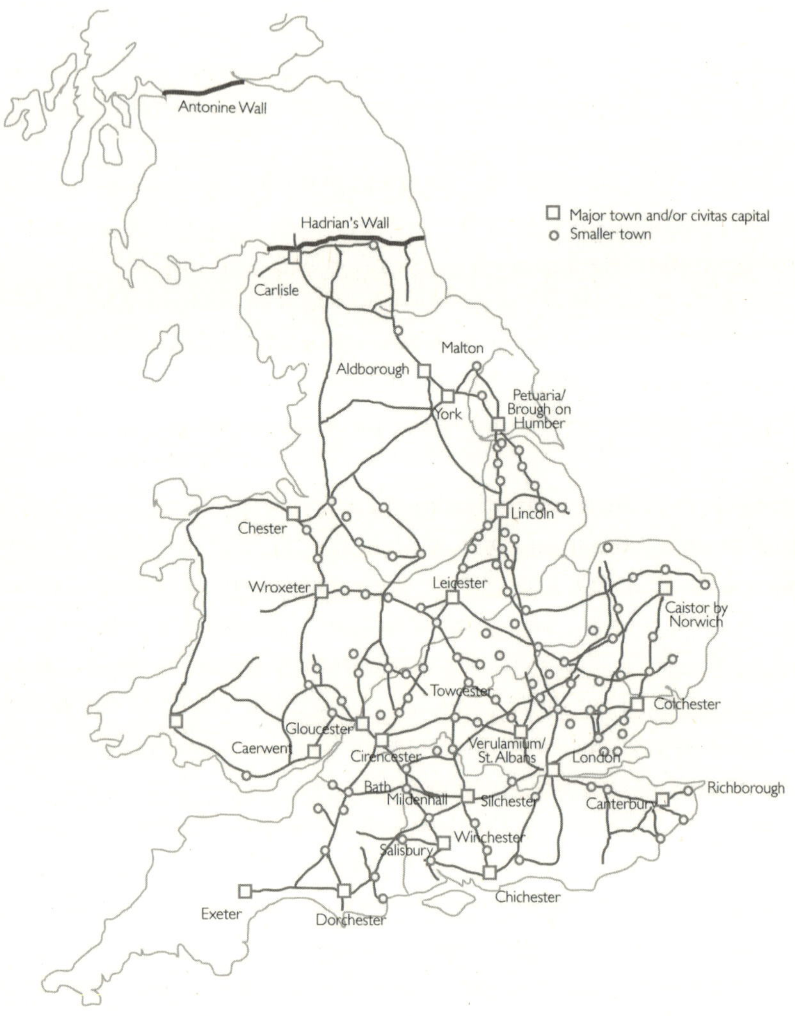

Figure 2. Roman Britain, key settlements, and roads.

Britain, The Historic Place Names of Wales project, The Prosopography of Anglo-Saxon England, Phillimore (Arthurian Period Sources), Oxford University Press (Malory, Works).

Chapter 1

Tribes, Rebels, Buckles, Militias and an Alliance

For a long time, the phrase 'the Arthurian Period' was used to describe the period following the end of Roman control in Britain. Some people still use it in that sense, and it is impossible to go in search of the truth behind Arthur without also going in search of the truth about the end of Roman Britain, a place that sounds like a united nation, but never really was.

Understanding what happened here in the first years of the fifth century has, as it turns out, proved almost as difficult and controversial as the search for Arthur. However, new work on the period may be leading us to a clearer understanding of one of the most important periods of British history.

The traditional narrative of the end of Roman Britain is built on the work of a key figure in this book, Gildas. We will return to him time and again because so much of what we think we know about the end of Roman Britain and the Arthurian period comes from him. Today, few Britons have heard of him, but he is the man who almost single-handedly wrote the story of the birth of England.

He was a British cleric writing sometime in the early sixth century. One of his main intentions was to castigate British rulers of the time for their sins and shortcomings. In the process of doing so, however, he also puts into writing his understanding of how Roman Britain ended. The key element to know about Gildas at this stage is that he thought the Romans left, and then rampaging, mainly Saxon, invaders violently destroyed the fabric of Roman Britain.

This was a narrative that was still largely accepted until comparatively recently. If you had been reading in the Victorian age something about the end of Roman Britain it might perhaps have been illustrated with pictures of a Roman legionary in 410 AD – dressed the same as the legionary in the illustrations of Romans invading Britain, since the Victorians were pretty uninterested in late-Roman military kit – kissing his British woman goodbye and departing across the Channel;[1] you could then think of Saxons – perhaps dressed in something furry as Saxons and Vikings were often depicted in the Victorian period – slaughtering some toga-clad Briton in a neat Roman villa.

There are a few elements of truth in all this, but we are quite sure now that the end of Roman Britain looked rather different.

For a start, while troops were leaving Britain, kissing their women goodbye, and heading across the Channel, many of them were Roman only in the broadest sense. They were dressed as the late Roman troops dressed, and not like extras in *Ben Hur*, *I Claudius* or *Gladiator*, and they started heading across the Channel long before 410 AD.

Many Victorians, perhaps because they were also keen on their empire-building, liked to see Roman Britain as a well-run province of Rome, full of Britons embracing the culture of the empire-builders and peacefully becoming contented, productive citizens of the empire.

In fact, a lot of Britons had a much less enthusiastic attitude towards Rome and Roman culture. Apart from Dacia, Britain was pretty much the last part of Europe added to the empire and the first to leave it. Despite making several attempts to do so, the Romans never managed to conquer Caledonia and did not even attempt to invade Ireland. Consequently, during the centuries of Roman occupation, Rome was forced to keep large numbers of troops garrisoned there. Even within the area of Roman control, for large numbers of Britons, particularly in the west and north, daily life was not that much changed from what it had been before the arrival of Rome.[2]

Britons did not give up their identities just because they paid taxes to Rome, and the emperor's head was on their coins. When the Romans arrived in Britain they found a sophisticated tribal system. There was some flexibility, but broadly speaking, Britain was divided up into the domains of various regional groups, with their own hierarchies and cultures. Rather than try to replace this, the Romans did what they had done elsewhere, as in Gaul, and adopted it as the basis of their civil administration. The tribes would become *civitates* while the tribal structure and many elements of the tribal leadership system probably remained in place.

Famously, Boudica rebelled against the new system. Gildas was still well

Figure 3. Some of the main tribes of Britain.

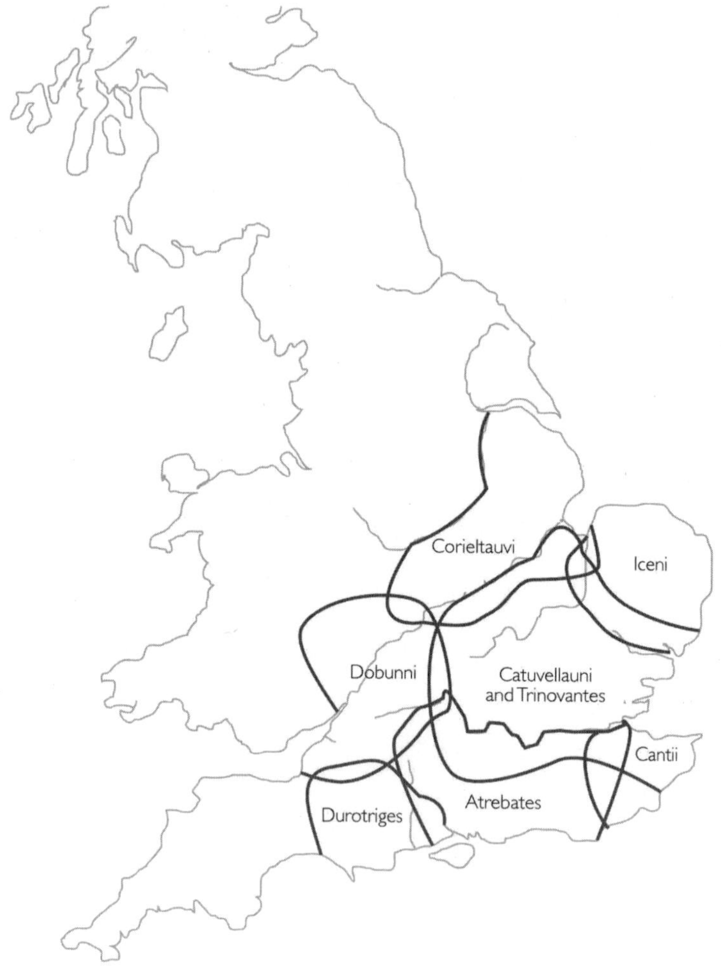

Figure 4. Distribution of pre-Roman tribal coinage, showing roughly where the tribal borders were. (From Cunliffe 2005 and Portable Antiquities Scheme)

aware of her in the sixth century and being a bit of a fan of the Roman Empire, refers to her as the 'deceitful lioness'.[3] It is even possible that her name lives on in some place names today. The Roman fort called the Lunt, built probably during the campaign against Boudica's rebellion is at Baginton, which means Badeca's farm. Bottisham which is pretty much where ridge routes crossed from Catuvellauni territory into that of Boudica's Iceni was originally Bodekesham,

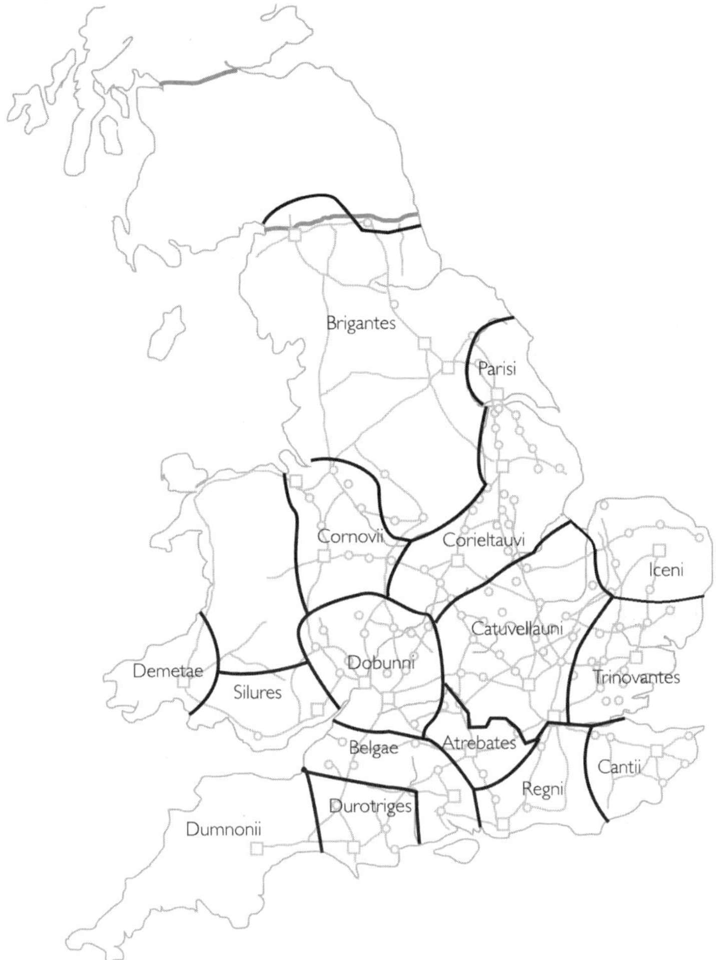

Figure 5. How the *civitates* of Roman Britain, administrative units mainly based on tribal territories, may have looked.

Bodec's settlement.[4] The similarity of names is not in itself enough to suggest a link to Boudica, but the combination of locations and rare names makes it at least worth considering whether this might be more than a coincidence.

Generally, existing tribal identities remained in place under Rome. As a result, under Rome, Britons' inscriptions still refer to themselves by their tribal identities, as members of Catuvellauni, or Belgae etc. Roman Britain, as a unified whole, never really existed. A lot of it was never very Roman, and rather than a united Britain, it was divided into tribal areas, and, by the end of the Roman period, was also divided into at least four different provinces. There even seems a possibility that in the last years of Rome, Britons were re-emphasizing their British identities. In the fourth century, temples were built within several of the old hillforts, such as Lydney, and Maiden Castle next to the capital of the Durotriges tribe, that must have been such a symbol of tribal heritage. A type of brooch, portraying a British Celtic warrior on a horse seems to have been sold at some late Roman shrines in Britain. Many these have been found a few miles from Mancetter (Roman name Manduessedum, derived from *mandu* meaning horse and *essedo* meaning war chariot) a possible location of Boudica's last battle.[5]

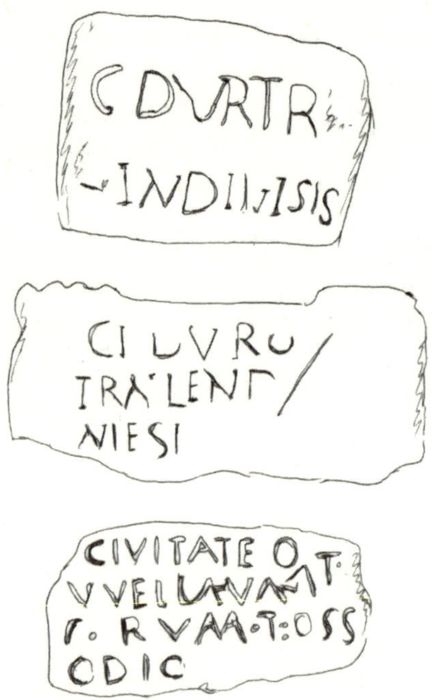

Figure 6. Building stones from Hadrian's Wall, showing building done by construction units from the *civitates* of the Durotriges and Catuvellauni.

It could be argued that invading Britain was a huge Roman strategic blunder, one that would ultimately destroy – or certainly play a large role in destroying – the Western Roman Empire.

If Rome had managed to conquer the whole of Britain and Ireland, and had managed to crush resistance, then it could have withdrawn its troops and sent them elsewhere. Instead, a large part of the Roman army remained for centuries. And as it happened, because of that, and because the Channel kept the island somewhat separate from the European mainland, Britain became an ideal area for Roman troops to organize rebellions against Roman authorities in Europe.

Already, in the late second century, military commander Clodius Albinus had declared himself emperor and led an army south across the Channel to establish himself on the imperial throne. He failed. His army was defeated in an extraordinarily large and bloody battle by the forces of rival emperor Septimius Severus at the Battle of Lugdunum in 197, and Clodius Albinus ended up dead.

In the third century, Britain joined the rebel Gallic Empire which had separated from the rest of the empire, and in the latter part of the century, after the end of the Gallic Empire, a military commander called Carausius established himself as a rebel emperor in Britain. He was then assassinated in 293 and was succeeded by another rebel emperor, Allectus. Allectus did not last long. In 296 a Roman army crossed the Channel and invaded Britain again and Allectus was killed in the fighting.

It would not, however, be long before another rebellion started in Britain. In 306, Constantine declared himself emperor in York and led his army south into Europe.[6] He, of course, was successful in seizing the imperial throne. In 312 he defeated his rival Maxentius at the Battle of the Milvian Bridge and marched into Rome. He would make the empire Christian and change the world forever.

In 383 Magnus Maximus – who appears in later Welsh medieval legend as Macsen Wledig and who would be claimed, on the ninth century Pillar of Eliseg, as an ancestor of the kings of Powys – declared himself emperor in Britain and took his army south across the Channel. The Roman army in Britain by now consisted of a mix of fighters from a wide variety of locations from across the empire and included quite a lot of troops born and brought up in Britain. Magnus Maximus had a lot of initial success. In the summer of 383 he defeated the army of emperor Gratian in fighting near Paris and established himself in Trier as emperor of the west. However, in 388 eastern emperor Theodosius, along with Valentinian II, rival to Maximus, invaded from the east and defeated the army of Britain's rebel emperor. Maximus was captured at Aquileia in northern Italy and executed.

Finally, in 405, discontented troops in Britain acclaimed a series of rebel emperors in quick succession, first Marcus, then Gratian, and then Constantine who is now known to history as Constantine III. Yet again, a Roman army headed south from Britain to fight other Roman armies in Europe.

Figure 7. Coin of Magnus Maximus.

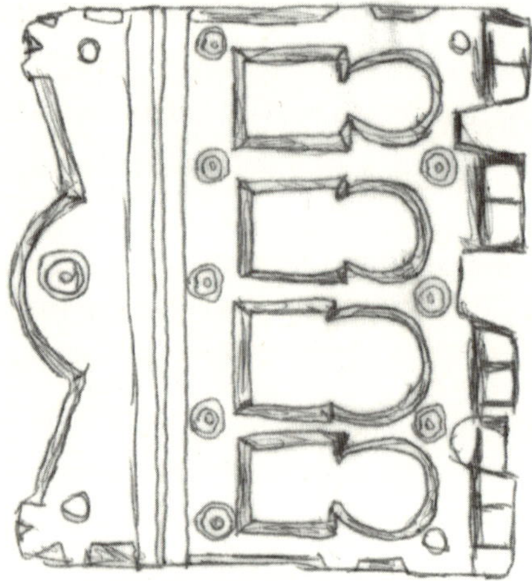

Figure 8. Buckle plate, possibly of British manufacture, found at Aquileia, Italy, where Magnus Maximus suffered his final defeat. (After Buora)

Constantine III had initial success and established himself at Arles, in southern France, as emperor of much of the west. He sent his British-born Gerontius into Spain to fight loyalists to the previous regime; Gerontius then rebelled against Constantine and set up his own emperor, another Maximus. Somehow amidst the chaos of Roman civil wars, a large band of Vandals, Alans and Suevi, who had managed to get into the Empire across the Rhine frontier, now travelled across Gaul into Spain. There they established their own kingdoms, largely free of Roman control. It was the start of the process that would see similar kingdoms established elsewhere in the western Roman Empire until the Empire itself ceased to exist. Constantine III himself, however, was not in any position to worry too much about all that. After losing his son Constans in fighting against Gerontius, the rebel emperor found himself besieged in Arles by his rebel general. At this stage, yet another Roman army, this one loyal to the emperor Honorius in Italy, turned up. Gerontius retreated, and Constantine was captured and executed.

The date often given for the end of the western Roman Empire is 476; however, Britain was long gone from the Empire by then. It is easy when, for instance, looking at reconstructions of life in a Roman villa in Britain to think of Britain

Figure 9. Coin of Constantine III.

as an integral part of the Empire. In reality, Britain was a vulnerable outpost on the Empire's northern border, threatened for much of the Roman period by raiders on three sides, from Ireland, from north of Hadrian's Wall, and from across the North Sea. If you look at the distribution of where Roman military buckles have been found in northern Europe in the third (see the so-called Viminacium buckle type) and fourth centuries, you can see a swathe of this material found along the Empire's borders in the Netherlands, Germany, Hungary, Austria, etc. When you look at Britain, the distribution patterns along the northern border, eastern and southern costs, and parts of the western coast are similar to those in the border zones of mainland Europe. In some sense, the whole of Roman Britain was by now a border zone.[7]

Already in the third century, the Romans were building coastal defences,

Figure 10. Buckle of British manufacture found in southern France, close to the location of Constantine III's campaigns. (After Aurrecoechea Fernandez 1999)

large fortresses spread along Britain's eastern and southern shore, and at London, a large defensive wall was built along the riverbank. The threat from raiders increased through the fourth century. In 367 something described by contemporary historian Ammianus Marcellinus as the Barbarian Conspiracy occurred in Britain.[8] It is not entirely clear what happened but it seems raiders from several directions attacked Roman Britain at about the same time, and, in the ensuing chaos, the Roman army in Britain seems to have ceased being a unified, effective military force. One senior Roman commander in the coastal area, Nectaridus, was killed. The Dux Britanniarum, Fullofaudes found himself surrounded. Many troops deserted; some may even have cooperated with the raiders. A type of weighted spear butt in use in Ireland and Scotland in the late Roman and early medieval period, and these days called door-knob spear butts due to their appearance, has been found fairly widely scattered across Britain; it is possible this could be linked to the events of 367.[9]

A Roman expeditionary force from mainland Europe had to be sent across the Channel to restore order. It did so, and the Roman army in Britain was formed once more, but whatever had happened seemed to have changed Roman Britain fundamentally.

Before 367, troops in the distant outpost of the Empire that was Roman Britain were still wearing kit that had gone out of use by Roman forces in mainland Europe decades previously. The expeditionary force of 367 brought with it new kit, of new design. On their knife belts, many of the troops that came across the Channel wore buckles decorated with animals, with dolphins, with lion heads and with dragon heads. The belt sets were bright and showy. In addition to the buckles, there were belt plates, belt stiffeners and strap ends that fitted on the end of the belt that went through the buckle loop.[10]

The troops stationed on Hadrian's Wall and in Wales were too remote to adopt these new designs, but elsewhere, in what is now southern and eastern England, the new kit spread among the military. What is even more significant is that it wasn't just the military now wearing knife belts, civilians were wearing them too. Ordinary Roman civilians did not wear belts and did not carry knives. Only government officials and soldiers did.

Yet in the period after 367, these buckles and other belt fittings, and local versions of them appear on civilian sites across the east and south of

Britain. Military-type knives are also sometimes found. The conclusion seems inescapable. In 367 the Roman army in Britain had shown itself incapable of defending civilians, and consequently, civilians were forming militias to defend themselves.[11]

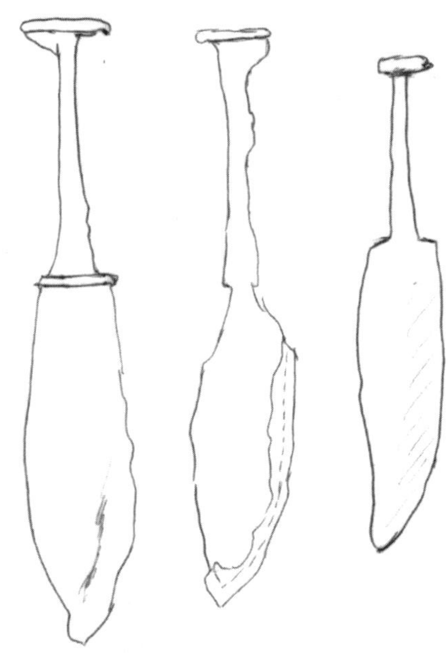

Figure 11. Late Roman military knives. (After Clarke 1979)

We can even perhaps see what one of the militia commanders looked like and guess at his identity. A unique buckle, found at Longbridge Deverill, shows a detailed portrait of a man, flanked by lions and wearing what looks like scale armour and a cloak.[12] Nothing quite like this has been found anywhere else in Britain or the Empire, and it seems likely the man was a militia commander, particularly since the buckle was found not far from an enormous Roman villa (mostly unexcavated) with mosaics that have been linked in terms of design and quality to the finest of the Dobunni Cirencester school of mosaics.[13]

Something like all this seems to have happened in north-western Spain, another remote part of the Empire where there was much violent chaos at about the same time; there civilian men were buried with similar new belt fittings and with knives and spears, so we know they were probably designed for combat. Interestingly, a few of these British belt fittings have been found on mainland Europe in locations associated with the wars of Magnus Maximus (a buckle plate from Aquileia[14]) and Constantine III (a buckle from Argeliers in southern France, and a buckle from Iruña/Veleia in Spain[15]); implying that some British militiamen joined the expeditions to Europe or troops had re-equipped themselves with British kit before setting off.

However, these British belt fittings can tell us even more about what was happening in Britain in the last decades of Roman rule. There are two aspects of them which seem particularly significant in trying to understand what was going on. Firstly, these buckles and belt fittings are not all the same across Britain. The early ones are similar, but soon regional design groups appear. In the third century, many troops on Hadrian's Wall were wearing the same kit as could be found on troops in Rome's distant eastern frontier in what is now Syria and Iraq.[16] By the end of the fourth century men in different parts of Britain were wearing different military kit. Some had birds on them, little eagles or hawks; some had Christian symbols, peacocks (symbolic of paradise and immortality) and gryphons, and some had intricate geometric designs linked to Celtic pre-Roman decoration. Some had human heads, perhaps severed heads, a pre-Roman Celtic symbol. When you look at the distribution of these different design groups they seem to link to different tribal, or *civitas*, areas and different provinces within Britain. It suggests that the new militias in Britain were regional militias supplied and probably organized and commanded by local regional authorities.[17]

What is equally significant is that while early British buckles and belt fittings manufactured in the period after 367 were like those worn by Roman soldiers, by 380 or 390, many of the British designs outside London and the south-east had diverged from the Roman designs. There were no birds, peacocks, gryphons, Celtic designs or human heads on the original Roman buckles.[18]

Some of the British buckle dolphins had started to look more like the carnyx, the traditional Celtic war trumpet.[19] In particular a new type of buckle had emerged in which the heads of horses (a traditional symbol of political and military power) appeared mounted above the dolphins that represented Roman design.[20] At first, both horse heads and dolphins were carefully modelled and clearly defined, but increasingly the horse heads took prominence over the dolphins until the dolphins disappeared from the buckle loops entirely.[21]

At the same time, something else was happening to another element of military kit in Britain. Along with the military belt, another key element of late Roman official and military dress was what we now call crossbow brooches. They are called this because they look a little like crossbows and they were worn on the shoulder as cloak brooches, but also as a symbol of military or official status, rank and power.

A different type of brooch, the penannular, had a long history in Britain and was sometimes worn by soldiers. Such brooches were mainly very plain, small types. However, sometime in the late fourth century, a new type of penannular brooch was used in Britain. This type, now known as the Type E penannular, featured elaborate, facetted, somewhat zoomorphic terminals, like the terminals on some military crossbow brooches. The distribution of this type, often in military areas, suggests these new British brooches were also now frequently being worn by soldiers and officials, probably in place of the Roman crossbow brooches. Then, in the early fifth century, these penannular brooches grew large (often about six centimetres across) and the zoomorphic terminals developed even further, to the stage where they often look like Celtic horse heads. These are known as Type F penannular brooches. In terms of sites where Type Fs are found, the biggest proportion comes from Roman military sites, and we know from early medieval Irish texts that large penannular brooches were often symbols of high status and authority.[22]

What we appear to be seeing here is, firstly, a process where central authority was disappearing in Britain and being replaced by regional and tribal powers reasserting themselves, and, secondly, a process where Britain outside the south-east was beginning to distance itself from Rome.

You may be asking yourself why, at a time when they were threatened by raiders from overseas, the Britons would be distancing themselves from the power that had traditionally protected them from such threats. The answer seems simply to be that the taxpayers of Britain decided that such defence as Rome still offered them was no longer worth what they were paying for it.

It is likely that by 410 few major Roman military units remained in Britain. Magnus Maximus and Constantine III had stripped out the best units and taken them to mainland Europe never to return. Gildas specifically laments that Maximus had taken from Britain all her soldiers and armed squads, all her commanders and the best of her young men, never to return.[23] That was before Constantine III assembled men for his (ultimately) failed expedition. A somewhat disputed passage in the historian Zosimus suggests that maybe the emperor Honorius told the cities of Britain to organize their own defence.[24] More clearly, Zosimus states that Rome did nothing to stop raids on Britain and that this prompted the Britons to arm themselves, throw off Roman rule, and fight the raiders themselves.[25]

Sometime around 409 or 410 Britain walked out of the Empire. Politically, Roman Britain had ended. Culturally, it had not. Roman money, Roman urban life, Roman villas, Roman industries and everything else that culturally made up what we call Roman Britain did not end in Britain overnight, but end it did, and not because of rampaging Saxons because by the time the Saxons turned up in large numbers most of the culture of Roman Britain was long gone. So what happened to cause one of the greatest cultural and economic dislocations in the history of these islands?

Over the past decades, people have suggested a wide variety of possible causes. A favourite with many has been the suggestion that the end of government taxation and spending in Britain caused a crisis that collapsed the economy. Another idea put forward by some is that a plague could have devastated Britain. Others have suggested that a cooling of the climate in the early fifth century could have caused an agricultural crisis.

All of these could have had a significant effect on Britain in the period after the end of Roman control and maybe they did. However, if we look at instances in history where we know such events happened and where we know more about the results, it's hard to find examples where such events had the kind of effect on a country that we see in the archaeological record of fifth-century Britain.

For instance, the Black Plague killed huge numbers in England in the fourteenth century and led to the total abandonment of some villages. However, the England of 1400 was still recognizably the same place with much the same culture that it had in 1300. The so-called Little Ice Age hit Britain in the Middle Ages and early modern period. The Thames froze over at times. However, the Little Ice Age did not destroy the economy and totally change the culture. There have been very many economic crises around the world over the centuries and there are still plenty today. However, humans are flexible and adaptable, and such crises rarely have a huge, long-term cultural effect.

Occupation on most Roman-period sites, often after a period in which the buildings become dilapidated, either ceases or becomes archaeologically totally or partially invisible. Advances in archaeology are allowing us to detect small signs of early post-Roman occupation on more sites than before, but still, the contrast between fourth- and fifth-century Britain is vast.

The reality is that, historically, the only set of events that has come close to causing the sort of cultural and economic dislocation seen in Britain in the period after the end of Roman control is persistent, widespread warfare. As already discussed, we know that during the fourth century raiders, particularly from Caledonia and from across the North Sea, but also from Ireland, had a significant effect on Britain. Some of the raiders may even, occasionally, have reached far inland.

There is an interesting debate over the question of where St. Patrick was living when he was abducted by Irish raiders. The Confession of St. Patrick says that his father, Calpurnius, was a decurio in a Roman town and that he was abducted from the family's villa at Bannavem Taburniae. No such place is known but the details suggest a town in the more culturally Roman parts of Britain and there was a town called Bannaventa on Watling Street, north of Milton Keynes and south of Rugby. If you take Bannaventa as the actual name, and assume Bannavem Taburniae is split in the wrong place, something that easily happened in early hand-written manuscripts, then you get Bannaventa Burniae. Burnia seems conceivably similar to the later north-eastern kingdom name Bryneich, Birneich, Bernicia, which appears to mean land of the mountain passes. As it happens Bannaventa is right in what we now call the Watford Gap, home to M1 services of the same name, and called Gap because it is a gap between two areas of high ground which was a communications route even before Watling Street arrived there.

However, apart from the events of 367, it seems likely that the effects of this raiding were mainly felt in the north and coastal areas, particularly along the North Sea coast and the Channel coast. There is some evidence, for instance in Sussex, that vulnerable coastal communities were in trouble in the late fourth century.[26] However, it seems hard to imagine that such, mainly coastal, raiding on its own could have destroyed the culture and economy of Roman Britain. If persistent warfare did cause the changes seen in Britain in the fifth century, it must have come from within.

A common scenario throughout history is the failed state scenario where the sudden removal of central power leads to a power vacuum in which a country fragments as regional leaders fight for power and to establish control over population centres and natural resources. In recent times we have seen this happen in, for example, Afghanistan in the period after the Soviet withdrawal;

in Yugoslavia after the death of Tito removed a key unifying factor; in Somalia after the collapse of the central government; and in Libya after the killing of Gaddafi. The war in former Yugoslavia was too short to create the kind of dislocation seen in fifth-century Britain, and in Libya, oil wealth keeps the economy going despite the country having been sliced up by militias. In the 1990s, Afghanistan and Somalia experienced a huge dislocation of the society and economy.

So, could something like this have happened in post-Roman Britain? It seems probable. The crisis may have been a complex one, as crises often are, with plague, climate change and economic difficulties playing a part, but violent political fragmentation was almost certainly a key element.

As discussed earlier, most Britons in the late fifth century probably did not see themselves as Britons, but instead as members of their *civitas* and tribe. Among others, they were Iceni, Brigantes, Catuvellauni, Atrebates, Durotriges, Dobunni, Dumnonii and Silures.

There was also separation on a provincial level. We are not exactly sure how the provinces were organized and where their boundaries were, but Lincoln, London, Cirencester (or Gloucester) and York seem to have been provincial capitals. This is based on an inscription from Cirencester and the fact that bishops from London, York and probably Lincoln were present at a synod of the Church in Arles in 314. We know the names of four provinces in late Roman Britain: Britannia Prima, Britannia Secunda, Flavia Caesariensis and Maxima Caesariensis, and there is a fifth province name mentioned, Valentia, the status of which is unclear. There is no general agreement on what the map of provinces in late Roman Britain looked like, but it is generally assumed that each province consisted of several *civitates* and that the provincial borders did not cut across their borders.[27] For simplicity's sake provinces will be referred to by their capital, thus London Province, or Lincoln Province.

There is evidence of extensive inter-tribal warfare in the pre-Roman period. Caesar for instance says that British leader Cassivellaunus had been involved in constant warfare with other tribes, and it's hard to think that the huge number of hillforts built in Britain before the arrival of Rome were there just for decorative purposes. The borders between tribes were probably never very fixed in the pre-Roman period and the years of Roman occupation, involving

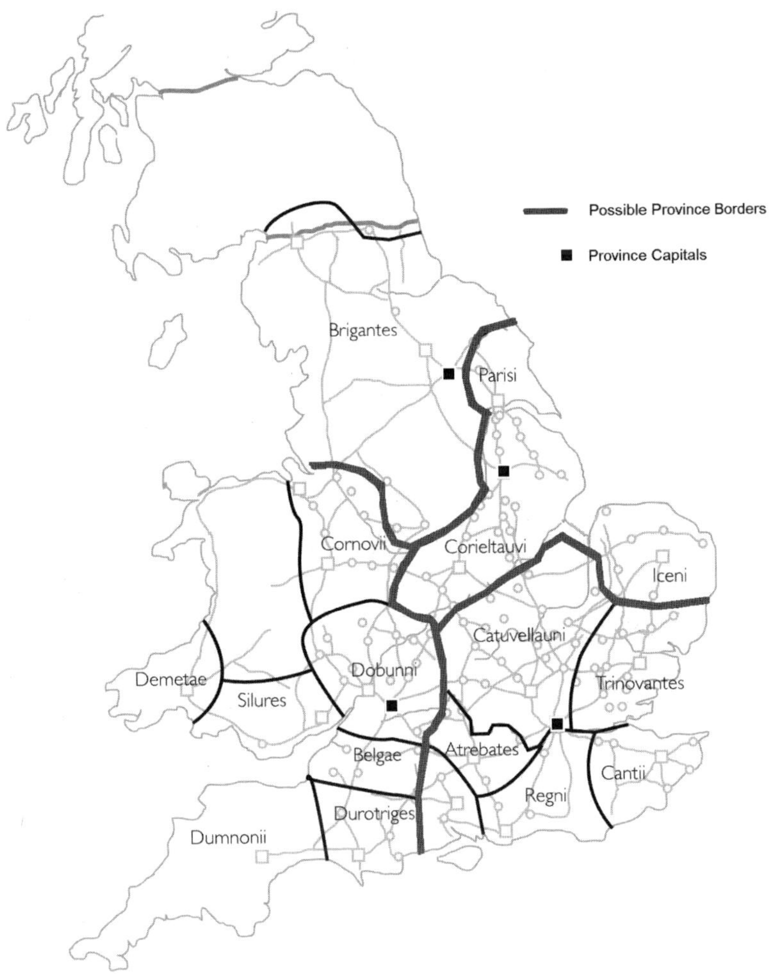

Figure 12. What the provinces of late Roman Britain may have looked like.

extensive economic integration and movements of populations, would probably have blurred those boundaries even further, so if fighting to establish borders did occur, there would have been plenty to fight about.

Gildas, in writing about the end of Roman Britain and the period after it, makes regular references to civil wars. During his account of the chaos surrounding the end of Roman Britain, he describes Britons fighting external enemies and fighting each other over food resources. He accuses Britain of being weak at repelling foreign enemies but formidable in civil wars. He says of the rulers of his time that they fight wars, but unjust wars against their fellow Britons. He accuses one of the rulers, Maglocunus, of depriving many other rulers of their kingdoms and their lives.[28]

In addition, as already discussed, it seems that by the end of Roman Britain, some regional militias were in existence, in addition to whatever elements of the Roman army remained. So, we now need to look at who might have been fighting whom, and where.

Figure 13. Distribution of Geometric Plate Horsehead type buckles and linked fittings, and of Peacock Plate Horsehead type buckles and linked fittings, showing a possible Dobunni–Corieltauvi alliance. (Laycock. Data sources: Portable Antiquities Scheme, Hawkes & Dunning, Appels & Laycock etc.)

As mentioned earlier it seems that a difference in kit provision developed in the last years of Roman rule between the south-east of England, or London Province, and the neighbouring areas, Lincoln Province, to the north, and Cirencester Province. Put in tribal terms this is a difference between the Catuvellauni/Trinovantes confederation which formed the core of London Province, and the Corieltauvi, who were the core of Lincoln Province and the Dobunni, who were the core of Cirencester Province.

Buckles and belt fittings in London Province remained much closer in design to the Roman originals.[29] By contrast, in both Lincoln and Cirencester Provinces, the very distinctively British horse head buckles, with their distinctively British buckle plates, were adopted. It seems conceivable that this difference is significant. London Province was geographically closest to mainland Europe, contained London, the biggest, most Roman city in Britain, and was more Romanized than any other part of Britain. Judging from the distribution of official Roman crossbow brooches there were probably also a significant number of official troops in East Anglia, which might have given the locals more confidence in the protection provided and less inclination to develop an extensive independent militia but would have left them less protected when the troops were withdrawn.[30]

We know from Zosimus that some Britons rebelled against Rome. It seems possible that Lincoln Province and Cirencester Province were more enthusiastic rebels than London Province. Generally, the motifs on buckle plates and strap ends of the horse head buckles in Lincoln and Cirencester Provinces are different and distinct, with the Dobunni favouring geometric designs, and with designs based on peacocks, gryphons and a tree of life appearing in Corieltauvi and surrounding areas. However, a few strap ends have motifs from both provinces;[31] this may have represented an alliance between Lincoln and Cirencester Provinces, between Corieltauvi and Dobunni, against the Catuvellauni, Trinovantes and others of London Province.

When added to existing tribal boundary disputes, such a fundamental difference of opinion about Britain's links with Rome could have been a major motivation for civil war.

We know that by the end of the fifth century, the part of Britain still held by the Britons had fragmented into separate kingdoms, mostly based on the tribe/*civitas* structure of Roman Britain. It also seems likely that we can see the beginning of that fragmentation process in the last years of Roman rule.

It is notoriously difficult to find archaeological evidence of ancient warfare, particularly of the sort of low-intensity, persistent, long-term inter-tribal border warfare that would have occurred at the end of Roman Britain. However, there is some evidence of the huge economic damage it would have caused.

In a phenomenon unparalleled elsewhere in the Empire in terms of extent and intensity, the end of Roman Britain saw lots of people bury large quantities of gold and silver and then fail to return to collect the hoards. This phenomenon occurs not just in coastal areas but deep inland as well and can only indicate large numbers of people fleeing or being killed.[32]

There is specific evidence suggesting a barrier emerged at this time between London Province and its neighbours. Coins minted after 402 continue to make it into Britain in very small numbers but very few of them are found far beyond the borders of London Province, suggesting the severing of internal trade and travel contacts.[33] Closing the border between London Province and its neighbours would have done huge damage to the economy of Roman Britain cutting across such vital trade routes as the Thames, Watling Street and Ermine Street.

And a fascinating new analysis of coin finds by site in the late Roman period has produced some very interesting data.[34] One interpretation of the data might suggest that in the last years of Roman rule, the economy of London Province, particularly the areas north of the Thames, could have been in severe trouble. Whereas in previous periods, the area had seemed prosperous, with plenty of coinage, fairly suddenly, towards the end of the Roman period, the amount of coinage in use in the area seems to have diminished significantly compared to Lincoln and Cirencester Provinces. It suggests that London Province was already in deep economic trouble by the time Britain left the Empire, and the other provinces would soon end up in a similar state as trade and industry collapsed and Britain fragmented into small warring kingdoms.

A scenario where regional militias, in a power vacuum after the rebellion against Rome, sliced up Britain and sliced up the economy seems the most viable explanation of the end of Roman Britain as we have come to know it, and we do seem to have some hard evidence for this.[35] It is a very important step forward in understanding the context of Arthurian Britain.

Chapter 2

Saxons, Quoit Brooch Style, Ambrosius, the Dobunni and Droitwich Salt

Traditionally the arrival of the Saxons is dated in 449, and our understanding of what happened next is based on a combination of Gildas, the *Anglo-Saxon Chronicle* and the *Historia Brittonum*.[1] Gildas, without dating the event and without naming any of the participants describes how a British 'proud tyrant' (most early manuscripts of Gildas omit a name for this figure) invited three boatloads of Saxons into the country to fight for him against his northern enemies, only to find that after a pay dispute the Saxons rebelled, seized land and invited more of their compatriots to land in Britain and settle the island.[2] Bede identifies the 'proud tyrant' as Vortigern, sets the landing in Kent and identifies the leaders of the Saxons as Hengest and Horsa. The *Historia Brittonum* elaborates on the theme of Vortigern's betrayal by Hengest and Horsa and the ensuing battles.

There is nothing inherently improbable in this narrative. Employing newcomers from outside the Empire as troops was standard for many late-Roman commanders. It was also not unheard of for such newcomers, having been employed by the Romans, to then turn against them. Alaric who sacked Rome in 410 had served in the Roman army. However, before we explore the story of Vortigern and his unwise recruitment campaign, we need to look north of the Thames where something little known, but just as significant, seems to have been occurring at much the same time, or perhaps even earlier.

In the previous chapter we noted how research on coinage in that part of London Province suggested that the economy there may have been in deep trouble at the end of the Roman period. We also explored the possibility that this might have been due to a civil war against other provinces and tribes.

There is a particular type of Anglo-Saxon brooch, known in Britain as a Supporting Arm Brooch, which is generally thought to have arrived with the earliest Anglo-Saxon immigrants and then to have fallen out of use.[3] Most seem to have been worn by women, but some types were also worn by men. They are often dated to the first half of the fifth century which suggests that people wearing them were around at about the same time as Hengest and Horsa or before. And while these brooches used to be extremely rare in this country, metal detectorists have found more in recent years.

Almost none has been found in Kent, but a few have been found in Lincolnshire and the south, with the majority found in a swathe across eastern areas, particularly across parts of the territory of the Catuvellauni and Trinovantes tribes in London Province.[4] In fact, the main grouping of these brooches is in roughly the same area which seems perhaps to have been in economic crisis at the end of the Roman period. Unlike with Kent, we have no historical narrative for what was going on here, so it is impossible to know whether these new settlers were taking deserted land in an impoverished area, seizing land from the locals, or being given land by local leaders who hoped, in return, for revenge on their British enemies to the north and west. Considering the appearance of very early Anglo-Saxon cemeteries at places on the borders of Catuvellauni and Trinovantes territory, including on their western border, the scenario of local leaders inviting the Saxons in may be the more realistic one. Whatever happened, it meant that a huge strategic chunk of Britain in the centre and east of what is now England may have started becoming culturally Anglo-Saxon almost before any Britons had started resisting the westwards advance of the newcomers.

And so to Kent and one of the key questions: if he existed, who was Vortigern? Neither Gildas nor the *Anglo-Saxon Chronicle* answer this question but there are hints in later sources and trying to get a clearer picture of Vortigern is important for our understanding of fifth-century Britain.

For a start, despite the Hengest and Horsa narrative taking place in Kent,

Vortigern does not seem to have been a ruler of Kent alone. Indeed, he may not have been a ruler of Kent at all. His connections seem to be more with the west of the country, perhaps with Dobunni territory.

The *Historia Brittonum* which we will consider in depth later, because of its nature as a key source for Arthur, states that Vortigern was descended from Gloui, who, the text says, founded Gloucester. Gloucester was one of the key cities of the Dobunni. William of Malmesbury refers to victory by Cenwalh of Wessex at a place he called Wirtgernesburg, or Vortigern's fort. This is thought by many to be the same battle as that located by the *Anglo-Saxon Chronicle* at Bradford-on-Avon. As it happens, an amazing late Roman villa, near an older hillfort, has been excavated at Bradford-on-Avon, with a Christian baptistery and a building for cattle and farm stores designed to look outwardly like another villa.[5] It's the sort of place where Vortigerm, or someone from his family, might have lived. The Pillar of Eliseg claims Vortigern as an ancestor of the kings of Powys, a Welsh kingdom that emerged on the western borders of Dobunni territory. A territory in Wales called Gwrtheyrnion is named after him and at the end of his life he is said to have fled westwards. Various sites are claimed as his destination but one of the contenders is the hillfort at Little Doward near Ganarew on the western borders of Dobunni territory.

If Vortigern was ruler of the Dobunni and perhaps in some sense overlord of the whole of Cirencester Province, it would make him a very powerful figure. It would not, however, necessarily make him ruler of distant Kent.

He could conceivably have acquired some kind of status as overlord of Kent. The *Historia Brittonum* refers to Vortigern making decisions about Kent without consulting its ruler, a man the text names Guoyrancgonus or Gwyrangon.

However, if it is not simply a matter of two incompatible traditions emerging from the mists of the fifth century, which it may be, then the answer to this puzzle may perhaps be found in the special status of Richborough in Kent.

Hengest and Horsa are said in the *Anglo-Saxon Chronicle* to have landed initially at Eopwinefleot and *Historia Brittonum* explicitly mentions the Isle of Thanet as the location for much of the action involving Hengest and Horsa. Eopwinefleot is traditionally identified as Ebbsfleet. Ebbsfleet is now close to Ramsgate, but much more significantly, in terms of the fifth century, it is very close to Richborough, the site of the Roman fortress of Rutupiae.

Richborough is one of the most important sites of Roman Britain.[6]

It was the main base for crossing the Channel. It was in some sense, the Dover of its day – although Dover itself was, of course, also an important Roman-period port and military base. It is likely Roman invaders first arrived near here when they landed in Britain and soon after Claudius sent his legions ashore, they built a fort and supply base here. At one stage the Romans had a huge triumphal arch there probably celebrating their conquest of this island. In the late third century, as the threat from seaborne raiders increased, a huge, more modern fort was built, one of the so-called Saxon Shore forts. When Roman generals led their armies into Europe attempting to conquer it, many of their troops travelled via Richborough. At the end of the occupation of Britain, due to its strong links to Europe, Richborough may easily have been one of the last places held by troops loyal to Rome.[7]

And there are plenty of signs in the archaeological record of how Richborough's position gave it special status in Roman Britain even in the last years of Roman control here, and even beyond that. For instance, while the coin statistics for the rest of London Province suggest serious problems in the last decades of Roman rule, the numbers found at Richborough remain large.[8] Belt fittings associated with Cirencester Province and the Dobunni are rare in London Province, but a cluster has been found in Richborough and the vicinity.[9] Legio II Augusta had been stationed at Caerleon in southern Wales, in Cirencester Province and just beyond the western borders of the Dobunni, during much of the Roman occupation of Britain. However the *Notitia Dignitatum*, a document that records the location of military units in the empire sometime around the late fourth century or early fifth century, indicates that the Prefect of Legio II Augusta had by then relocated to Richborough. There is a sense here that the Richborough area, in the post-Roman era, may have retained, or perhaps resumed, some contact with western areas linked to Vortigern, which the rest of London Province had lost.

Trying to understand the nature of Hengest and Horsa and those who may have arrived with them is also interesting and useful in attempting to understand how Arthurian Britain developed. Gildas refers to the arrivals he describes, as Saxons. However, there is evidence that suggests those who first arrived in Kent were ethnically and culturally rather more diverse than that.

The *Anglo-Saxon Chronicle* references to Hengest are perhaps not the only references to this warrior. The Battle of Finnsburh or Finnsburg is mentioned both in Beowulf and in a document called the Finnsburg Fragment. Accounts of the battle indicate that at Finnsburg, in Frisia (mainly now in the Netherlands), sometime in the mid-fifth century a warrior called Hengest fought alongside Danes, against a force of Frisians and possibly Jutes.

A lot of the warbands that roamed the Empire in the fifth century were perhaps quite ethnically and culturally diverse, as various groups teamed up, separated and then teamed up again.

There is a particular design group of metalwork, mainly belt fittings and brooches, that appears in Kent at pretty much the same time as Hengest and Horsa are said to have signed up with Vortigern, and it is tempting to link the two phenomena.

The design type is known as Quoit Brooch Style (QBS), after the spectacular quoit brooches that are such a feature of it.[10] It seems to be based on chip-carved late Roman military belt fittings that were widely found in the fifth century, both in the border zone within the empire and in the coastal area north and east of the Empire that stretches through the Netherlands, Germany and part of Denmark, the coastal areas from where most of those settling in Britain in the fifth century came. However, there are other cultural elements involved in QBS. It seems to have been manufactured mainly in Kent and was probably made by British craftsmen, used to British belt fitting design, and, therefore, incorporating elements of that. Rosettes somewhat like the wheel design for the shields of *Secunda Britannica* (assumed by many to be a late name for Legio II Augusta) as shown in the *Notitia Dignitatum* are also a feature. In short, it appears to be what you would

Figure 14. Quoit Brooch Style brooch from Howletts. (After Suzuki 2000)

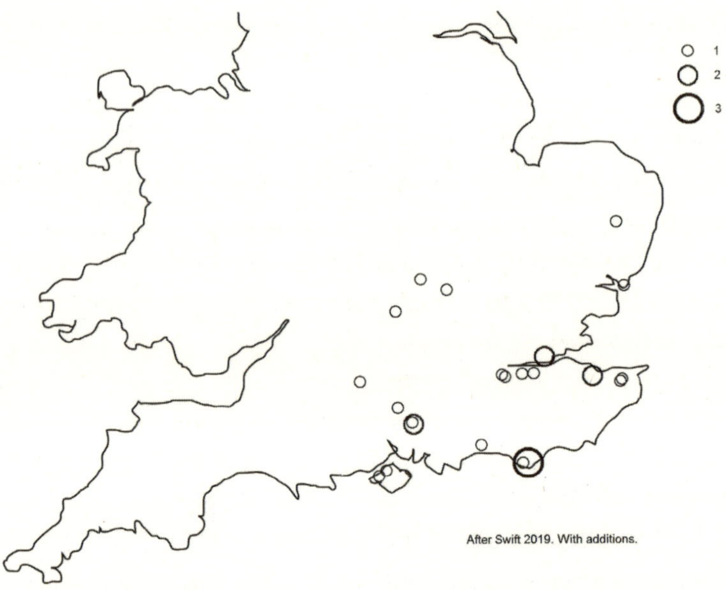

Figure 15. Distribution of Quoit Brooch Style belt fittings. (After Swift 2019, with additions Laycock)

expect Hengest and Horsa's people to be wearing if they were kitted out in Kent by the metalworkers of a British king.

If it is correct to link QBS to Hengest and Horsa, then the distribution patterns of QBS also perhaps allow us to deduce something about their activities in Britain.[11]

QBS distribution, for instance, does seem to suggest some form of coastal defence still being operative and perhaps manned by the troops of Hengest and Horsa, or similar newcomers. There are clusters of the material at some key strategic locations, like Mucking on the Thames, Lyminge and Lympne (near the Saxon Shore fort at Lympne), Alfriston (near the Saxon Shore fort at Pevensey) and Meonstoke (near the Saxon Shore fort at Portchester). There is QBS material from Highdown which is not a Saxon Shore fort but a hillfort near the coast and pretty much equidistant between Pevensey and Portchester.

In his account of the Saxon rebellion against the '*superbus tyrannus*' Gildas describes 'the fire' spreading from sea to sea and reaching the western ocean. This, at first sight, seems incompatible with the *Anglo-Saxon Chronicle* and *Historia*

Figure 16. Quoit Brooch Style buckle and buckle plate from Bishopstone. (After Suzuki 2000)

Figure 17. Quoit Brooch-style fitting from Kingsworthy. (After Suzuki 2000)

Brittonum which tie their narratives more to Kent. However, some of the battles mentioned in the *Anglo-Saxon Chronicle* cannot be located with total certainty and it is, of course, possible that Gildas was exaggerating or mistaken. The spread of QBS material is interesting in the context of all this. It does not spread quite as far as 'the western ocean'. However, it does spread along the Channel coast as far as the Solent. And it does spread inland as far as Pewsey in Wiltshire, about thirty miles from the Severn River estuary, and as far north as Aylesbury in Buckinghamshire. If the spread is somehow linked to the rebellion of Hengest and Horsa it could just about bridge the gap between the accounts of Gildas on the one hand and the *Anglo-Saxon Chronicle* and *Historia Brittonum* on the other.

The *Anglo-Saxon Chronicle* names Vortigern as the opponent of Hengest and Horsa in one battle and gives the Saxons two victories out of four without specifically assigning any victories to the British. The *Historia Brittonum* names Vortimer, son of Vortigern, as the main British opponent of the Saxon rebels and claims he defeated them two times out of four with the victors in the other battles unspecified. By contrast, the account of Gildas, the most reliable of the sources and the one written closest in time to the actual events mentions no specific battles and no British victories against the Saxons until he mentions a victory by British forces under the command of one Ambrosius Aurelianus. One excellent aspect of Ambrosius Aurelianus is that he is a significant named character universally accepted as having existed, rare in the historical fog of fifth-century Britain, and for that reason (and the fact that many have suggested he is the prototype for Arthur) he is worth considering in some detail.

Unfortunately, the information Gildas gives us about Ambrosius Aurelianus is both somewhat scant and somewhat confusing.[12] The writer calls him 'a modest man', says that his parents, who had been killed in the chaos, were clad in purple, says that he was the only one of the Roman people who had come through the storm alive and that his (unnamed) descendants had in his time, greatly degenerated from their ancestral greatness. Gildas also adds a complicated statement about the date of the victory of Ambrosius Aurelianus. There is no universal agreement on what he is saying, and Bede, for instance, seems to have a different understanding of it, but the most logical understanding of the best version of the text we have today seems to say that the victory took place forty-four years and one month before the British victory at the Battle of Badon Hill and that the year of Badon was also the year Gildas was born.

We will be looking in depth at Badon later in the book because *Historia Brittonum* attributed the victory there to Arthur. Unfortunately, the only specific ancient date we have for Badon is one in the *Annales Cambriae*. There the date of Badon is usually interpreted as being sometime around 516, but Badon could have taken place across a range of dates either side of 516 depending on exactly how the dating in the document is understood. Forty-four years before 516 would date the victory of Ambrosius Aurelianus to 472. The *Anglo-Saxon Chronicle* dates Hengest's last victory in 473 and then lists an Anglo-Saxon landing and victory in Sussex in 477. Meanwhile, in mainland Europe, the Western Roman Empire came to an end in 476. Apart from this, none of these dates is very certain, but it's worth mentioning them to get a sense of the context in which Ambrosius Aurelianus was operating.

We will also return to the question of the descendants further on in this book, but it clearly suggests that there was some kind of dynasty descended from Ambrosius Aurelianus in existence at the time Gildas was writing. The question of what Gildas is trying to say about the ancestry of Ambrosius Aurelianus is a difficult one.

The Western Roman Empire was probably still in existence when Ambrosius Aurelianus defeated the Saxons, so it seems best to interpret the comments about him being the only Roman left alive as indicating he was the last major figure representing Roman continuity and values in Britain. Many have interpreted the reference to his parents being clad in purple as an indication they were of high rank within the Roman structure, but elsewhere Gildas describes blood as being purple-coloured and therefore, this could be a reference to the violent nature of their deaths and martyrdom.

It is hard to get more out of the words of Gildas on Ambrosius Aurelianus, so we have to look to other sources to get any real sense of who he was and what he did.

Some have tried to make a connection between the name Ambrosius Aurelianus and various people with the name Aurelius. Aurelius Caninus, one of the rulers criticized by Gildas, is one such character and we will discuss him further in Chapter 7.

Another is Aurelius Ursicinus. This is a name found on spoons in the hugely rich Hoxne hoard, which was buried in Suffolk in the early fifth century and never recovered. Ursicinus is also an interesting name here because it is from the Latin word for bear, just as Arthur is derived from the British word for bear. To add to the interest, another name on an item in the hoard is Euherius. Euherius was not a name in the late Roman period, so it seems to have been a spelling mistake for Eucherius or Eutherius. Another rich late Roman hoard from Suffolk is the famous Mildenhall hoard. On items from that, the name Eutherius is found, so the name in the Hoxne hoard is probably also Eutherius. Eutherius could conceivably become British Uther, and one of the silver items in the Mildenhall hoard shows rare depictions of a bear hunting, quite possibly in some kind of reference to Ursicinus. There was a unit of the

Figure 18. A late Roman gold belt buckle from the Thetford Treasure demonstrates the wealth of late Roman officials in this part of East Anglia.

late Roman army based in northern Gaul called the Ursarienses, the bears, who had a shield design of an eight-pointed star, rather like some of the designs found on bracelets in the Hoxne hoard. It all seems, at first sight, mildly intriguing.

However, it is unclear to what extent Aurelius and Aurelianus might be viewed as linked names in the fifth century. Certainly, in earlier periods they were separate names. It is possible that by the fifth century, the tendency for families – for instance in Gaul in the period, and some Welsh royal genealogies – to choose similar-sounding names might have linked Aurelius and Aurelianus but it would perhaps be unwise to use this as the foundation of any significant argument. In addition to this, Aurelius was quite a popular name in the Roman Empire. Also quite popular were names derived from Ursus.[13]

Historia Brittonum makes a few suggestions on the geography. In a rather confusing passage that involves dragons, the book says Ambrosius came from Glevesing, or Glywysing, an area of southern Wales, specifically from the Field of Aelecti, perhaps somewhere near the Palus Elleti of the Llandaff Charters, which is near the river Thaw.[14] It states that he allowed Vortigern's son, Pascent, to rule a part of central Wales called Builth and Gwrtheyrnion and says that he fought a battle called Guoloph against an unidentified character called Guitolinus or Vitalinus.[15]

The reference to Glywysing is interesting because the *Life of Saint Paul Aurelian* – with the same second name as Ambrosius – also gives the saint a south Wales origin. It says he came from Penychen, part of Glywysing and that his father was called Perphirius. The trouble is that Perphirius means purple and therefore, the writer of the *Life* may be deducing this name from the details Gildas gives of the parents of Ambrosius. Equally, the fact that Paul Aurelian probably did come from Glywysing could have been used by the author of *Historia Brittonum* to name an origin for Ambrosius Aurelianus in his story about dragons.

Or perhaps both are true. If the parents of Ambrosius Aurelianus were originally based in southern Wales, they would have had to move some distance eastwards to have been killed by Saxon rebels from Kent. One possibility that might make that feasible, is if the father of Ambrosius Aurelianus was connected with Legio II Augusta when, as seems to have happened, part or all of the legion moved from Caerleon in southern Wales to Richborough in the fifth century.

By contrast, the reference to Ambrosius having authority over Builth and Gwrtheyrnion is easier to accept, as is the Battle of Guoloph. Guoloph is usually identified with one of the villages now called Wallop, near Amesbury in Hampshire – though there is also a Lower Wallop in Shropshire and a Wallhope at Tidenham in Gloucestershire. Due to a Roman arrowhead, an unusually large (considering the small size of the Roman-period settlement there) cluster of late Roman belt fittings – including a Dobunni-type buckle and a rare fifth-century belt mount – and a rare post-Roman penannular brooch being found at Nether Wallop,[16] and due to it being the closest Wallop village to Danebury hillfort, this seems the most likely location for the battle. With the appearance of similar names in the genealogy of Vortigern, it tends to be assumed that Guitolinus had something to do with Vortigern, though this is far from confirmed, as similar names were quite common across the Roman Empire. The battle is thought to have taken place before the arrival of Hengest and Horsa in Britain.

It is, of course, possible that the families of Ambrosius Aurelianus, and indeed Arthur, came to Britain from abroad. Magnus Maximus, who was probably of Spanish origin, was adopted in Welsh legend as Macsen Wledig. Something similar could have happened to either Ambrosius Aurelianus or Arthur, or indeed both. For instance, a high-status burial in a mausoleum from the late Roman period from Gloucester is that of an officer or official whose origin was somewhere in Eastern Europe.[17] Burials at Lankhills, Winchester, show soldiers or officials arriving from the Pannonia region of central Europe in the late fourth century and establishing a community there.[18] This community may be linked to a type of punched decoration plate belt fitting which would suggest their presence across much of the west country, including some Dobunni areas.[19]

There is, however, other evidence that may perhaps tell us not only where Ambrosius Aurelianus operated, but how he operated, and might even tell us a bit about how he financed his operations.

The earliest form (c. 880) of the place name Amesbury, the nearest major town to the probable site of the Battle of Guoloph, is Ambresbyrig. The Byrig element means fort, but there has been much discussion of the Ambre or Ambres element. This element or something similar is found in a small group of names, divided mainly into two groups, an eastern group located in places like Essex, and a western group located in places like Wiltshire, Gloucestershire and beyond.

Conventional place-name etymology has provided several possible explanations for the Ambre element. There is the possibility that it may be a rare place name element meaning a bunting (a type of bird) or sorrel, or a measure of about four bushels. Or it may be a pre-Roman Celtic river name, though many of the Ambre names are either not on a river or are on a river called something else. The other explanation is that it is a personal name; very many, perhaps most, Anglo-Saxon place names include a person's name. The form of some of the Ambre place names does indeed suggest they contain a personal name. However, Ambre or Ambres is not an Anglo-Saxon personal name. There is a rare German name that is similar but there is no evidence of it over here. So, what's going on?

The place names in the eastern group include minor rural sites that might well be named after buntings, sorrels or bushels. The western group, which includes Amesbury, seems more interesting.

There is a long-running belief that Amesbury is 'the fort of Ambrosius'. A 1508 inscription in a book, for instance, refers to Amesbury as '*Ambrosii Burgi*'. Geoffrey of Monmouth links Ambrosius to Aurelianus and Stonehenge, in the parish of Amesbury. There were traditions linking Arthur to Tintagel and the hillfort at South Cadbury. Both sites turned out to be major fifth-century political centres. Though largely unexcavated, we know Amesbury was a major Roman-period site and there is a hillfort there too. A hoard of three slightly mysterious late Roman high-status silver Brancaster-type rings was found at Amesbury – one depicts a stag and bird, one shows a gryphon and one features four helmet heads. There is fascinating evidence of some activity at Stonehenge in the fifth century as well.[21]

Recently there has been more acceptance in the world of place-name etymology that English place names can sometimes contain Celtic personal names.[22] It is not a big distance from Ambrosius to Ambres or Ambre. The Welsh version of Ambrosius in *Historia Brittonum* is Embreis, which is pretty close to Ambres. Maximus becomes Macsen in Wales. Gerontius becomes Geraint.

In addition to Amesbury, with its proximity to Wallop, there are other interesting locations in the western group of Ambre place names. Three of these seem particularly interesting.

Amberley in Gloucestershire (Ambresleg in 1248) is about a mile from a Roman site at Woodchester. Amberley is the village next to it and has the Amberley and Minchinhampton complex of little-understood earthworks. Woodchester is not, however, just any Roman site, it is the site of perhaps the biggest and most magnificent Roman villa in Britain. The site was excavated in the eighteenth century, so details are somewhat sparse, but what we do know is spectacular. It contained quantities of marble statuary and a vast elaborate mosaic pavement that is perhaps the biggest known Roman mosaic north of the Alps, containing an estimated 1.5 million tesserae. It had a layout that made people suggest it should be regarded as some kind of official palace, perhaps the seat of the governor of a province. Mosaics at Woodchester are of the Cirencester school, linking it to the capital of the Dobunni tribe, and of the province. Much of the structure seems to have been fourth century but there is probable evidence of post-Roman occupation too, with mosaics being patched up or covered by cement. A late Roman military or official buckle was found. The walls of the medieval church built on the site follow the line of some of the villa walls, suggesting possible continuity in the post-Roman period between the villa and church. There is even a mysterious reference in the Brut y Brenhinedd to Arthur being crowned at Kaer Vudei/Uudei, and though this has usually been identified as Cirencester or Silchester, it has sometimes been suggested that it could be Woodchester (Uuduceastir 716–743, Wuduceaster 869).[23] About four miles distant from Woodchester is the

Dobunni's hillfort of Uley, which has within it both a Roman period temple and what is thought might be an early Christian basilica or monastic site with high-status finds like glass cups.[24] If you were looking for a location to link to Ambrosius Aurelianus, defender of Roman heritage and values, either from a family of high rank or who had attained high rank, who probably operated somewhere between the Welsh borderlands and Wallop it is hard to think of a more suitable location than Woodchester, with Amberley right next to it.

The next site is Amberley in Herefordshire (Ambresleye 1291). In the, admittedly rather old, book *The Place Names of Herefordshire* it is explicitly suggested that this may contain the name Ambrose.[25] Amberley is about a mile from a hillfort called Sutton Walls which is near the western border of what was Dobunni territory. Again, this is not any normal hillfort. Quarrying has removed much of the site, however; it is known that the Mercian king Offa had a palace that was probably in the hillfort or next to it. A unique ring of probable fourth-fifth century date, with a possible parallel at Barton Court Farm in a fifth century ring made from a very late bracelet, was found very close to the hillfort.[26] At Marden, about a mile from Sutton Walls on the other side of it a rare early post-Roman cemetery was found in the 1940s and excavated in the 1950s. Weapons are said to have been found. When one of the skeletons was radiocarbon dated, it was found to have a date of AD 340–540.[27] Sutton is an Anglo-Saxon name, however, Marden may be a British name, and it has an early form of Magewurdin (1177). This may be the previously unlocated Cair Meguaid mentioned in the *Historia Brittonum*. Or it may be Cair Maunguid, which has also been suggested to mean nearby Hereford[28] and which could be linked to the ancient name of the region around Sutton Walls, now found in Maund (Maund Bryan, Rosemaund, Whitchurch Maund.) Nearby is a Roman villa site at Wellington where signs of post-Roman activity have been found.[29] Sutton Walls is situated next to a key Roman road junction, with roads south to Gloucester and Cirencester and north to Chester, and with roads east to Doncaster and west to southern Wales. Again, if you were looking for a site connected to a fifth-century British military commander who operated somewhere between the Welsh borderlands and Wallop, it is hard to think of a more suitable location.

The third site is Ombersley (Ambreslege 706) in Worcestershire. It is very close to Droitwich near the northern border of what was Dobunni territory. More specifically, it is a couple of miles away from the site of Salinae, the pre-Roman and Roman salt works at Droitwich. A late Roman military spur, a high-status late Roman Brancaster ring, a spearhead, a military-type knife and two late Roman official strap ends come from the site of a deluxe, possibly government-controlled, villa there that was surrounded by defensive ramparts in the late third century. A coin of Honorius was found sealed under a floor at the villa suggesting fifth-century activity.[30] Three late Roman official crossbow brooches have been found near the Roman road north of Droitwich.[31] Salt production at Droitwich was probably state-controlled during the Roman period and would probably have come under the control of British authorities after that.

Salt production seems to have continued at Droitwich in the post-Roman period in the fifth, sixth and seventh centuries; you can still buy Droitwich salt today.[32] This is perhaps the only large-scale British industry, of any type, that continued in production throughout the chaotic period after the end of Roman rule and into the centuries beyond. It may, in that sense, be unique. The salt works were well-known to the author of the *Miriabilia*, a text often linked to the *Historia Brittonum*, who was well aware of the hot salt wells at Droitwich and referred to them.[33] Finds from the area indicate its importance in the period. For instance, a British penannular brooch of Fowler Type D7 (400–600) and about the most western example of a supporting arm brooch (420–480) have been found in the area, as was a very rare gold Merovingian tremissis (580–670) and an intriguing, and very rare, bear figurine which may or may not have anything to do with Arthur.[34]

These salt works were hugely valuable. The brine of the Dobunni at Droitwich had ten times as much salt in it as seawater. You can get two and a half pounds of salt from each gallon of Droitwich brine.[35] By the time the Domesday Book was compiled, Droitwich seems to have been producing over 1,000 tons of salt a year.[36] Salt was such an essential for flavouring and preserving food, and for other processes like the production of leather and dyeing cloth, that it was known in pre-industrial times as 'white gold'. A recent work has argued that two key factors in the emergence of Mercia as the dominant Anglo-Saxon kingdom in the seventh and eighth centuries were its control of Droitwich and

London and the taxes it could raise from both.[37] The fact that the word salary is derived from a Latin word that meant something like 'a salt allowance' for soldiers shows how valuable salt has always been. We still use phrases that signify the same. There is, for instance, 'worth his (or her) salt' and the phrase 'the salt of the earth,' a Bible quote which Gildas himself uses in his writing.

Droitwich is close to Worcester, a major Roman city and one where there is intriguing evidence of possible major late Roman and possibly post-Roman activity.

Again, if you were looking for a site connected to a British commander able to exercise control over large numbers of men and large distances between the Welsh borderlands and Wallop, and who can sustain that financially in a world where Roman Britain's complex and sophisticated economy had collapsed, then it is hard to think of a more suitable location.

So is all this just a coincidence? That is certainly possible. However, if it is not, then perhaps they might help us to construct a more detailed picture of who Ambrosius Aurelianus was and how he operated.

We mentioned the Dobunni *civitas* when looking at Vortigern. With Ambrosius Aurelianus they may be arguably even more significant, so we should take a more detailed look at them. We know the name of this tribe from various sources. The geographer Ptolemy mentions the name and states that Corinium, Cirencester, was their main city. The Ravenna Cosmography – known for having many spelling mistakes – mentions *Cironium Dobunorum*, Corinium of the Dobunni. A milestone from Kenchester in Herefordshire has on it RPCD, for *Res Publica Civitatis Dobunnorum.* A second-century diploma of a soldier serving in Pannonia with *Cohors I Britannica* identifies him as Lucco, son of Trenus, of the Dobunni.[38] A sixth-century gravestone found near Buckland in Devon is inscribed *Dobvnni Fabri Filii Enabarri*, which means either 'Of Fabr(i)us of the Dobunni, son of Enabarrus', or 'Of Dobunnus, the smith, son of Enabarrus'.[39] Either shows the name still in use long after the end of Roman Britain.

Most of what we know about the boundaries of the tribe comes from pre-Roman coinage which can reasonably be attributed to the Dobunni. Many of the coins – like a lot of pre-Roman British coins – have a horse on the reverse. Some of the coins carry inscriptions like *EISV*, *ANTED*, *CORIO*, *BODVOC*,

Figure 19. Coin of Bodvoc of the Dobunni.

CATTI and *COMVX*. *BODVOC* is a known Celtic name and it is assumed that most, perhaps all, of these inscriptions refer to rulers of all or parts of the Dobunni.

The rich salt works at Droitwich were in operation as early as the sixth or fifth century BC. Big tanks lined with timber were constructed where the brine from the salt springs was left to concentrate before the manufacturing process was completed by evaporation on ovens. The salt was then packed in briquetage containers for transport to consumers. The salt works would flourish in the Roman period. The Roman road network was laid out so that two or three Roman roads met there, and one of these roads would become known in the medieval period as a Salt Way.

The Dobunni also played a major role in coastal salt production. Sometime around the second century AD salt production decreased considerably on southern and eastern coastlines where it had been very important, and, by contrast, salt production increased considerably in the Central Somerset levels, so that, in the late Roman period, this was the main area for coastal salt-production.[40]

The Dobunni tribal territory could at a stretch be called rectangular, with a northern border stretching roughly from Tenbury Wells to Rugby, an eastern border from there to Basingstoke, a southern border to Burnham-on-Sea, and a western border back to Tenbury Wells again. It's a big area, that includes a wide variety of landscapes and the Severn estuary and much of the Bristol Channel, one of Britain's great water routes. Gildas specifically mentions the Severn, along with the Thames, as one of the two great waterways of Britain, that brought wealth and trade to it, as the text puts it, 'like two arms'.[41]

The major cities of the Dobunni in the late Roman period were Kenchester, Worcester, Gloucester and Cirencester. Bath is attributed by Ptolemy to the *civitas* of the Belgae, whose capital was at Winchester. This does not correspond with pre-Roman tribal and cultural reality, so if the Romans really did give Bath to the Belgae it would almost certainly have created a territorial dispute between the two states at the end of Roman Britain. An entry in the *Anglo-Saxon Chronicle* for 577 which mentions British forces from the cities of Bath, Cirencester and Gloucester at the same battle, suggests that in the post-Roman era the Bath region belonged to the Dobunni again.

In the early Roman period, the Dobunni adopted less Roman culture than some of the areas of Britain further east, and even in the late Roman period, parts of the west and north of Dobunni territory still looked less Roman than a lot of other places in Britain. However, by the fourth century, Cirencester had become, after London, Roman Britain's second most important city and, as already mentioned, probably the capital of the province of Britannia Prima. By then the *civitas* contained a significant number of major industrial sites (for instance, Droitwich and the ironworking region in and around Worcester) and large, wealthy villa estates.[42]

There is also evidence that the Dobunni were well-prepared for whatever violence occurred in the decades before and after the end of Roman control here and probably did a largely successful job of protecting themselves from it.

We have already mentioned the horsehead buckles that appear in Britain in the last decades of Roman rule. There are two main categories of horsehead buckle and one of them, categorized now as Hawkes & Dunning 1b Geometric, seems, judging by its distribution, to have been largely manufactured and worn by Dobunni (by that section of the Dobunni who wore Roman-type kit). The buckles themselves originally have horseheads over dolphins, but later examples, perhaps produced toward the very end of Roman rule, have just the horseheads. The buckle plates that went with buckles are long and often beautifully decorated. Some buckle plates feature a line of cross-hatched diamond designs.[43] Others incorporated complex wheel, or rosette, designs that perhaps have links to the wheel associated with the Celtic thunder god

Figure 20. Buckle plate design of a type regularly found in the Dobunni areas. After (Hawkes & Dunning, *Soldiers and Settlers in Britain*, 1961)

Taranis, or to a sun symbol, or to late Roman shield designs, or to Celtic crosses.[44] The regular and standardized nature of manufacture suggests a well-organized kit factory probably managed by the *civitas*. An intriguing little aspect of the distribution is a bulge out from Dobunni territory into Belgae territory near Winchester, the *civitas* capital, a bulge that happens to incorporate the Wallops, likely site of the battle involving Ambrosius Aurelianus at Guoloph. (One of the buckles from Nether Wallop has some similarities to a type perhaps associated with the Atrebates and Belgae.[45])

Another type of buckle plate is found in some Dobunni areas. These consist of plates decorated simply with circles and other patterns of punched dots. The buckle plates seem to have been cheaply and quickly made, probably at a manufacturing site at Ickham near Richborough. Reinforcements seem to have arrived, probably from eastern Europe, in the late fourth century and seem to have re-equipped at Ickham before moving west.[46]

Most British militiamen in the late fourth century and in the fifth century were probably armed with spears, knives and shields. The well-equipped would have had swords. There is evidence, however, that suggests that fighters in Dobunni territory were, in addition, equipped with a specific type of weighted dart used by the late Roman army. This is the *plumbata*, and they are rarely found outside military contexts, yet a number have been found on civilian sites in the territory of the Dobunni, at Kenchester, Nettleton and Cirencester. The northern neighbours of the Dobunni, the Cornovii, seem to have been quite well equipped too. No less than nine of these darts have been found at their capital, Wroxeter.[47]

The result of all this is perhaps visible in the distribution of hoards of silver and gold from the period around the end of Roman Britain. Since these hoards were never collected by their owners, they present evidence of wealthy people who have become refugees, or were killed, or both. In the east of the country, they seem to mark out an area of particular vulnerability, in London Province. In the west, by contrast, the comparative scarcity of such hoards from the wealthy Dobunni territory seems to show that it was much less vulnerable.[48]

The Dobunni were powerful at the end of Roman Britain and seem to have remained powerful afterwards. For instance, there is evidence that suggests the amphitheatre at Cirencester was turned into a fortress in the post-Roman period (some have suggested this could be the origin of the story of King Arthur's Round Table). The *Anglo-Saxon Chronicle* entry for 577 describes an army from Wessex under Cuthwine and Ceawlin defeating three British kings, Conmail, Condidan and Farinmail at Deorham (now Dyrham) and then capturing Gloucester, Cirencester and Bath. It indicates that over 150 years after the end of Roman Britain, the Dobunni were still sending armies into battle.

High-status burials from the early post-Roman period have been found in Dobunni territory. A mausoleum containing three burials was found under St. Mary de Lode, a church next to Gloucester Cathedral,[49] and there is a local tradition that the earliest Christian church in Britain was on this site. Under Worcester Cathedral, a burial from this period was found where the buried person had gold braid round the head.[50] If you were looking for the burial of Ambrosius Aurelianus or members of his family, these are the sort of places you might look.

There is also an interesting discussion to be had about the extent of Dobunni power and influence in southern Wales in the late Roman and post-Roman period. The distribution of pre-Roman Dobunni coinage suggests that Dobunni power in that period extended almost as far as Caerleon and Caerwent. A horsehead buckle and buckle plate of a type closely linked to the Hawkes &

Dunning 1b Geometric designs of the Dobunni has been found at Caerwent.[51] And in the post-Roman period the kingdom of Glywysing emerged between the Tawe and the Usk. Glywysing is said to be named after a fifth-century founding king, Glywys. There is a suspicion though that both names ultimately derive from the Roman period name for Gloucester: Glevum. Glywysing, for example, could come from the word Glevenses, the people of Gloucester. If so, then the *Historia Brittonum*'s indication that Ambrosius Aurelianus came from Glywysing is perhaps not incompatible with links to the Dobunni. Glywys is said to have dedicated himself to religion later in life and moved to Cornwall, where Penryn's church of St. Gluvias (note the similarity of changes in Glevum to Gloucester) is said to be named after him.

There is even a rather battered fifth- or sixth-century gravestone from Aberhydfer near Trecastle north of Glywsying[52] and not too far from a place named in the Llandaff Charters as Deri Emreis (the grove of Ambrosius).[53] Some of the inscription is now lost and the first name looks too short for Ambrosius but the second name could conceivably be Aurelianus.

All in all, when the evidence is examined, there is a logic in seeing Ambrosius Aurelianus as a man who based his power on the *civitas* of the Dobunni.

Is it then possible to locate the site of his victory over the Saxons mentioned by Gildas? The short answer is no. However, it is tempting to wonder about a location near Ambrosden. The 'hill of Ambre or Ambres' is located a couple of miles from the Roman town of Alchester on the Roman road leading west from St. Albans to Cirencester. There are Anglo-Saxon burial mounds. The site is on the eastern borders of the Dobunni and pretty much on the north-western borders of QBS distribution (finds at nearby Aylesbury and Brackley). Nearby are Horsenden and Horsendon Hill, the names of which contain the (very) rare Anglo-Saxon personal name Horsa.

Another possible path to finding Ambrosian battlefields is to 'follow the standards'. It is fairly well known that some late Roman forces (and probably some post-Roman forces) carried a type of standard called the *draco*. It was essentially a windsock, designed like a dragon, and fixed at the top of a pole which flowed out, like a live creature, when air flowed through it. The Romans adopted them from the Dacians and then brought them to Britain. Being a *draconarius*, a draco standard bearer, was regarded as a great honour. What is less widely known is that we may have elements of the uniforms of three British *draconarii* from the end of the Roman period. There are three strap ends from belts of the period which show what are almost certainly British *draco* standards. These three strap ends are unique and fit into no other design group. It is therefore not unreasonable to think they may have belonged to actual *draconarii*. If so, they would have been prestigious, specially made and carefully guarded items. No *draconarius* would lose such an item lightly. On the other hand, such an item could easily be lost in combat. One of these *draco* strap ends was found at Richborough.[54] Another was found at Winterbourne Gunner, a few miles from Amesbury and a few miles from the Wallops.[55] The third was found at Gussage St. Michael in Dorset, roughly between the late Roman or post-Roman linear defences of Bokerley Dyke and the hillfort of Badbury Rings where there is some evidence of early post-Roman activity; it is often suggested as a possible site for the Battle of Badon Hill.[56]

The *draco* is sometimes suggested as the origin of the Welsh dragon (and is probably the origin of the mysterious so-called s-dragon symbol that appears on some Pictish stones). Another possible influence on the origins of the Welsh dragon is the crouching gryphons that sometimes appear on Dobunni belt fittings. Their posture is very similar to that of the Welsh dragon.

Before going any further through the archaeological evidence of the period, we should take a more detailed look at the historical sources for Arthur and the period.

Chapter 3

The Sources: The *Historia Brittonum* and Arthur

The earliest account of Arthur's career is found in a mysterious book known as the *Historia Brittonum* – the History of the Britons. In this, we are told that in the second generation after the Saxon invasion, Arthur, alongside the kings of the Britons, fought against the Saxons. He was victorious in twelve battles, culminating in the Battle of Badon Hill, in which he overthrew 960 men in a single charge.[1]

The locations of the battles are by no means obvious, and we shall look at them in detail later in the book. There are battles on rivers, on hills and in a forest. One is fought in the City of the Legion. Another is in the Fort of Guinnion, where, we are told, Arthur carried the image of the Virgin Mary on his shoulders and by her power and the power of Jesus Christ, he was able to put the pagans to flight and inflict great slaughter upon them.[2]

It is worth noting that some of the battle sites are very similar to the locations where Gildas said the Britons had held out: high fortified hills, dense forests and the cliffs of the coast.

Arthur's status is not clear. He fought with the kings of the Britons, but he was the 'leader of battles': *dux bellorum*. Late accounts would be certain that Arthur led the other kings of the Britons, that he was some kind of king of kings. This was the firm view of late medieval stories like the *Le Morte d'Arthur*, where kings and the sons of kings sit at Arthur's Round Table. In

Historia Brittonum, just before Arthur, Ambrosius ruled as king or great king among the kings of the British people.[3] After Arthur, Mailcunus, king of North Wales, rules as 'great king among the Britons',[4] so it is a concept with which the writer is familiar. The fact that he does not say Arthur is such a king may well be significant. In the rest of *Historia Brittonum*, the title *dux*[5] is used to mean only one thing – a Roman general. It is even used similarly elsewhere, in contrast with the 'kings' of the Britons. It is most reasonable to suppose the writer means something similar here, that Arthur is a general working for, or with, the kings of the Britons in a way analogous to that of late Roman military commanders.

Beyond this, we enter a realm of mystery and speculation. We do not know who wrote *Historia Brittonum*, or when or why. We do not know what most of his sources were.

It is incredibly rare for written works of the ancient and medieval world to survive in manuscripts of their own time. The letters from Vindolanda, on Hadrian's Wall, or papyruses from Egypt are extremely unusual exceptions. Far more often, ancient sources, whether the Commentaries of Julius Caesar, the New Testament or the works of Bede, only survive in manuscripts from many years, often centuries, after the time they were composed. In the intervening period, the works have been copied from one manuscript to another, usually by Christian clerics, usually monks. The possibility for error, addition and deliberate omission is always present. This means that historians must invariably look beyond the physical manuscripts and at the texts they contain for clues as to their origin, provenance, and content.

Some of the sources we use from this period exist in single manuscripts, others in manuscripts more or less faithfully copied from originals. This is not the case with *Historia Brittonum*. There are over forty surviving manuscripts, and the differences between them are often quite significant. The work is not a single narrative but consists of chapters of very marked differences, genealogies, lists, lives of saints, chronological calculations and passages which sound like folktales. This meant it was easy for a scribe to insert or leave out material or rewrite passages for consistency. The manuscripts can be grouped into five families or 'recensions' derived from particular versions. There has been much scholarly debate over what the 'original' text would have contained. Some argue that the fullest version is the 'The Harleian Recension', found in the oldest surviving manuscript. This was named after the famous eighteenth-century collector, Edward Harley, Earl of Oxford, after whom Harley Street in London is also named. The library he and his father built forms one of the founding collections of the British Library, adding to the prestige and accessibility of the manuscript. On this assessment, the other recensions would be more stripped down and edited versions, removing material only of interest to its original writer and his patron. Other scholars argue the exact reverse, that only the material common to all the recensions can be derived from the original version to which scribes at different times and places have added material of interest to them and their patrons. In this case, the Harleian would represent the extreme outgrowth of this tendency, with much material not found elsewhere. And, not surprisingly, there are intermediate theories, with the original text composed of material now found variously among the recensions.

Fortunately, this is not a major issue for us, as the Arthurian battle list exists in all the recensions but one. And that outlier is just a single incomplete manuscript which breaks off before it reaches the point where Arthur would be found. Furthermore, there is only one major discrepancy – whether the eleventh battle was fought on a hill called Agned or a place called Breguoin/Bregion/Bregomion. Other material from *Historia Brittonum* that can be used to contextualize and compare the Arthurian battle list does, however, vary to a greater or lesser degree from recension to recension.

Later in the book, we shall consider possible locations for Arthur's battles. The first thing to note is that, unlike most place names in *Historia Brittonum*, those on the list are by and large opaque, not important locations when it was written. Only one of them, the City of the Legion, seems an important location. Gildas had said that two early Christian martyrs had been citizens of the City of the Legions[6] and that the place of their martyrdom was now cut off from the Britons by the division of the island with the Saxons. Bede had described a sixth-century battle at Chester, which he says was called the City of the Legions in Latin (using a slightly different form than Gildas or *Historia Brittonum*), and that the British called it 'Carlegion'.[7] Bede's battle is a great defeat of the Britons, and the argument that some historians make that it is this very battle which has been misplaced into the Arthurian list seems very unlikely. However, by the time *Historia Brittonum* was written, another Welsh town was also being called the City of the Legion, Caerleon in Gwent. Another obvious battle location is 'the wood of Celidon'.[8] Caledonia had been a name the Romans had applied to Britain north of their walls, effectively modern-day Scotland.

These two battle locations alone should be enough to demonstrate that the list is intended to be read as referring to widespread campaigns rather than a localized defence. A city of the legion, no matter where, could hardly be near a Caledonian wood, explicitly an area outside of Roman control. The frame the writer gives (the son of Hengest, leader of the first Saxon settlement, coming down from the north of Britain to found the kingdom of the men of Kent) gives a sweep of the length of the country, but again one where the city of the legion at least is not in either the beginning or the end location.

The context *Historia Brittonum* gives to Arthur is important. The history covers a very broad sweep of time. It begins with the arrival of the Britons, the ancestors of the modern-day Welsh, in the aftermath of the Trojan War. The island is named after their leader, Brutus or Britto, who is linked both to the illustrious Trojans and to the founders of Roman Britain. The Britons arrive before even the foundation of the Kingdom of Israel, in the early first millennium BC. The English, by contrast, are very recent arrivals. The latest event covered seems to be the death of Ecgfrid (Ecgfrith King of Northumbria[9]) dated by Bede to 685.[10] This nearly 1,700-year span is, however, misleading. Half of *Historia Brittonum*, and the most narratively detailed sections of its content, deal with Britain in the fifth century. It is in this context, at that time,[11] that the Arthurian section is placed, synchronized with the generation of the son of the first Saxon leader Hengest and before the next event dateable from Bede, the arrival of Ida, founder of the Northumbrian Angles royal dynasty, in 547.[12]

The overwhelming importance to the writer of these 100 years clearly signals his intention. This is the watershed between the time when Britons dominated the majority of the Island of Britain, albeit sometimes under the rule of the Romans, and the time when the majority of the island was ruled by Angles and Saxons. By the ninth century, Britons were confined to the peninsulas of the west, Wales, Devon and Cornwall and parts of the North West. In Bede's *Ecclesiastical History of the English People*, the Angles and Saxons are God's chosen people, and the defeat of the Britons was an inevitable part of God's plan. He portrays the Britons as cowardly, traitorous and shirkers of their responsibility to bring Christianity to the heathens. *Historia Brittonum* denies this. The Britons share the same origin as the Romans, whose part in God's plan was clearly established. They were Christians centuries before the Angles and Saxons appeared on the scene. Vortigern, the leader who first invited the Saxons to settle in Britain, might have been a bad apple, duped by lust, but it was Saxon treachery at a peace conference which proved his undoing. Far from neglecting their missionary duty, the Britons had provided St. Patrick, who had brought the whole of Ireland to Christianity, and many miracles besides. Most importantly, the Britons had fought back, and they had been victorious. Vortigern's son Vortimer had fought and beaten the enemy in four battles, but he was followed by Arthur, who defeated them in twelve.

At the Battle ofBadon Hill, *Historia Brittonum* says Arthur overthrew 960 men in a single charge 'and no-one laid them low save he alone'.[13] Many historians see this, and by extension, the rest of the Arthurian battle list as mythological in its hyperbole, and thus unworthy of consideration. This is supposed to set up Arthur as a mythical superman who could destroy whole armies in single combat. Even given the tendency for exaggeration by Dark Ages writers, this may not be how the author intended it to be read. It was commonplace, then as now, to ascribe the feats of an army to its commander. The *Anglo-Saxon Chronicle*, if read literally, says that in 508, the West Saxons 'Cerdic and Cynric slew a Welsh king, whose name was Natanleod and five thousand men with him'.[14] This is, of course, around the same 'legendary' time as the Arthurian battles. But the battles in the *Anglo-Saxon Chronicle* after the time of the composition of *Historia Brittonum* continue to be described in the same way: in 833 'King Egbert fought against twenty-five ships' companies at Carhampton, and great slaughter was made there'.[15] If Arthur was leading a charge in which 960 Saxons were overthrown, the claim is modest compared with the totals ascribed to the Saxon leaders. If we look at the report of Badon Hill in context, it is clear that the statement 'no one overthrew them save himself alone' is not meant to exclude Arthur's troops (they have never been mentioned) but his partners, the kings of the Britons. In previous battles, they had fought together, but in this final charge of the last battle, the glory went to Arthur alone.

The fact that Arthur fights alongside the kings of the Britons is another indication that the battles are widespread rather than localized. This raises a question which will be crucial to our analysis of the period, and which we have already considered to some extent, but about which we know little from the written records: Britain had long had different tribes, *civitates* and provinces but when did it fragment into several kingdoms?

As Gildas presents it,[16] there was one single Proud Tyrant, albeit aided by a council, who allowed the Saxons to settle in the eastern part of Britain. No mention is made by Gildas, of his tribal or *civitas* origins, but it is clear this figure is seen by him as having some kind of broad power. The tyrant settles the Saxons as a response to attacks from the Picts (from the North) and the Scots (from the West). That his authority extends over a significant part of Britain is confirmed when the Saxons revolt over disputes about supplies, and ravage from shore to shore, laying low all the *coloniae*.[17] One of those would have been Gloucester. They hold other Britons, not just those in their immediate area of settlement, responsible. The rally under Ambrosius involved survivors 'from all directions'.[18]

Historia Brittonum tells more or less the same story. There is one tyrant, Vortigern, who can settle Saxons in Thanet and the rest of Kent but in times of trouble can retreat to the 'farthest borders of his kingdom', in Gwynedd.[19]

However, by the time Gildas writes,[20] there are more than five tyrants (he directly addresses five but indicates others exist). One of those, Vortiporius, is explicitly assigned to a region, Dyfed,[21] another, Constantine, is connected to Devon and Cornwall[22] and later tradition, exemplified by *Historia Brittonum*,[23] located Maglocunus in Gwynedd.

This fragmentation was based on existing tribal divisions, but the creation of a specific set of separate kingdoms must have occurred in quite a short space of time. Gildas's chronology of the revolt stretches over four generations. Ambrosius's parents were killed in it and some people witnessed both the revolt and the rally under Ambrosius. Ambrosius's grandchildren are contemporaries of Gildas. In the intervening generation 'kings, public [officials] and private persons … kept to their own stations'.[24] One of these good kings was the father of the tyrant Vortiporius. This is very much the scenario *Historia Brittonum* suggests too, after the revolt there are multiple 'kings of the Britons', all united in a purpose, with a public official, a dux/Roman-style general also keeping in his proper station.

Historia Brittonum gives one more indication of the fragmentation. After the death of Vortigern, his surviving son Pascent is allowed to rule the countries of Builth and Gwerthrynion by permission of Ambrosius, king (some recensions clarify 'Great King')[25] among the kings of the British nation. A genealogy of Pascent and his descendants down to the writer's contemporary 'Fernmail, who now rules'[26] suggests that either Pascent or his son Briacat are among the 'kings of the Britons' fighting alongside Arthur.

Presumably the writer of *Historia Btittonum* is thinking of a similar situation he has found in Muirchu's *Life of St. Patrick*, possibly an eighth-century work, summarized between the Pascent material and the Arthurian battle list. In this, the saint encounters various regional kings of the Irish, but also a single High King who has a higher status than them.

Another piece of evidence that this is the model the writer is using comes earlier in the book. He frames his narrative of Vortigern and the arrival of the Saxons within a hagiography of St. Germanus. Indeed 'the book of the Blessed Germanus' is the only source text he specifically cites.[27] Before his encounter with Vortigern, Germanus encounters a wicked king, a strong tyrant, named Benli. The tyrant is destroyed by the saint and replaced with a faithful servant named Catel. 'All his sons were made kings and from their seed all the region of the Powys men are ruled up to today.'[28] The Germanus story is brought to its close immediately before the St. Patrick material, so we can presumably count the kings of Powys among Arthur's allies.

We are fortunate to have independent contemporary corroboration about two British kings from the fifth century. St. Patrick wrote a letter 'to the soldiers of Coroticus'.[29] He writes of Coroticus's tyranny and his temporal kingdom, indicating he is a king of some kind, as well as a military commander. His iniquitous acts have made him a companion to the Picts and the Scots (the Irish), indicating that he is a Briton. Muirchu's *Life of St. Patrick* clarifies this.[30] Later tradition would make Coroticus a king of Strathclyde. Patrick refuses to number the soldiers among his fellow citizens (the Britons) or as fellow citizens of the holy Romans, which perhaps suggest he is thinking of Coroticus being from a more Romanized part of Britain than this. Coroticus and his men have been attacking newly baptized Irish Christians and taking them as slaves.

Far away from Patrick, in 460 Sidonius Apollinaris, Bishop of Clermont in the south of France, wrote to a leader called Riothamus, complaining that his Britons, 'a crowd of noisy, armed and disorderly men'[31] were drawing away some of his friends' slaves to join them. As with Coroticus, we have to use a later source to confirm that Riothamus is a king of the Britons. This is provided by the sixth-century writer Jordanes, who explains that Riothamus had arrived two years earlier in the Loire valley with a large army of Britons coming in ships 'by way of the Ocean'.[32] They were driven south after a defeat by the king of the Visigoths. Gildas also tells us that, in the wake of the Saxon revolt, some of the Britons sailed to lands beyond the sea rather than be slaughtered or submit to the Saxons,[33] before Ambrosius organized the resistance.

As Gildas tells it, after the Saxon revolt, the Britons banded together under Ambrosius Aurelianus and challenged the Saxons to battle. 'From then on the victory went now to our countrymen, now to their enemies ... this lasted right up till the year of the siege of Badon Hill, pretty well the last defeat of the villains and certainly not the least.'[34]

Although the details are different, the basic framework of the Saxon wars in *Historia Brittonum* accords with that presented by Gildas and Bede. The area where it most differs is not that of naming Arthur, but how it presents Ambrosius. It says much more about Ambrosius than about Arthur. The author knows him both by his Latin name and as Embeis Guletic,[35] suggesting he featured in British tradition too. He appears as a fatherless child and as the son of one of the consuls of the Roman people, he is a native of Mais Elleti in Gleguissing, the region of South Wales between Gower and Gwent, he has prophetic powers and goes on to rule western Britain, being described as 'king among the kings of the British nation'.[36] Just about the only thing we are not told about him is that he rallied the British to fight against the Saxons. If we did not have Gildas's testimony that Ambrosius was an 'ordinary man'[37] of the Roman race responsible for the first phase of the resistance against the Saxons, he would almost certainly have been regarded by historians as a figure of myth or folklore. By contrast, the treatment of Arthur is much more sober.

Considered by itself, the picture *Historia Brittonum* paints is broadly in accordance with what we know from Gildas. The rally of the Britons under Ambrosius Aurelianus was followed then and in the next generation by Britons fighting against the Saxons, up to the Battle of Badon. According to Gildas it was a time when the kings of the Britons and public officials, which presumably includes military officers, kept to their stations. There is nothing particularly outlandish about Arthur fighting twelve battles, particularly as we don't know over what period of time the battles were fought or the scale of the battles, other than Badon. The *Anglo-Saxon Chronicle*, written in the ninth century, ascribed seven battles to a fifth- or sixth-century West Saxon leader, Cynric, including one with British casualties of 5,000, over a supposed career of sixty-one years, making the Arthurian battle list perhaps less exceptional. Something Gildas tells us, and which both the *Historia* and the *Chronicle* ignore, is that during the period both sides scored victories and the balance alternated between the Britons and the Saxons. Even so, we can wonder just how successful Arthur was, fighting four battles on the River Dubglas and another as far west as the City of the Legion is likely to be. There is, moreover, no evidence the author of *Historia Brittonum* or that of the *Annales* had read Gildas. You might think, therefore, that the existence of Arthur as a leader of the kings of Britons in this period was a relatively uncontentious proposition.

Far from it. Since the 1970s there has been a concerted academic effort to remove Arthur from the picture of fifth- and sixth-century Britain altogether, and to denigrate the sources that refer to him. The first, and possibly most significant, counter argument is that Gildas doesn't mention him. This was also seen as problematic in the Middle Ages when stories in which Arthur encountered Gildas were circulating. It was explained that a feud between Arthur and one of Gildas's brothers had caused the writer to remove Arthur from his account. In reality, this is very far from a convincing argument.

Granted, if Arthur's name had appeared in Gildas, there is no doubt he would be accepted as a historical figure, however many legends were later attached to him. The same, after all, happened to Ambrosius, linked in *Historia Brittonum* to a miraculous birth, hidden dragons and prophesy, yet accepted as a real historical individual. The converse, however, is simply not the case.

There are countless real characters who are either unnamed or completely unmentioned by Gildas. These would include the usurper Constantine III, who oversaw the end of Roman rule in Britain, St. Germanus, the child, or children of Ambrosius, along with a plethora of mentioned but unnamed characters like the illustrious teacher of Maglocunus, the royal youths killed by Constantine, the good father of Vortiporius and so forth. In fact, only eight Britons are named in the whole of the book, three martyrs killed in the great persecution and five tyrant contemporaries of Gildas. No historical secular Britons are named at all by Gildas. Ambrosius, the exception who proves the rule, is specifically identified as, in some sense, a Roman, and fits conveniently into Gildas's scheme of the Britons alternately receiving help from and being rejected by Romans. Not being named by Gildas is hardly an argument for a character's non-existence.

Historians critical of the concept of Arthur as a war leader after the rally under Ambrosius grasp for alternative explanations. One is that the author has assigned battles of other commanders and aggrandizes the figure of Arthur. The famous Battle of Badon, from Gildas, is suggested as one. Gildas could be read as saying that Ambrosius himself led the fight back to the victory at Badon.[38] On the other hand, no medieval writer, not Bede nor the *Historia* nor any other author, whether they had heard of Arthur or not, attributed that battle to Ambrosius. Attention to Gildas's text makes it clear he thought the final victory came in the generation after Ambrosius, which is precisely as the first historian to use his work, Bede, interpreted it.

Another suspect battle is the one at the City of the Legion. Bede did know there was a battle at that location in about 603. It is also reported in the *Annales*. Bede is unequivocal that this battle was a catastrophic defeat for the Britons, with 1,200 casualties including a large number of monks praying for Christian victory. It seems extraordinary that the *Historia* would have ignored this and pretended it was a victory. It surely would have raised questions from any reader of Bede about the veracity of the rest of the account. It seems obvious that more than one battle might have been fought at the same location, and that the site of British resistance in the late fifth or early sixth century would need to be overcome by English armies of a later generation. In fact, for instance, the *Annales* does include a 'second battle of Badon' 150 years after the first one.

A parallel suggestion is that the battles are from legend or mythology, and not historical to any era. The Battle of the Wood of Celidon is likened to a medieval poem *Kat Godeu,* 'The Battle of the Trees', in which trees and shrubs are the actual participants and Arthur is mentioned obscurely in passing. Another earlier poem about Arthur's men, called *Pa Gur,* 'What man', says the mythological figure Manawidan, son of Llyr, was at Tryvruit (Tribuit).[39] In both these cases, the legendary material, even if connected, comes later – the famous war leader Arthur gathers other heroes to his ambit, a process which is evident throughout the Middle Ages.

Both the misplaced historical and mythological battle arguments fail to explain the majority of the battles, which are utterly obscure, not historical campaigns in search of a leader nor the subject of legendary tales. And neither explain the figure of Arthur himself. It is suggested that he too is a mythical superman, plucked from legend or association with mysterious landscape features, and given spurious historical life by the author of the *Historia,* who is then followed blindly by all later sources presenting him as a Saxon-fighter of the fifth or sixth centuries.[40]

There is no evidence for this whatsoever. There are no pre-existing references to a mythological Arthur.

Two reasons have been advanced for the *Historia* placing Arthur and his exploits in the narrative. Elsewhere, where characters like Catell and Pascent appear, it is to justify the positions of contemporary rulers. This is emphatically not the case with Arthur, who is not given a home base in the *Historia*, nor does he feature in genealogies. Instead, it is argued that the writer has an intention of telling the providential or God-directed history of the Britons, which requires such a figure at this point. Just as Patrick is likened to Moses, so, like Moses in the bible, he must be followed by a war leader analogous to the biblical Joshua.[41] It is not clear why this is not made explicit if it is the author's intention – he gave 'four ways Patrick is like Moses' – nor is the analogy carried through to any of the details of Arthur's campaigns. Joshua is not a defender but a conqueror of a hostile land, he is not associated with twelve battles. Key features of his campaigns, like bringing down the walls of Jericho, are not referenced. The two exploits of Arthur carrying the image of the Virgin Mary and overthrowing 960 men have no parallel. Joshua is once called '*Dux Belli*', 'Leader of War', in the Book of Judges, reminiscent of the description of Arthur as '*Dux Bellorum*', 'Leader of Battles', but that is all. The *Historia* was aware that Joshua's usual title '*Iudex*', 'Judge', had been in use as a synonym for British kings in the past, and indeed Gildas seems to use it in that way too. So why would he not use it for a Joshua-like Arthur? If Arthur is like any Biblical figure, it is Judas Maccabeus, or indeed the Judges or kings of Israel and Judah. When Gildas was looking for biblical analogues to the Saxon invasion, he likens the Saxons to the Assyrians, and compares a good king of the Britons, the father of Vortiporius, with Hezekiah,[42] who fought against them.

Slightly more convincing than the very strained Moses–Joshua argument is the idea that the *Historia* needed to support its overarching contention that the Britons were guided by God. They had worked to convert pagans and heretics and had resisted valiantly the attacks of the Saxons. Lapses had been the result of a few bad apples like Vortigern, not, as Bede would have it, a whole people who showed themselves unworthy of God's protection. Thus, the account of Vortigern's folly and sin is mitigated by the character of his son Vortimer, fighting four victorious battles against the revolting Saxons. Perhaps Arthur was invented by the *Historia* to plug a similar gap; although the resistance is initiated by the 'Last of the Romans' Ambrosius, the victories are won by the British Arthur. An inconvenient Roman leader would hardly prove the point that God worked through the Britons or that they had responded militarily to the Saxon invasions.

Unfortunately for this argument, the *Historia* does not support a clear distinction between a Roman Ambrosius and a British Arthur. Although Ambrosius claims his father was a consul of the Roman Race[43] (consul is one of the *Historia*'s words for emperor), this is no more than a nod to Bede's 'of royal and famous name'.[44] The author does everything he can to anchor Ambrosius's identity as a Briton. Despite Ambrosius's claim to Roman blood, this is contradicted earlier in the story when he is presented as the product of a virgin birth to a British woman, that he is a native of Maes Elleti in Glywyssing, he is a 'king among the kings of the Britons' and that he has a British name 'Embreis Guledig'. The author, in short, seems to bend over backwards to avoid the implication that Ambrosius is a Roman, in contrast to

Gildas and Bede who are explicit that he, in some sense, is. On the contrary, he is fairly explicit that Ambrosius isn't. We are told that Vortigern is under pressure from fear of the Picts, the Scots and the Romans, and also from fear of Ambrosius, as though those are four distinct categories of enemy.

On the other hand, it is not clear at all that Arthur is a Briton. He has no geographical origin – he is not Arthur of anywhere, nor is he linked genealogically to any kingdom. Far from concluding that his 'Celtic' name made it obvious he was a Briton, a contemporary reader might just as easily have concluded that he was an Irishman. All the other Dark-Age men we know of called Arthur were Irish or of Irish extraction. The first known to history, from the sixth century, is Arthur, son of Aedan Mac Gabran of Dal Riada, mentioned in the seventh-century *Life of Saint Columba*.[45] Bede describes his father as 'King of all the Scots [Irish] living in Britain'. The next, featuring first in the Harleian Genealogies, is Arthur map Petr of Dyfed, presented as a great-grandson of Gildas's Vortiporius. Dyfed was heavily settled by the Irish and its ruling dynasty was presented in Irish sources as having been expelled from Ireland. Possibly the opening, 'Then Arthur fought against them in those days with the Kings of the Britons' was intended to signal that he was not, in fact, a Briton himself. The reality of Irish settlers in some British areas is not in doubt. Fifth-century Irishmen have memorials among the Romano-British of Wroxeter[46] and Silchester,[47] impeccable locations for potential 'Kings of the Britons' resisting the Saxons. Furthermore, *Historia* described Arthur as '*Dux Bellorum*',[48] when *Dux* had only previously been used in the book to describe Roman generals. It might have led a reader to assume that, while Ambrosius was British, a king among the kings of the Britons, the next commander, Arthur, was a Roman. In reality, the Roman generals of the fifth century were, more often than not, drawn from warlike barbarian tribes rather than being native Romans. Some had been mentioned elsewhere in *Historia Brittonum* and Hengest is shown playing exactly this role for Vortigern in his war against the Picts and Scots. Far from a British figure invented or plucked from elsewhere to demonstrate the providential role of the Britons (unnecessary as Ambrosius has been furnished with British credentials), it is quite possible Arthur is being presented as a barbarian, Irish military commander in Roman style.

It was equally unnecessary to invent a British Arthur because the kings of the Britons were also included as those fighting the Saxons. There undoubtedly were kings of the Britons at the time, and likely their names were remembered by their people. Many names of supposedly fifth- or sixth-century kings of the Britons were recorded in genealogies in the tenth century, and two, Pascent and Briacat, are already recorded in a genealogy in the *Historia*. Either of them could have been used as a convenient 'British leader of Battles', just as Pascent's brothers Vortimer and Categirn were used earlier if the writer had needed them. The only convincing reason for the *Historia* using the name of Arthur as that of the military commander is that pre-existing traditions had already placed him in that position.

Which brings us back to the fundamental question of when *Historia Brittonum* was written, and what were its sources.

Exactly when *Historia Brittonum* was written is not clear. It refers to 'The fourth year of King Mermin'[49] as if that is the present. This character, known in modern Welsh as Merfyn 'Ffrych' (The Freckled) ruled in North Wales from the 820s to the 840s. Another calculation seems to place the present as AD 859. A ruler described as 'ruling now' is given a family tree showing him to be in the twelfth generation (say 360 years) after the mid-fifth century. A preface found in some manuscripts describes the writer as 'a disciple of Saint Elbodugus',[50] a figure recorded elsewhere as dying around 809.[51] It seems safe to conclude that *Historia Brittonum* was composed in the early ninth century, a context we shall examine later.

We should set aside immediately any idea that the writer of *Historia Brittonum*is is simply a fiction writer, making up material to suit his purpose. Not only is that an exceedingly rare activity in the ninth century, but it is also readily apparent that he is constrained by many pre-existing sources. One clear piece of evidence for this is the variety of different dating systems he uses. Some dates are given as AD, after the birth of Jesus. This is familiar to us, largely because it was the system pioneered by Bede. He used this throughout his *History*, even including a useful list of AD dates at the end. But this was a relatively new system and was not by any means the universal standard in the fifth, sixth or seventh centuries. *Historia Brittonum* gives examples from practically every rival system. There are dates 'After the Passion',[52] counting from the rather more securely dated year of Jesus's death. There are dates 'from the creation of the world',[53] using calculations from the Old Testament. Dates are attached to the nineteen-year cycle fundamental to calculations of the date of Easter.[54] Some 'dates' are given as calculations of intervals between them. Two pre-Christian dating systems are also used. One is the consular system, used in the Roman Empire for centuries. Every year two consuls were appointed, and the year thereafter is known by their two names. The date of the Passion (apparently) is given as 'The two Twins, Furius and Rubellius'.[55] The coming of the Saxons is given as 'When Gratian ruled for the second time with Eqitius' and as 'In the consulship of Felix and Taurus'. Finally, *Historia* also dates by regnal years, dating from the start of the reign of a particular ruler. Bede confirms this was standard among the Angles in his time. Many of the dates are contradictory, not helped by likely miscopying and attempts to harmonize and update them between different manuscript families and individual manuscripts. The Arthur section simply begins 'At that time …' referencing a character, the Saxon leader Hengest, last heard of ten paragraphs earlier.[56] The individual passages are also of very different types: There are prose narratives, interspersed with numbered lists, like Arthur's battles, and genealogies, with rather perfunctory links between them.

We can well suppose that a writer, unconstrained and following only their imagination or focusing on a single source, for instance, Bede's *History*, would have been able to avoid these inconsistencies. He could very easily have put positive glosses on Bede's material, and hung other material, like the Arthurian battles, on the already established framework of AD dates. The fact that he does not do this is a very strong indication that previously existing sources are the basis of his narrative. What might they be?

The preface identifying the writer as 'Nennius, disciple of St. Elbodugus' is the only place where a detailed description of the author's intentions and sources appears. As explained earlier, we do not know if this preface was part of the earliest manuscript, dropped out by certain recensions with no interest in Nennius or a desire to claim themselves or someone else as the author. Alternatively, it could have been added at a later point, to address the question of provenance, either with outside knowledge of the original author or just by doing what we are doing, speculating around the form and content of the different sections. The preface starts by criticizing his predecessors. He is writing down extracts 'that the stupidity of the British people had cast out, for the scholars of the Island of Britain … set down no record in books'.[57] This is not true. Bede himself, giving his sources as a combination of writings and traditions, specifically cites 'Gildas their own historian'.

The most frequent suggestion for the provenance of the battle list is that it is derived from a Welsh praise poem. Praise poems listing battles exist for various Welsh leaders, including some from the sixth and seventh centuries. We know for certain that such poets existed at the time, as Gildas castigates the tyrant Maglocunus for preferring not to hear the praises of God or melodious church music 'but the empty praises of yourself from the mouths of criminals who grate on the hearing like raving hucksters, mouths stuffed with lies and liable to bedew bystanders with their foaming phlegm'![58] Whether the surviving poems derive from contemporary material or indeed whether they predate the Arthurian battle list is a matter of debate. The praise poems themselves do not have much in common with the Arthurian list. None of them gives numbered battles, for instance, but they do include battles on hills, rivers, forests and so on.[59] One argument is that the reference to Arthur bearing the image of the Virgin Mary on his shoulders rests on a mistranslation of the Welsh *iscuit* (shield). Read as the very similar *iscuid* (shoulders).[60] This seems strange, as the writer of *Historia Brittonum*, presumably a native Welsh speaker, leaves Welsh versions of Latin names in his work, including in the list, and evidently saw nothing odd about the image being on Arthur's shoulders – a device on a shield to easily be described in this way. The same phrase 'on his shoulders' also occurs in the *Annales Cambriae*, referring to a cross carried by Arthur for three days at Badon, and continued to be used by writers through the Middle Ages. Of rather more significance is the fact that in Welsh, many of the battle names would rhyme. *Dublas* rhymes with *Bassas*, *Celidon* rhymes with *Guinnion*, *Legion* with that and with *Bregion*, if that is the correct reading of the eleventh battle, and *Badon* with them too. If *Yscuit* were the original word, it would rhyme with *Tribuit*. It is surely unlikely that the original names of a commander's battles all just happened to rhyme[61] – it seems probable that the rhyme is a mnemonic device, for argument's sake a poetic device, and a Welsh one at that.

By way of comparison, the praise poem for seventh-century king

Cadwallawn[62] assigns him fourteen battles in a military career which, based on Bede and *Annales Cambriae* must have lasted less than ten years, and we know ranged from locations in his native Gwynedd up to Bernicia, corresponding potentially to the spread of Arthur's battles from the City of the Legion to the mouth of the river Glein.

The Harleian recension of *Historia Brittonum*, which continues beyond the Arthurian battle list, tells us that at the time of Ida of Northumbria and Mailcun of Gwynedd (Gildas's Maglocunus) 'Talhaern Tataguen, was famous for his poetry and Neirin and Taliessin and Bluchbard and Cian, who is called Gueinth Guaut, were all at the same time famous in British Poetry'.[63]

Poems survive that are attributed to two of those poets, Taliesin and Neirin (Aneirin is the modern form of his name). These works do indeed touch on Arthur. Those attributed to Taliesin cover several centuries, by the language and the content. The earlier are in praise and lament for sixth century warriors and are indeed from exactly the context *Historia Brittonum* gives them, the sixth century, after the arrival of Ida in Bernicia. However, those which mention Arthur are demonstrably later works, and are much more mythological in theme, including the aforementioned one about battling trees.

Aneirin is different. The poem attributed to him, *The Gododdin*, commemorates warriors of the Gododdin tribe, from the area around Edinburgh, who have died fighting at Catraeth, assumed to be Catterick in Yorkshire. They have passed through a Bernicia as yet not under Angle control, so in the period Arthur's battle list is set, or just after. There is a later version of the poem and an earlier version, itself composed of earlier and later material. The mention of Arthur comes from the very earliest stratum and thus the poet's original work. One fallen warrior is described thus: 'He brought down black crows to feed before the wall / Of the city, though he was no Arthur'.[64]

Exactly why the poet made the comparison is not clear. It may be nothing other than the fact the warrior's name 'Guaurthur' rhymes with Arthur, but we are told that he was one of the mightiest of men, that he single-handedly slew 300 men, that he was extremely generous (Arthur would also be so described) and that he fought at a Roman city or fortification (the word in the original, *Cair*, means that).[65] These are traits that Arthur is given in the battle list – he fights Saxons coming from the north in the time before Bernicia fell to the

Angles, he is a mighty warrior killing three times three hundred adversaries, he fights at a Roman city and a fortification – some versions of the battle list even translate the City of the Legion with the same word *Cair*. The poet Aneirin knows no other material from *Historia Brittonum*, nor does *Historia Brittonum* know of the Gododdin expedition, but both sources know the same sort of things about their subject and, in the case of the poet, seem to know it in the late sixth century. One obvious way the poem reads is that Guarthur is a superlative warrior but just not as famous as Arthur. That Arthur is 'famous' literally goes without saying. The *Gododdin*, *Historia Brittonum*, the *Wonders of Britain* and *Annales Cambriae* all introduce him without ever troubling to explain who he is. It is also very possible that the poet is distinguishing Guarthur as an ordinary warrior rather than a leader. The only other place in *the Gododdin* where the poet uses the same comparison 'though he wasn't…' '*cen ne bei…*'[66] is to tell us that a fallen warrior's father 'wasn't a *Guledig*' – the high title used in *Historia Brittonum* for Ambrosius '(Great) King among the kings of the Britons.'[67]

The additional material in the Harleian Recension has been widely used by historians to determine its context. This is on the assumption that, because it is found in the oldest surviving manuscript, it is closest to the original. The Harleian follows the Arthurian battle list with a 'Northern History' which presents a direct alternative to Bede's version of the history of the Angles of Northumbria and stresses the important rule of the British ruler of Gwynedd. The dating of the present to 'The fourth year of King Mermin' directs the reader, too, to the context of the establishment of a new Gwynedd Dynasty under the king known as Merfyn Ffrych (Mervin the Freckled) and his desire to connect his rule to heroic leaders of the North Welsh past. If, however, this material is a later, next-generation, addition to the original text of the *Historia*, then its original context would be the rise and westward expansion of King Offa's Mercia. Mercia had been an ally of the kings of North Wales. In the later years of the eighth century, Offa of Mercia expanded his power, in particular pushing the frontier westward beyond the Severn Valley to the dyke which bears his name, and which substantially still forms the border of England and Wales. *Annales Cambriae* dates these wars to the 770s and 780s. The final fall of the kingdom of Powys, the British kingdom which had dominated the upper Severn Valley, fatally weakened by the loss of those eastern territories, is given as around 822. The *Historia*, of course, includes the origin myth of the kingdom of Powys and of its neighbour Buelt. It is surely likely that many of the locations linked to the British resistance in the fifth and early sixth century are ones which during this period ended up on the English side of this frontier, their identity lost to the Britons and submerged under English placenames.

The additional material is, however, extremely useful in expanding the picture we have of Arthur as a historical figure. Beyond the 'northern history' presented as part of *Historia Brittonum*, the other materials have their own characteristics, and some are also preserved elsewhere. The first is known as *Annales Cambriae*, the Annals of Wales, a list of events year by year, two of which mention Arthur. The next is a group of Welsh genealogies, the second of which includes the name 'Arthur'.[68] Comparison with the first (they concern the mother and father of a character, Ouein, dated by the preceding annals to the mid-tenth century) suggests that this Arthur is too recent to be ours if his place in the genealogies is correct. The genealogies are followed by a list of 'all the cities of all Britain',[69] twenty-eight of them, some of which reoccur in Arthurian contexts. Of possible importance to the battle list are two cities of the Legion, *Cair Legion* and *Cair Legeion guar usic*, the latter being Caerleon on Usk and the former, by elimination, Chester.

Finally, there is a list of the wonders of Britain, the *Mirabilia*. This concludes with a list of Irish wonders, but the first part deals with wonders primarily in Wales, with a focus on the south and east of Wales, the River Severn and its estuary. Two of these refer to Arthur. Their locations are explicit. The first is in the country of Buelt (Builth) where there is a pile of stones built by 'Arthur the Soldier',[70] called Carn Cabal. The topmost stone bears the footprint of Arthur's dog Cabal, made when he was hunting the boar Troynt. In Ercing, thirty-five miles away in modern Herefordshire, is the wonder of Licat Anir. This Anir was the son of Arthur the Soldier, who killed him and built a tomb there. The author of The Wonders has personally tried to measure the tomb and found it impossible to get the same measurement twice.[71] The son's name is usually 'corrected' to 'Amr',[72] forming an etymological connection to the Gamber River, as a spring, presumably the source of the river, rises beside the tomb.

The only other wonder connected to a named individual is a tomb in a church built by St. Illtud, fifty miles from the Arthurian wonders, on the Gower Peninsula. These wonders are the first clear indications of any sort of 'King Arthur's Country', but both seem connected with domestic activity, not with wars against invaders.

Although the wonders are accompanied by pieces of folklore, this gives no reason to doubt that Arthur was real, any more than that Illtud was a real Dark-Age cleric. Folklore and legend linked to real characters and events were very much in the idiom of historians of the period. The wonders attributed to Arthur are no more than would be expected from a writer in Dark-Age Britain. No one doubts Bede's account of the death of Oswald of Northumbria at the Battle of Maserfelthin in 642. But Bede devotes most of his account to describing wonders such as the cure of a sick horse which rolled onto the spot where Oswald was killed, or the man whose house burnt down except for the beam where his cloak, touched by the mud of the site, had hung.[73] Tombs of varying lengths were not considered impossible. The stone sarcophagus made for King Sebbi of the East Saxons was too short: 'as the bishop stood by, together with Sigeheard … the son of the royal monk as well as a large crowd of men, the sarcophagus was found to be of the right length to fit the body.'[74]

Paradoxically, the *Mirabilia* show how misguided the argument is that Arthur was a mythological super-being transformed by those writers into a mundane historical character. The *Mirabilia* are later than the battle list, not its source, and calls Arthur no more than a soldier and relates to mundane activities, killing his son and hunting, no matter the mysteriousness of the wonders themselves. The author of the *Historia*, just as much as Bede and the author of the *Mirabilia*, thought they lived in a world surrounded by wonders, both in the past and in the present. They did not feel any need to rationalize or explain away the wondrous to make their accounts 'more believable' as history. The writer of the *Historia* had just described two fifth-century tyrants destroyed by fire from heaven, mysterious fighting serpents unearthed by the power of prophecy from beneath a collapsing fortress, a bishop who had lived to 120, raised the dead, drove out demons and had blessed an innumerable flock of multicoloured birds,[75] before turning to Arthur the war leader. The author of the *Mirabilia* says he has personally tried and failed to measure the tomb of Arthur's son and tested a magical homing plank, as well as testifying to a nearby stone altar levitating off the ground.[76] The writer of the *Annales* faithfully recorded, from an Irish source, before he entered Badon, that Bishop Ebur had died aged 350.[77] It is inconceivable that any of the writers, faced with a mythological Arthur battling with animated trees or aided by a mighty folkloric ally, would have made such little use of the information. Arthur killed a large number of men in a single charge, but otherwise, his feats are unexceptional – carrying an image of Our Lady or a cross on his shoulders. Placing him in the late fifth century or early sixth century would be even more puzzling. The *Historia* covers the whole sweep of British history from the fall of Troy. A mythological character could have been placed anywhere in the text rather than in the already crowded fifth century.

Just about all the other characters in *Historia Brittonum*'s account of the fifth century are real people from that era, St. Germanus, St. Patrick, the Proud Tyrant and the first Saxon settlers (their names, Vortigern, Hengest and Horsa may, a sceptic might argue, be legendary, but the *Historia* takes their names and deeds primarily from the impeccable historian Bede). The one character aside from Arthur we cannot directly vouch for is Vortimer, but he hardly seems likely to be a figure of mythology. The most mythological material in the whole of this section, with a magical fatherless child, wizards and fighting serpents interpreted as prophetic dragons, is assigned to the perfectly historical figure of Ambrosius.

Before we turn to the next source, *Annales Cambriae*, we ought to mention a little about Arthurian dates. The battle list does not have a date beyond 'at that time', which may refer to the time of St. Patrick, which immediately precedes it, or the last time the Saxons were previously mentioned. It ends with a period of Saxon recuperation which lasts until the reign of Ida, first king of Bernicia. The Harleian Manuscript has more material about Bernicia, suggesting it placed the arrival of Ida shortly before 560.[78] Bede, writing earlier from Bernicia, dates it to 547.[79] The battle list is therefore set before those dates. What dates it comes after is more complex. *Historia Brittonum* has two different calculations for the coming of St. Patrick to Ireland, AD 405 and AD 438. In the section about Patrick, he says first that Patrick preached Christ to foreign nations for forty years, and then that he preached in Ireland for eighty-five years, meaning that if his 'at that time' for Arthur is connected to Patrick, we have a range of 445, 478, 490 or 518 for his intended date. If, on the other hand, we infer Arthur's 'at that time' is connected to the arrival of the Saxons, *Historia Brittonum* provides us with a plethora of dates for that event, and Bede and the *Anglo-Saxon Chronicle* give others.

Firstly, Gildas places the arrival of the Saxons after a desperate plea from the Britons to a man of Roman power on the continent, called Agitius, whom they address as 'consul for the third time'.[80] This is usually taken to be the Roman military commander Aetius, who was consul for the third time in 446. Bede took the arrival of the first Saxons as happening between three and ten years after this. Gildas then gives a date involving the Battle of Badon Hill. Some have argued he is dating Badon as happening forty-four years before his time. Bede took him as saying the Battle of Badon had happened forty-four years after the Saxons arrived, thus between 493 and 500. However, the probable meaning of the original text is that Gildas was dating Badon forty-four years and one month after the victory by Ambrosius and that he, Gildas, was also born at that time.

On the other hand, a late fifth-century source, *The Life of St. Germanus* by Constantius of Lyon (a neighbour and contemporary of Sidonius Apollinaris), records a visit by St. Germanus to Britain. His mission was to confront British heretics, but he also encounters an attack by Picts and Saxons.[81] There are no actual dates in this source, and Bede incorporated the details after his own account of the arrival of the Saxons. *Historia Brittonum*, as mentioned, makes use of a book of the Blessed Germanus to have the saint encounter Vortigern. However, *Historia Brittonum* has also discovered that Germanus visited Britain in 429 and provides earlier dates for Vortigern and the arrival of the Saxons which harmonize with this, giving dates twenty years earlier than those of Bede. *The Life of St. Patrick* also connects St. Germanus's mission with Patrick. Two Gallic chronicles, preserved in manuscripts contemporary with the *Historia Brittonum*, also opt for the earlier date of 441 for the Saxon takeover of Britain.[82]

There is really nothing to be said for these competing dates. Gildas may be wrong about the circumstances of the appeal to Aetius, Constantius may be wrong in placing the Saxons he and Sidonius were aware of in their own time as invaders of Britain decades before (when according to Gildas it was Picts and *Scots* who were invading). Only Bede adopts and uses consistently a single dating system, the AD dates we are familiar with. All the other writers use different systems and discrepancies creep in because of it. *Historia Brittonum*, for instance, makes use of After the Passion (the death of Jesus) dates, an event the AD system places in AD 33. (Although the After the Passion system places this event in about year AD 29.) This approximately thirty-year discrepancy is a constant possibility with any dates given. For example, *Historia Brittonum* says the fourth year of Vortigern's reign was in the Consulship of Felix and Taurus 'the 400th year from the *Incarnation* of Jesus',[83] that is AD 400, when in fact the consulship is in AD 428–429 and the '400th year' must therefore relate to the Passion.

It is exceedingly rare in this period to be able to date archaeological sites and finds anywhere near twenty-nine years or even fifty years of each other, meaning we are very unlikely to be able to pin down Arthurian dates with any certainty. Archaeologists working on Roman sites in Britain are used to having the evidence of coinage to work with. As long as the coins are undisturbed, we know that anything deposited above them must be later than the date the coins were minted. Coins are effectively small inscriptions securely dated to a particular emperor. This is supplemented by inscriptions which may also carry a date or datable material. None of the British rulers of the early Dark Ages issued their own coins. Although we know coins were in use (we are told so by both Gildas and Patrick) they must have been very old ones, primarily from the last time garrisons in Britain were paid. We can see this moment archaeologically. In AD 403 the mint of Rome produced a bronze coin with the inscription *VRBS ROMA FELIX*, 'Happy City of Rome'. Essentially, this issue never reached Britain.[84] It is hardly surprising that the non-arrival of the 403 coinage was quickly followed by a succession of revolts over the next six years. Later coins did make their way to Britain, including one dated 480–93, but on nothing like the scale to suggest regular shipments.

Another convenient dating tool for archaeologists is the pottery sequence. Changing tastes in design and manufacture can be traced through the incredibly durable medium of pottery fragments. Sequences can be constructed and, better still, cross-referenced with other contemporary finds, particularly coins. This is the reason for the huge significance of so-called Tintagel ware (after its main find spot in Britain). This pottery can be dated precisely because it originates from the Eastern Mediterranean, where it is found in association with coins and other datable evidence from the Eastern Roman Empire. That these fragments include ones from storage containers for relatively perishable imports like wine and olive oil means we can be reasonably clear its appearance in Britain is indicative of activity within its range of 450–530 or 475–550. These are still obviously very broad ranges of time and not ideal for the fine dating a historian would like.

It seems clear too, that although the date of a coin can establish the time it was minted, it cannot date the time it was deposited. A clumsy modern coin dealer could drop an AD 403 Roman coin, but it would only prove that his shop had been built after that time if discovered by a future archaeologist, not that the shop was a Roman building. This can be proved archaeologically. By comparing the latest dated coins in deposits of Late Roman coins in Britain with the other coins in the same context, it has been established that a coin minted in the fourth century was on average over forty-three years old when deposited. These old, reused coins compound the difficulty of dating when a coin from the 390s could easily be found in the context of the 430s.

Radiocarbon dates, typically accurate to plus or minus eighty years, are very useful for identifying, if there is doubt, whether remains which can be dated are from the Iron Age or the late Anglo-Saxon period but are of no use at all in determining whether Saxons arrived in the 420s or the 450s.

All this means that archaeologists often fall back on dates derived from history (not all of which themselves are necessarily well-founded), such as dating 'Roman' remains to before the 'End of Roman Rule' in 410 (a reasonably secure date for the end of Roman rule, but not for the end of Roman culture) or Saxon remains to 'After the arrival of the Saxons' in 449 (not a particularly accurate date for the arrival of the Saxons or their cultural items).

We have digressed to look at these dates because we are about to encounter some more. In the Harleian Manuscript, the *Historia Brittonum* is immediately followed by a list of years. These are known for convenience as 'The Annals of Wales', *Annales Cambriae*. These are marked out in three columns, each line starting with the abbreviation 'An' for '*Annus*', 'Year'. Decades are marked with

Roman numerals. The page starts with 'From the year the English came to Britain and were welcomed by Vortigern to Decius and Valerian are sixty-nine years'[85] as if this marks the start of the sequence, but there is no Consulship of Decius and Valerian (Decius was consul in 486 and 529, Valerian in 521,) while previous calculations suggest the author was thinking of a date around 497. None of these dates seem connected with the start of the Annals, which are therefore usually considered alone. The first entry, in year nine, is that 'Easter was altered on the lord's day by Pope Leo, Bishop of Rome'.[86] This seems to refer to a circular letter from the Pope dated 453, which will serve as a convenient marker for the time being.

The first two columns deal, sparsely, with the births and deaths of Irish ecclesiastics. The death of St. Patrick is recorded in year 13 (457) for instance. These continue into the third column, with the birth of St. Columba and the death of St. Brigit in year 77 (521). This framework, unsurprisingly given its contents, derives from the Ulster Annals, perhaps contemporary with *Historia Brittonum*, but in this case, continues into the mid-tenth century. Of vital importance to us, however, are the two entries on either side of that relating to St. Columba, for they both concern Arthur. It is worth noting how significant this is. Arthur is the only secular figure referred to in the first hundred years of the annals. No other material from *Historia Brittonum* is included here (St. Patrick is from the Ulster source, not the *Historia*). The information is thus independent of the *Historia*, despite appearing in the same manuscript. The first is in Year 72 (516) 'The battle of Badon, in which Arthur carried the cross of Our Lord Jesus Christ for three days and three nights on his shoulders, and the Britons were victorious'.[87] This corroborates *Historia Brittonum*'s attribution of the victory at Badon to Arthur, and is reminiscent of the idea of Arthur carrying a Christian symbol or object 'on his shoulders' at Castellum Guinnion, but if it were merely copied from the *Historia*, it is odd it does not include the details from it. Or indeed record the Castellum Guinnion battle separately. There are, after all, eight completely blank years in the column immediately above it, to fit in other battles. Interestingly, the three days of the battle remind us that Gildas had referred to Badon as a siege.

Even if there were some connections between the Badon entry and the battle list, the next entry, in year 93 (537) is completely new material. '*Gueith*

Camlann in which Arthur and Medraut were slain and there was a plague in Britain and Ireland'.[88] *Gueith* is a Welsh word meaning 'strife' and is used elsewhere in the *Annales* to mean battle. For instance, Bede's Battle of Chester appears as '*Gueith Cair Legion*'.[89] Unlike the other battles, Camlann retained a presence in Welsh tradition.

There are two further entries in the *Annales* which may be significant. Ten years after Camlann is a great plague in which Mailcun, king of Gwynedd (Gildas's Tyrant Maglocunus) dies. This is only thirty-one years after Badon, which contradicts the reading of Gildas's book suggesting that the writer and Maglocunus are both alive forty-four years after the battle. However, the annals entry is simply a result of substituting the original victim of the great plague in the Ulster Annals (*Finn mac Telduib*) with Mailcun and may mean nothing more than the knowledge the tyrant died in a plague. Twenty-three years later (570), the death of Gildas himself is recorded.

Fifty-nine years after the death of St. Patrick seems rather long for the 'at that time' of Arthur's campaigns culminating in Badon. We do not know how the compiler synchronized the Arthurian dates with the Ulster material. Nor can we be sure where the chronology is intended to be anchored. For example, the Battle of Chester (year 169) is ten years later than we would expect it to be from Bede, who dates it to 603. If that 'Gueith Cair Legion' is connected, then possibly Badon is intended to be in 506 and Camlann in 527. And there are plenty of other adjustments which could be made if we had any reason to know any of the dates with certainty.

Welsh tradition is fairly agreed that Medraut and Arthur were adversaries at Arthur's final Battle of Camlann. Civil wars among the Britons are endemic when Gildas writes. The idea that Arthur was involved in wars with other Britons becomes commonplace, as we shall see. One of the wonders concerns Arthur killing his son. Gildas is explicit that some of the British civil wars are between close relatives. He also accuses contemporary tyrants of setting aside their first wives, which could point to reasons for rifts with their children.

Historia Brittonum presents a convincing picture of Arthur as a British war leader of the late fifth or early sixth centuries, with at least some of his activities on or beyond the eastern borders of modern Wales. Other early sources, the Wonders, the *Annales* and the *Gododdin* also give material which harmonizes with this. There is nothing intrinsically implausible about this and nothing whatsoever to make us think Arthur is a figure from a different context, historical or mythical, misplaced to this time and place. We shall therefore be including consideration of the material from these first sources to refer to Arthur as we examine the rest of the evidence for Britain in this period.

Chapter 4

The Sources: Gildas and The Destruction of Britain

Alongside the tantalizing glimpses offered by written sources from some centuries later, and the small amount of archaeological evidence available, we do possess one invaluable source from Britain at the time which illuminates what 'King Arthur's Country' was really like.

This is the work of Gildas. Gildas identified himself as a cleric who was neither a bishop nor a priest.[1] Documents and quotations attributed to him on monastic practice,[2] and later accounts of his life make it reasonably clear he meant that he was a monk. He says he was born in the year of the siege of Badon Hill,[3] the battle *Historia Brittonum* described as Arthur's culminating victory. Although Gildas considered himself unworthy of the role and says he had wrestled with himself for ten years over it,[4] he now set himself the task of an Old Testament prophet. He believed he was watching the imminent destruction of his country. He could discern how this had come about and he now had the means to divert it. So, he composed a book we know as *De Excidio Britanniae*, 'On the Destruction of Britain'. Britain was beset by enemies, of whom he reckoned the worst were the pagan Saxons, comparatively recently settled in the eastern part of the Island, from where they had previously spread death and destruction from sea to sea. Although a British rally in the previous two generations had managed to defeat the Saxons, the siege of Badon Hill being one of the last and one of the greatest victories over them, their threat remained. Instead of maintaining unity, readiness and, above all, devotion to the Christian faith, the British leaders had turned inward. Civil war was endemic, vice ubiquitous, the lessons learned at such cost by their fathers and grandfathers forgotten.

Now Gildas set out to admonish his contemporaries, religious and secular, named and unnamed, for not only ignoring the imminent destruction of Britain but by their actions actively hastening it. As well as direct denunciation and prophetic warning to his contemporaries, Gildas also devotes some time to explaining how Britain has arrived at this position. His view of history, based on his close study of the Bible, was that there were cycles. When patterns, either in the time of the ancient Israelites or in the recent history of the Britons, God's 'Latter-day Israel',[5] repeated themselves, it was clear what the future must hold.

When the Israelites turned from God and fell into sin and civil war, God had warned them through his prophets. When they did not heed the message of these holy men, God had sent a fierce warlike pagan menace from the east, the Assyrians, who had ravaged to the western sea, destroying the northern kingdom, Israel itself. Gildas is explicit. The Saxons are the Assyrians,[6] the Britons are the Israelites. The southern kingdom, Judah, was given a respite, it was given more warnings, it ignored them too. The result was the conquest of the Holy Land by the Babylonians, the enslavement of the Jews. The analogy was quite clear to Gildas. His country was poised between calamities and only wholesale repentance by the leaders of Britain could avert its final destruction.

Gildas was sure that British history itself revealed this message too. He presented a broad narrative from pagan pre-Roman antiquity, up to the present day. Surely it had been characterized by the same cycles, times of degeneration, followed by divine admonitions, plagues, invasions and the like. The Britons, like the Israelites, had doubtless turned to mighty foreign powers for help, sometimes temporarily successful. But only when they turned to God, united, and standing up for themselves had they truly been victorious.

Gildas did see part of his work as being that of a historian. Bede, the historian of the Anglo-Saxons, recognized Gildas as his British counterpart and made use of his book.[7] Like any good historian, Gildas examined trends and patterns as well as individual episodes. Family trees, year by year chronologies and the founding of individual kingdoms did not interest him, meaning that his work reads very differently from the other sources we are considering. Some things he undoubtedly did know, names in particular, he does not include, probably in part to make the analogy stand out better.

Unfortunately, his history does contain errors. He confesses he does not have access to any British historical materials, which he thinks were meagre anyway, but are now either destroyed or taken abroad by exiles. His guide to what 'must have happened' is scripture, church history from the continent and the situation among his contemporaries in Britain. His view of what happened to end Roman rule over the island and what occurred in the century or so which followed is, in places, distorted.

He presents the Romans as all-powerful conquerors who had 'won the rule of the world'[8] before turning their attention to the subjugation of remote Britain but sees them as always remaining an essentially overseas people, from lands of wine and olive oil, forever hankering for their homeland. After thinking Britain subdued, they would return to their warm homes in Italy. Britain would revolt, or be attacked, then they would come back, wreak vengeance, fight back invasions, and then go home again. Gildas never sees indigenous 'Romans' or 'Romano-Britons' as long-term inhabitants here. The inhabitants of Britain are Britons, or 'Fellow Citizens'. The Romans are foreigners. Britain was, for a time, rated as 'Romania',[9] all its precious metals stamped with the image of Caesar, but by the end it was 'Roman' in name only 'not by law and custom'.[10] Even this ended when the usurper Maximus removed the entire Roman army to further his wicked ambitions on the continent. In reality, we know from continental sources that Maximus left the island in 383, and Roman rule continued for a generation more, under Roman usurpers or direct rule.

It is with this flawed understanding of the Romans and their rule that Gildas makes his biggest errors. He takes it for granted that barbarians could only attack and settle on an island where the Romans were not present, so he assumes that big defensive structures, whether earthworks or stone fortifications, could only have been put up after the Romans ceased to have a permanent army stationed here. The Picts, therefore, must have settled in the North of Britain, formerly the undivided home of Britons, after Maximus. The earthworks must have been British responses, feeble and doomed to fail, while Hadrian's Wall and the Saxon Shore forts must have been put up by temporary Roman relief forces in the last hundred years or so. Logical as the inference is, given Gildas's parameters, these are so wrongheaded that they have sometimes led to Gildas being dismissed almost entirely as both a historian and a reliable witness to Dark Age Britain.

Gildas's historical account, especially of the century or so leading to his own time, has been subjected to much scrutiny. It is, however, only a sixth of his comparatively short book. The majority of what Gildas writes is specifically directed at his contemporaries, by name or by analogy. He reminds them of their grandfathers, their fathers, their uncles and the experiences they had. His view of the past is derived from his present, projecting realities of the world he and his fellow Britons inhabit back into the past. For example, it is uncontested that Gildas lives on an island where the north is inhabited by hostile Picts. This is irrespective of the fact that he believes they arrived there from overseas about forty years after the time of Magnus Maximus. So, when he says the Picts, though an ever-present menace, are prevented from further attacks by the Roman stone-built wall, garrisoned now by native Britons trained in Roman military methods, we are potentially reading very interesting evidence of the world of the late fifth or early sixth centuries.

What does Gildas tell us of the world he lives in? He starts his book outlining the situation of Britain, an island approximately 800 miles long and 200 miles wide, with headlands and bays. 'It has the benefit of the estuaries of a number of streams, and especially two splendid rivers, the Thames and the Severn, arms of the sea along which luxuries from overseas used to be brought by ship.'[11] This feeling that Britain is in decline from a prosperous past is something he insists on. When and why this period of prosperity occurred is clarified later. It happened after an appeal to a powerful Roman man on the continent, identified as the Roman *Magister Militum* Aetius in 446, was rejected. The Britons instead 'trusting not in man but in God'[12] fought back against the Picts and the Scots (from Ireland), from bases in mountains, caves and thickets. The British victory was followed by a brief period when 'the island was so flooded with an abundance of goods that no previous age had known anything like it'. This period of abundance was ended by a 'memorable plague',[13] itself divine punishment for civil war and sin. This in turn was followed by the arrival of Saxons.

We do know that overseas luxuries were still arriving in Britain in Gildas's day, so he must mean that they are now confined to the more coastal areas rather than moving inland. The fact that only the southern estuaries are mentioned may be significant. Gildas continues, Britain 'is ornamented by twenty-eight cities and a number of castles, and well equipped with fortifications – walls, castellated towers, gates and houses'.[14] These cities, at least since the Saxon revolt, and possibly since the first Pictish invasions, are no longer inhabited as they used to be. Exactly what Gildas means by 'cities' (*civitates* is his word here) is not clear. Although Gildas uses the word *cives* or 'citizens' as a frequent synonym for 'Britons', his *cives* have fled to 'steep fortified hills, dense forests and cliffs on the sea coast'.[15] If anything characterizes fifth- and sixth-century British sites like Tintagel, Cadbury, Cadbury-Congresbury and Alt Clut, it is precisely this kind of refuge location, so different to Gildas from the *civitates* the *cives* should be living in.

Technically, in the vocabulary of the Roman government, the *civitates* were county-type administrative units. They took their name from preexisting Celtic tribal units and were presumably roughly of the same extent and in the same location as those tribes. By Gildas's time, the word had come, more usually, to refer to the major urban centre in that unit, and hence is the origin of our word 'city'. This is clearly how Gildas thinks. He distinguishes between *civitates* and fields, his description of them always includes urban features. In his Latin version of the Bible, it is the word used for the 'cities' of the Holy Land. The fact that he thinks Britain has twenty-eight of them means he must also be including settlements which were not area capitals, since there were only about sixteen of these.

What of his 'castles'? The word Gildas uses, *castella*[16] (singular *castellum*), is indeed the origin of our word 'castle'. But Gildas has plenty of words for structures which were purely military. He refers to *munitionibus*,[17] 'fortresses', and you can see *deserta moenia*[18] – deserted city walls – which are old Roman structures, decorated by carvings of pagan deities. A stone wall (Hadrian's Wall) has *arcis* or 'citadels'[19] for its garrisons. On the south coast, there are *torres per intervalla*[20] or 'towers at intervals' protecting it. These structures still stand, they are the massive fortifications of the Saxon Shore forts. They are archetypal 'castles' in modern English, but are scarcely innumerable, like Gildas's *castella*. They are clearly different in scale, too, from what our word 'tower' conveys.

It is more likely that by *castellum*, Gildas means a settlement which is smaller than a *civitas*. In the Latin Bible, it is a word used for villages like Bethany to distinguish them from the City of Jerusalem. Gildas specifically distinguishes them from fortifications.

Gildas uses two other words for a town, but whether they are synonyms for *civitas* and thus included in the list of twenty-eight is less clear. Did he intend his readers to think of them as different, in size or function, or was he just using a variety of words for 'town' to vary his prose? One is *urbs* (plural *urbes*). Outside Britain, he uses the word of large cities, like Aquileia,[21] where Maximus is killed, and Antioch where St. Ignatius was Bishop,[22] are both *urbes*. In Britain, he says there is a *Legionum urbs*, 'City of the Legion', which two early martyrs were citizens. The three towns in Roman Britain which had legions based in them were York, Chester and Caerleon. None of these was technically a *civitas*, though Bede would later call Chester the Civitas[23] of the Legion. Unfortunately, the idea an *urbs* means a big city is complicated when Gildas describes the wall (Hadrian's Wall) as running from sea to sea, between *urbes*.[24] If he only means the settlements at each end, then only the one at the west end, Carlisle, *civitas* capital of the Carvetii, is of any large size and importance. The passage reads as though the wall connects several of them, not just two.

The other word Gildas uses is *colonia*. Technically a *colonia* was a specific large town where army veterans were settled. There were four in Britain: York, Gloucester, Lincoln and Colchester (the last two preserving the 'col' in their modern names, showing the status was, in some sense, recognized into Anglo-Saxon times). Gildas says that all of them were laid low by battering rams during the Saxon revolt.[25] They had walls and towers, as well as houses. They were seen by the Saxons as potential providers of their monthly military allowances and as homes of the leaders who could supply then. Specifically, Gildas says their inhabitants included the leaders of the church. One further settlement, Verulamium (modern St. Albans) is mentioned as the place where early martyr St. Alban himself was a citizen.[26] It presumably counted as a *civitas* to Gildas.

All Gildas's references to cities relate to earlier periods in British history. They have not been inhabited as they formerly were since the Saxon revolt. The only settlement, perhaps, connected to one of Gildas's contemporaries, is the bear's stronghold or *receptaculum ursi*'[27] of which tyrant Cuneglassus is enigmatically charioteer. Whether this is where he lived, is the site of one of his victories or a geographical location within his kingdom is impossible to say, but it seems smaller than a town or city.

Briefly, we can conclude that Gildas did have a concept of what archaeologists call a hierarchy of settlement. At the top are the *coloniae*, seats of secular and church government. These are destroyed and perhaps deserted in Gildas's time. Next are the *civitates*, including some *urbes*. *Urbes* seem to include Carlisle and one of the legionary centres. *Civitates* include towns which are smaller than the regular *civitas* capitals, since there are more of them. They are deserted, or at least not inhabited as they used to be. Below them are *castella*, villages or small towns. At the bottom of the ladder are the fortifications, including towers and walls.

It is important to note that, even when the towns of Roman Britain were fully inhabited, and even more so once they had been devastated and abandoned, most of the population, over 90 per cent, lived in the countryside. As Gildas puts it,

> Like a chosen bride dressed in a variety of jewellery, the island is decorated with wide plains and agreeably set hills, excellent for successful agriculture, and mountains especially suited to varying the pasture for animals. Flowers of different colours underfoot made them a delightful picture. To water it, the island has clear fountains, whose constant flow drives before it snow-white pebbles, and brilliant rivers that glide with gentle murmur, guaranteeing sweet sleep for those who lie on their banks, and lakes flowing over with a cold rush of living water.[28]

So much for the physical situation of Britain, but what does Gildas have to say about how his homeland is governed? The first thing he tells us, in his introduction, lamenting his own unworthiness for the task of admonishing his sinful countrymen, is that Britain has governors 'if not more than she needs, at least no fewer'.[29] Exactly what he means by this is not clear. He later tells us that all the governors of Britain were removed by Maximus. The word he uses on both occasions is *rector*.

We have a very interesting document called the *Notitia Dignitatum*, which lists the officials, civil and military, of the late Roman Empire.[30] It explains how the officials should be addressed and who they report to. Its actual date is not clear, and duplicate entries for military units show it was a live document, responding to changes. In Britain it must deal with the last years of the fourth century since the full Roman administrative system is still in place. Civil administration in Britain is under the control of the Prefect of Gaul. The Diocese of Britain, comprising all of Britain south of the Wall, is delegated by him to a viceroy or *vicar*. These administrative terms (*rector*, *vicar* and *diocese*) were appropriated by the church for its own structures, where they survive in use to this day. The Vicar of Britain or 'the Britains' (meaning British provinces) would have been based in London. The diocese was divided into five provinces. Maxima Caesariensis and Valentia had higher-ranking governors than the other three, Britannia Prima, Britannia Secunda and Flavia Caesariensis. We do not know where Valentia was. It could have been the renaming of one of the other four, erroneously duplicated in the *Notitia*, or that it is a subdivision of one of the others, possibly Maxima Caesariensis, considering the rank equivalence. Maxima perhaps included the south-east and London, Flavia the eastern lowland to the north, Britannia Prima the west and its promontories and Britannia Secunda the North. The Britannias were the bases of most of the military units. It is the governors of these provinces who are the rectors.

If we are to believe Gildas's story of the Proud Tyrant and the settlement of the Saxons, we might have to infer that something like the Diocesan government persisted at that time. The Proud Tyrant could settle Saxons to fight the Picts and the Scots, primarily threats to the northern province. The Saxons' homes are in the eastern part of the island,[31] according to Bede in what would be another province, perhaps Maxima Caesariensis. Gildas is not as precise as this, but he does indicate that Verulamium is now cut off from the

Britons by the partition of the island with the Saxons.[32] On the other hand, when the Saxons fall out with the Britons over supplies, their response is to ravage from sea to sea, so into Britannia Prima, laying low all the *coloniae*, one of which is Gloucester.

In Gildas's time, however, there no longer seems to be a diocesan government. His statement that Britain has many *rectors* indicates it has at least devolved to a lower tier. Britain, for Gildas, is unequivocally the whole island, not a Roman diocese.

We do know that *rector* was a title in use on the island both before and after Gildas. Although the *Notitia Dignitatum* has a different title for the governor of Britannia Prima, one of them, Lucius Septimius, set up a column in Cirencester, perhaps the provincial capital, describing himself as 'Rector of the First Province'.[33] In the poem *Gododdin*, set in the mid-sixth century and, according to some linguistic experts, containing elements dating back to the time, one of the warriors, Tudfwlch, has *rector*[34] as one of his epithets. He is from Edinburgh, and his other epithets 'helmsman', 'rampart' and 'citadel' do not suggest he holds an official Roman title, but it indicates the title carried prestige.

One possibility is that by 'rectors' Gildas means both secular and religious leaders, in this case, the bishops. He goes on to denounce sinful or ineffective bishops. He clarifies that by no means are all the bishops bad, even though they have not risen to the challenge of denouncing his contemporaries as he has. One of his major criticisms of the bishops and priests is that they have bought their positions from the tyrants. Their general money-grabbing disposition is shown when they rejoice if they find a single denarius.[35] In what is now an incredibly obscure criticism, but one which must have seemed significant at the time, Gildas complains that candidates who cannot find any of their upright colleagues to ordain send messages abroad, go overseas to get promotion, and then return in triumph.[36] None of this remains in the legends and hagiographies the Welsh preserved later in the Middle Ages. In these, the bishops stand up to the tyrants, none is appointed by them.

It is staggering to contemplate just how much information was lost about the church in the late Roman and post-Roman period in Britain. Britain had bishops under the Christian Roman Empire. Two bishops of London and a bishop of York turned up at a meeting of Western religious leaders. Where the sees of Gaul maintained unbroken lists of their bishops before and after the fall of the Roman Empire, with bishops like St. Martin of Tours and St. Germanus of Auxerre continuing to be revered, the sees of Britain did not. Gildas writes as if there are a considerable number of bishops, some bad, some good, more numerous it seems than the bad kings, who are addressed individually by name. The twenty-eight *civitates* may be the seats of bishops. At the very start of the seventh century, Bede records seven British bishops turning up for a conference with Augustine, the newly arrived missionary to the English.[37] There were eight *civitates* in Britannia Prima. This again is not the impression that the later lives of the Welsh saints give. In them the bishops are few, the bishoprics all newly founded in the sixth century, none of them are pre-existing sees from the time of the Romans.

It is Gildas's censure of the secular rulers of his time which stands out most clearly. Five of them are addressed by name. Gildas gives a variety of titles to the secular rulers, starting with *rector*, and as far as we can tell these seem to be synonyms to vary his prose. Thus, they are kings (*reges*), princes (*principes*), leaders (*duces*) and tyrants (*tyranni*). He does not make the same distinction between *duces* and *reges* which *Historia Brittonum* makes. He starts his section on his contemporary Britain with a general denunciation which paints a vivid picture of Britain in his time:

> Britain has kings but they are tyrants, judges but they are unjust. They frequently plunder and terrorize, but do so to the innocent; they defend and protect people, but only the guilty and thieves; they have many wives, but they are whores and adulteresses; they swear constantly, but their oaths are false; they make vows but almost immediately tell lies; they wage wars, but only civil and unjust ones; they chase thieves energetically all over the country, but love and even reward the thieves who sit with them at their table. They distribute alms profusely, but amass immense mountains of crime for all to see; they take their seats as judges, but rarely seek out the rules of right judgment, they despise the harmless and humble but exalt to the stars … their military companions, bloody, proud and murderous men, adulterers and enemies of God … they keep many prisoners in their

> jails who are more often loaded with chafing chains because of plots than because they really deserve punishment. They hang around the altars swearing oaths, then shortly afterwards scorn them as though they were dirty rocks.[38]

Though Gildas clearly views these kings in a negative light, this passage shows the same pattern of British kingship described in the *Gododdin* and other early Welsh poems, and in the medieval Arthurian accounts. The Arthurian tales give some of the most famous accounts of adulterous wives, Guinevere and Isolde, and of course the adulterous military companions of the kings, Lancelot and Tristan. Although not usually mentioned in the romances, there was a persistent tradition that Arthur himself had more than one wife – when his grave was supposedly discovered at Glastonbury in the twelfth century, it came with an inscribed cross identifying Guinevere as his second wife.[39] The Welsh Triads claimed Arthur had three wives.[40] Perhaps that might provide a context for the conflict between Arthur and his son, revealed in the Wonders of Britain. There is unanimity in the later sources that Arthur does indeed chase thieves across the country and does defend people. Generosity among the rulers is praised, with Arthur singled out as more generous than the three most generous men on the island.[41] In the *Gododdin*, the warrior compared to Arthur is praised not just for his warlike prowess, but also for his generosity.[42] The later legends were certain that Arthur had succumbed to a civil war, and it is possible the *Annales Cambriae* intended that, giving Arthur's last battle a Welsh name and having him die alongside a Briton.

It is not clear that king (*rex*) and judge (*iudex*) are simply synonyms in this passage, as are the various words Gildas goes on to use for priests when he comes to denounce them. The distinction between kings and judges as similar, but not identical, types of rulers is one that Gildas was familiar with from the Bible. That all the rulers have judicial functions is clarified by Gildas – 'they sit in judgment but rarely seek out the rules of right justice'. The *Codex Justinianus*, the Roman Law code roughly contemporary with Gildas, gives *iudex* as a synonym for provincial 'rector'.[43] *The Gododdin* uses the loan word *iudex* in the form *Ut*[44] for one of its warriors, just as it preserved 'rector' as a title. *Historia Brittonum* refers to an ancient proverb 'whenever *iudices* or *reges* are spoken of, "He judged Britain with the three islands".[45]

Many of the themes in the denunciation are taken up by Gildas again when he turns his attention to the individual tyrants. The first, Constantine, is immediately denounced as a swearer of false oaths in a church context. So it may be that Gildas is simply lumping together the crimes and sins he intends to highlight. The overall picture is, nonetheless, hugely revealing.

One aspect that might pass unremarked is that the kings are military leaders, and their companions are fellow soldiers. This is exactly what St. Patrick said about the companions of Coroticus.[46] That this would be the norm for the government of Britain for at least the next thousand years obscures how innovative it was in this period.

Under Roman rule, although the Vicar of the Britains had some troops at his disposal, the main military units were separate from, and indeed independent of, civil structures. The commanders reported to the *Magister Militum* (Master of Soldiers) in Gaul. Three commanders were enumerated in the Diocese, their commands cutting across *Civitates*. The most senior was the *Comes Britanniarum* – the Companion (or, as the title would become in the Middle Ages, Count) of the Britains. He held the mobile reserve which was intended to be used to support the static commands, to defend against unrest or respond to invasions. Next was the *Comes Litoris Saxonicii*, the Companion or Count of the Saxon Shore. He controlled the frontier garrisons and their fortresses along the east and south coasts, as the name suggests, against the Saxons. Finally, the *Dux Britanniarum*, the leader (or, as it would be in the Middle Ages, duke) of the Britains, who commanded the troops and forts of the North Frontier, particularly Hadrian's Wall, against attacks from the Picts. Such at least was the official position according to *Notitia Dignitatum*.[47]

We know there must have been more to the defence of Britain than this. There are many forts in the west of Britain which do not have a designated commander. Whether an office has been accidentally dropped at an early stage of copying, whether it was commanded by one of the usurpers, such as Maximus or Constantine III who took their troops over to the continent, or whether there was localized control of these forts, or perhaps some of them had been abandoned by this time, we do not entirely know.

Elsewhere in the Western Empire, powerful landowners, villa dwellers who provided leadership in the towns, supported private armies to protect their social position and wealth. On the western fringes of Britain, however, we do not generally see this. It is an area where urban and villa life did not really take hold. Instead, as Roman rule collapsed, local magnates appear to have refortified hill forts from the pre-Roman Iron Age, and sometimes added new earthworks of presumably defensive character. It is conceivable this replaced formal Roman military structures in the west.

Another source of military power may have been settled barbarian groups, the *Foederati*, enjoying rights to land and supplies in return for their military service. Nothing of this, however, appears in the official record of *Notitia Dignitatum*.

Gildas refers frequently to military subjects. It is not always easy to know what aspects derive from his own time and which from his literary sources. The Latin translation of the Bible he uses and his literary upbringing, which seems to have included studying Vergil, provide vocabulary which may be misleading. He views the Britons as fundamentally ignorant in matters of warfare, deriving all their military practice from the Romans. Thus, the Romans advise the Britons to arm themselves with the *ensis* (sword), the *hasta* (a spear which could also be thrown) and the *pelta* (a light skirmisher's shield).[48] These are contrasted with the *gladius* (a short stabbing sword), and the *scutum* (a large rectangular shield) that he describes being used by the Romans.[49] Along with these, they provide training manuals, or perhaps just instructions, on how to use them. The *ensis* and *hasta* are explicitly to be used by the contemporary tyrants Constantine[50] and Maglocunus.[51] Gildas writes very evocatively about cavalry warfare in Roman times.[52] Contemporary tyrant Cuneglassus is called a rider or horseman of many. He is also called a charioteer and described as fighting with weapons peculiar to himself, whatever that means.[53] The only formation described is the battleline,[54] though the military activity at Badon Hill is called a siege.[55] Fighting men are identified as soldiers (*milites*)[56] fighting for booty or reward.

Gildas's view of how his island is threatened and defended is surprisingly accurate for the late Roman Empire, if we dispense with his demonstrably inaccurate impression of the timescale and sequence which produced them. He portrays a Britain ruled by *rectores*. The backbone of its defence is the Stone

1. British horse and hider brooches, perhaps evidence of the inhabitants of late-Roman Britain celebrating their British heritage.

2. Statue of the Emperor Constantine in York, from where he set off to conquer the Roman world. Late-Roman Britain was a land of rebels.

3. A relief on the Arch of Constantine in Rome showing fourth-century troops besieging fortifications.

4. Hadrian's Wall at Sycamore Gap. From territory north of here, the Picts invaded late- and post-Roman Britain.

5. The late-Roman walls of the Saxon Shore Fort at Portchester, part of the coastal defences of late-Roman Britain.

6. Buckle from Longbridge Deverill possibly showing a British militia commander of the late fouth century.

7. The Tetrarchs. Late-Roman statue of four emperors on a corner of St. Mark's Cathedral, Venice, showing how commanders in late-Roman Britain may have looked.

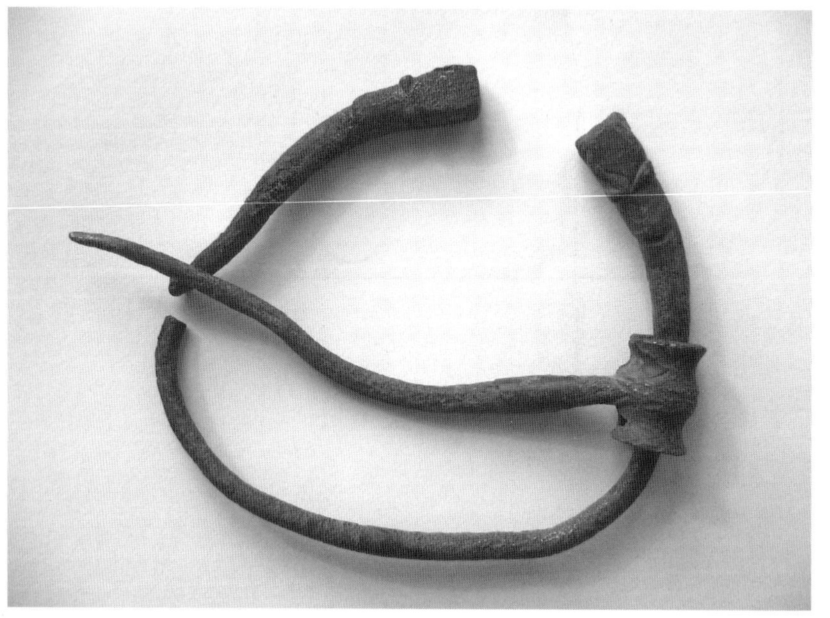

8. British Type F penannular brooch. British warriors were probably wearing cloak brooches like these at the end of the Roman period.

9. British militia horsehead buckle of the very late-fourth or early-fifth century. An alliance between the two main areas using such buckles may have been key in fifth-century Britain.

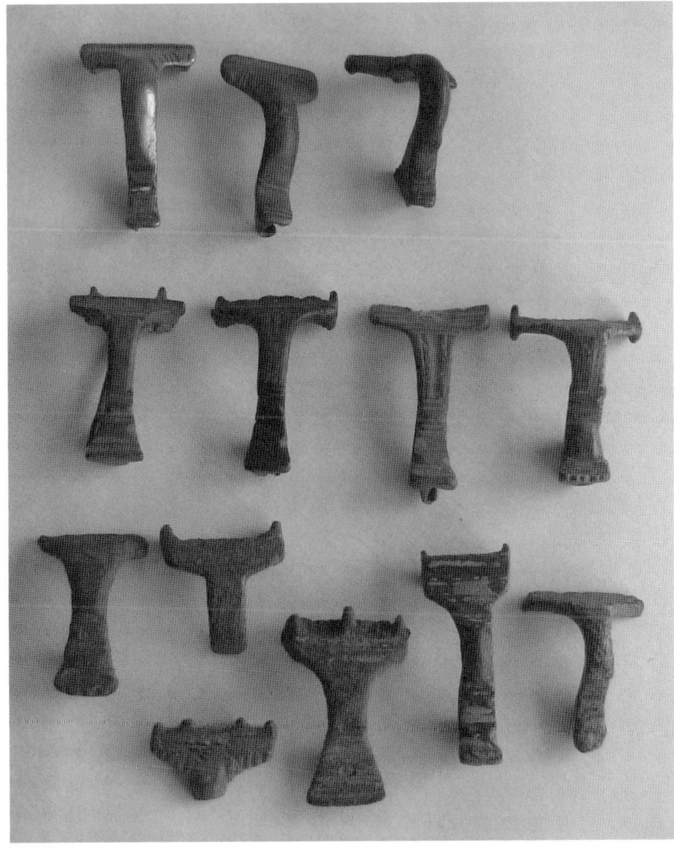

10. Supporting arm brooches. Very early evidence of the arrival of immigrants from across the North Sea.

11. A late-Roman brick font in Richborough fort.

12. The *Hugin* at Pegwell Bay, near Richborough, where Hengist and Horsa are supposed to have landed in 449.

13. A fragment of a Quoit Brooch Style strap end, with distinctive decoration. The distribution of Quoit Brooch Style items may reflect the spread of Hengist and Horsa's men.

14. A reconstructed brine pit on the site of a pit dating from the Roman period at Upwich, Droitwich. Droitwich saltworks were a vital resource in post-Roman Britain.

15. Left: Roman bath at Bath.

16. Below: Belt fittings with designs typical of those found in Dobunni territory. The Dobunni may have played a key role in the lives of Arthur and Penda.

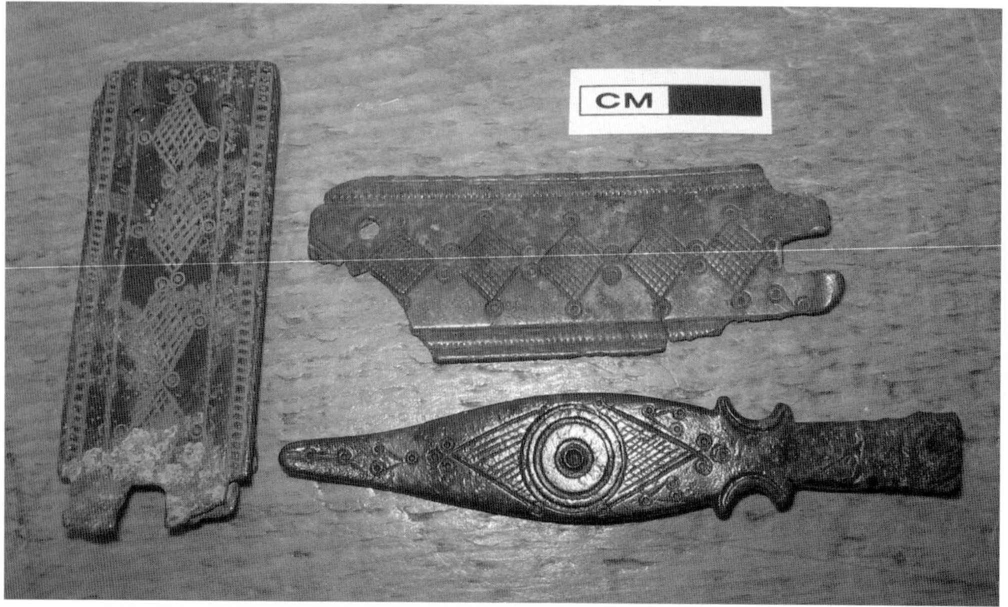

17. Above: Tintagel.

18. Left: Statue of Gildas in the Abbey of St. Gildas de Rhuys which claims he lived there in later life.

19. Above: British Type G penannular brooch from around the end of the fifth century, or later. The Arthur Brooch?

20. Ramparts of Cadbury Congresbury hillfort. Reoccupied in the post-Roman period, a significant site for Type G penannular brooches.

21. Looking from the ramparts of Cadbury Congresbury hillfort, across the Severn estuary to South Wales in the distance, showing how a kingdom could easily stretch from Somerset into Wales.

22. Left: The Drustan stone in Cornwall. Often thought to mention the Arthurian character Tristan and located south of the sites where a couple of Type G penannular brooches were found far to the west of the main distribution area.

23. Above: Roman gate at Lincoln in what would become the Kingdom of Lindsey, perhaps a key element in the alliances of Arthur and Penda.

24. The amphitheatre at Caerleon, a site often linked with King Arthur and on the eastern edge of King Arthur's Country.

25. Right: The Roman walls of Caerwent, near Caerleon.

26. Below: A Church at Talgarth dedicated to St. Gwendoline, a member of the family of King Brychan, a key figure along with Arthur in *The Life of St. Cadoc*.

27. The banks of the Triffrwd, near Talgarth.

28. The plain beside the Triffrwd, near Talgarth. A probable Arthurian battlefield.

29. Badbury Rings hillfort. A possible site of the Battle of Badon.

30. Cadbury Castle hillfort, at South Cadbury, reoccupied in the post-Roman period and thought by some to be Camelot.

31. Site of the Battle of Heavenfield fought in 635, and the church of St. Oswald.

32. A cross marking the site where Oswald is said to have raised his battle standard, preparing to fight Penda's British ally, Cadwallon of Gwynedd.

33. Portrayal in mosaic of the court of the Byzantine emperor Justinian. Both British and Anglo-Saxon rulers of the early medieval period took some inspiration from the ruler culture of the Byzantine Empire.

34. The early Mercian church at Brixworth in Northamptonshire.

Wall in the North and the towers on the south coast. These are supplemented by lines of turf defence built by local labour. They are manned by local forces armed with spears, shields, and swords, but trained in the Roman manner. *Milites* and their *duces* defend against attacks. It is expected that Roman leaders overseas will support this with forces like the legion, used to bolster the frontier defences, and then by more mobile units of the fleet and the cavalry. The figure Gildas has the Britons appeal to seems intended to be Aetius, who really was the *Magister Militum* nominally responsible for the regular forces in Britain. The threats come from the Picts and the Scots (the Irish), and latterly from the Saxons, but also from internal revolts and usurpations. The solution of settling German federate troops to address these threats is fully in accord with late Roman practice.

Gildas, however, self-confessedly does not have access to historical material.[57] How has he come to this surprisingly accurate picture? In nearly every case, Gildas's view of what must have been happening in the past is simply a projection backwards of what is happening in his present. His understanding of history as essentially cyclical militates in favour of this interpretation. It might not be too great a leap to suggest that Gildas makes these assumptions about the defence of the island because they were in fact features of the present or of a past within living memory, as passed from one generation to the next, and maintained by the Britons. He is explicit there are *rectors* in his own time. He imagines the Roman emperor and senate of the past acting in ways similar to those of the Proud Tyrant and the Council, hearing regional appeals, responding militarily, rushing reserve troops to the threatened area, including by ship. Contemporary Britons were throwing up great earthworks, like the Wansdyke, in the area between two of the tyrants he locates. These are rarely intended against external invasions and must have been planned to some extent for local political reasons. This in turn might give Gildas the impression they were built irrationally, without an overall leader to coordinate them. The refuges of the Britons, high fortified hill and sea cliffs[58] are clearly evidenced in the archaeology of sites like South Cadbury and Tintagel. Hadrian's Wall, on the other hand, still had stone forts that were probably occupied or reoccupied at the time. Perhaps the counterattacks, legions and cavalry, are Roman because they are the methods most recently used by the only Roman Gildas has knowledge of, Ambrosius Aurelianus, and the Britons who succeeded him in the generation of Badon Hill.

Some issues might be clearer if we knew exactly from where Gildas was writing. Various suggestions have been made since the Middle Ages. Although an early 'Life' of Gildas has him writing in Brittany,[59] this is not the case for *De Excidio Britanniae*. In it, he is explicit he does not have access to the literary remains of the Britons which have been taken overseas,[60] which places him firmly on the island.

Gildas names very few locations in Britain. The named locations are: the River Thames (twice), the River Severn, Verulamium (St. Albans), the City of the Legions (most likely Chester or Caerleon), Dumnonia (Devon and Cornwall), Demetae (the people of Dyfed) and Badon Hill (location unknown or disputed). All those suggest a southerly location. Some less precise features are noted. The Saxons are in the eastern part of the island and Verulamium is mentioned specifically because the division of the island with the Saxons makes Christian access to his grave, and the place where he suffered, difficult. He mentions all the *coloniae*, saying they have all been devastated by the Saxons.[61] Colchester, Lincoln and York are all on the east side of the island. The only one in the west is Gloucester, slightly more north than Verulamium, on the Severn and not far from the upper reaches of the Thames, and on the most direct land route from Dumnonia to the Demetae. The only locations which do not fit with this pattern are the Stone Wall (Hadrian's Wall) and the associated Turf Wall. But whether Gildas knows these locations or has only heard of them is debatable. He thinks the Stone Wall runs between towns that happened to be there, rather than being a straight feature on which most of the settlements are subsequently sited. His idea that the Picts only settled to the north of the Stone Wall sometime between 388 and 446 would surely be called into question by anyone from that area and would be disputed by the Britons of the Gododdin who lived north of Hadrian's Wall.

Gildas claims recent knowledge of the tyrant Constantine of Dumnonia, describing a crime he has committed 'this very year'[62] and knowing for certain that he is alive. He is the first of the tyrants to be admonished and many commentators have seen a geographical scheme behind the denunciations – working northward to the Demetae then ending with Maglocunus, located since the time of *Historia Brittonum* in Gwynedd.[63] The five named tyrants denounced by Gildas are not the only rulers of Britain. Gildas says that some leaders, a tiny handful, have found the narrow path of Salvation.[64] Even the foremost of the tyrants is only 'higher than almost all the leaders of Britain in your kingdom'.[65] It might well be that Gildas writes from the land of one of those exemplary rulers, perhaps in the adjacent kingdom to Constantine.

The earliest 'Life' of Gildas says he was born in Strathclyde, a British kingdom at the mouth of the River Clyde.[66] In the twelfth-century version of his life this is updated to 'Scotland',[67] the Scots having taken it over in the intervening years. Gildas sees his contemporary Scots (the Irish) as overseas raiders 'readier to cover their villainous faces with hair than their private parts … with clothes'.[68] The later 'Life', however, suggests Gildas wrote his book in the Glastonbury area,[69] which fits in surprisingly well with these conjectures of his location from his work.

The first tyrant, Constantine, is described as a cub of 'the filthy lioness of Dumnonia'.[70] Most likely this is just a reference to his homeland, the *civitas* of Devon and Cornwall. In a similar way, the Saxons are described as cubs from the lair of a barbarian lioness,[71] meaning their Germanic homeland.

Constantine is no longer a young man – he put aside his lawful wife 'many years before'. His main crime, however, took place 'this very year' after he had sworn a terrible oath not to work his wiles on his fellow citizens. Dressed as a holy abbot, though wielding a sword and spear, he killed two noble youths in a church, where they were sheltering with their mother. This subterfuge was evidently necessary, as almost no man could handle weapons as bravely as they could.

That is all we learn about the identity of those youths. The fact that Arthur is not named by Gildas is often used as proof that Arthur did not exist. Now, we have to admit that if Gildas had named Arthur, his existence would be accepted by all historians, just as the existence of Ambrosius Aurelianus as a historical figure is now accepted without question. This even though Ambrosius is either absent (*Anglo-Saxon Chronicle* and the *Welsh Annals*) or the centre of fanciful stories of virgin birth and prophetic dragons (*Historia Brittonum*) in later accounts of the period. The converse, however, proves nothing. Only eight Britons are mentioned in the whole of Gildas's work. Three of them are the Christian martyrs of the Great Persecution, and the other five are these tyrants. The pages teem with unnamed characters, either from Gildas's time or from the generation which proceeded it. A majority occur in this section, denouncing the tyrants.

This in turn raises the question of why Ambrosius Aurelianus has been singled out for mention by name. He is, as Gildas indicates, in some sense a Roman, and the names of Roman leaders are dotted through the work, with Ambrosius the last of them. Interestingly, though, Ambrosius himself provides a link between the categories of named characters among the Britons. His parents, despite him being, in some sense, a Roman, are inhabitants of Britain killed in the Saxon revolt. Although Gildas is explicit that Ambrosius is a modest man, *vir modestus*, his comment that his parents 'surely had worn the purple'[72] has been interpreted by commentators, from Bede onwards, as specifically meaning they were of royal or imperial origin.

This may perhaps not be what Gildas meant. The last emperor he referred to was the usurper Maximus, and the rulers of Britain who succeeded him were 'anointed' by cruelty, culminating in the Proud Tyrant who invited the Saxons to settle. In fact, nowhere else in his book does Gildas use the imagery of wearing purple as anything to do with royalty. Instead, it often seems to be one of his images of Christian martyrdom. The aftermath of the Saxon Revolt in which Ambrosius's parents died saw 'holy altars, fragments of corpses, covered (as it were) with a purple crust of concealed blood'. The two noble youths killed by Constantine wear metaphorical purple robes, 'their purple robes touch' the altar where they were killed, and the purple of 'their coagulating blood'.[73] This is often how the word 'purple' is used in other Christian writings of the time. It is the colour of Christian martyrdom, dyed by the blood of the slain. In other words, Ambrosius's parents were killed in the revolt, and, whatever their rank, 'surely they wore the purple robes of martyrdom'. Thus, the naming of Ambrosius can point back to the three previously named characters, the British martyrs at the hands of the pagan Romans.

In a similar way, he points the reader forward to the named Britons of Gildas's day. Immediately after the fate of his parents, Gildas writes 'his descendants in our day have become greatly inferior to their grandfather's excellence'.[74] We shall be considering these descendants (*suboles* is the word Gildas uses) in more depth later. One possibility must be that they *are* mentioned, indeed possibly named, in this section. If not, they may be among the handful of good rulers, yet ineffective in power or deeds.

Constantine does have a Roman name. In reality, it had such power in Britain, where the first Constantine had been proclaimed emperor, that one of the usurpers, Constantine III, was allegedly declared here on his name alone.[75] Perhaps Constantine of Dumnonia still considered himself a Roman. Gildas uses the word 'citizens'[76] for Constantine's fellows, rather than 'Britons'. Archaeologically, the most important royal site in Dumnonia in the fifth and sixth centuries seems to have been the fortified peninsula of Tintagel. It encloses a larger area than any other fortified location of the time. Fragments of Latin have been found there, but more tellingly, the site, along with others in the *civitas* and neighbouring sites, is characterized by pottery from the Eastern Mediterranean. This originates from what had been the Eastern Roman Empire; we usually refer to it as the Byzantine Empire. These fragments were once the storage containers and tableware used to transport and consume Mediterranean luxuries like olive oil and wine, precisely the commodities Gildas identified with the Romans.

The next tyrant also has a Roman name, Aurelius Caninus, which seems superficially related to the name Ambrosius Aurelianus, but may well not be. He is being tarred with the same brush as Constantine, with fornication, adultery, and the plunder of civil war. He is a young man,

Figure 21. Grave of Cunaide from Cornwall, with complex inscription suggesting contact with continental Europe.

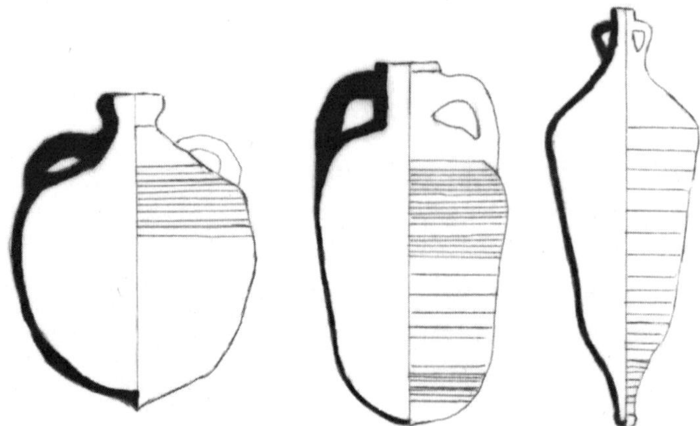

Figure 22. Types of East Mediterranean pottery imported into parts of Britain in the late fifth and early sixth centuries. (After Dark, *Britain and the End of the Roman Empire*, 2000)

and Gildas doubts he will live to old age. His 'brothers and his fathers [sic]' have already died young.[77] The latter are more of the unnamed characters of the former generation.

The third tyrant is geographically located, he is the tyrant of the Demetae,[78] the civitas of south-west Wales, the name that survives in modern Welsh as Dyfed. Although we do not know why Gildas lists the tyrants in the order he does, many readers have assumed a geographical logic behind it. If that is so, Aurelius may rule over one of the lands between the Dumnonii and the Demetae. The three *civitates* between them were the Durotriges, Dobunni and the Silures, with a fourth *civitas*, that of the Cornovii in the north.

None of those names lasted into later Welsh, although the *civitas* capital of the Silures, Venta Silurum, gave its name to the kingdom of Guent. The later Anglo-Saxons saw this as a location where British kings had ruled in the sixth century. The *Anglo-Saxon Chronicle* records the Battle of Dyrham in 577.[79] In this, three British kings were killed, and the cities of Cirencester, Gloucester and Bath came under Saxon control. Cirencester was the *civitas* capital of the Dobunni. It is usually seen as the provincial capital too, due to the presence of the column previously mentioned, put up by a rector of Britannia Prima. Gloucester was one of the *coloniae*, the veterans' cities Gildas had identified as targets of the Saxon Revolt, and the only one on the western side of the island, during an attack which burnt 'from sea to sea'.[80] The Cornovii had links with the Dobunni and their capital was at Wroxeter near Shrewsbury. We will return to the question of the location of Aurelius Caninus in a later chapter.

Figure 23. Tombstone of Voteporix from Castell Dwyran, often thought to be the Vortipor mentioned by Gildas as ruler of Demetia/Dyfed.

The Tyrant of the Demetae is called Vortiporius by Gildas. A memorial stone to a very similarly named figure 'Voteporix' was found in Dyfed. It dates from the sixth century and features a Christian cross in a circle with the Latin title 'Protictor'.[81] A protector in the late Roman Empire was an imperial bodyguard, though of course the term had its more general meaning too. It is assumed Voteporix the Protector is the same man as Vortiporius, though the names differ somewhat.[82] The spelling without the 'r' is confirmed on the memorial as not just a slip of the carver's chisel, as the stone also has an inscription in Irish, in the Ogham alphabet, which also begins 'Vote…' Here it is more likely that Gildas's 'r' is an error, and perhaps one produced by a later copyist influenced by the name Vortigern, in Bede.

Murder, rape and adultery characterize the villainous career of Vortiporius. His hair is already whitening, he is no longer a young man. He, interestingly, has inherited his position. He is the bad son of a good king. Gildas uses the analogy of sinful king Manasseh of Judah and his virtuous father King Hezekiah.[83] Hezekiah had withstood an invasion and siege by the Assyrians,

Gildas's chosen analogy of the Saxons. Vortiporius's father is therefore another of the unnamed Britons of the previous generation, when kings had kept to their station and had united in resistance against the Saxons.

The Harleian Genealogies feature Vortiporius, as Guortepir,[84] in the genealogy of Dyfed. It makes him the great-grandfather of a man called Arthur. This man is one of several characters given the name Arthur in the century after the Battle of Badon, which may be significant. The genealogy is derived from Irish material dealing with migration from Ireland to Wales, and the presence of the Irish in the area is confirmed by the Irish inscription on Voteporix's memorial stone. That this monument was already being connected with Gildas's tyrant in the tenth century is demonstrated by the inclusion of a character called 'Protector' as one of Guortepir's ancestors in the genealogy.

The fifth Tyrant related to North Wales from at least the ninth century, so by the same process used to locate Aurelius, it is often assumed that the fourth Tyrant, Cuneglassus, ruled somewhere between Dyfed (Vortiporius) and Gwynedd. Although not located by Gildas, plenty of circumstantial details are given about Cuneglassus. He is no longer young but has been wicked since his youth. He is a rider, even a charioteer, with many horses or riders. He fights with weapons special to himself, and wages war against his fellow citizens. He has put aside his wife, in favour of her sister, ignoring the condemnation of the holy men who surround him.

Gildas says his name means 'tawny butcher'.[85] It really means something like 'blue/grey hound', so the exact point Gildas is making isn't clear. Some colour words are not that precise in this period. The *Gododdin* poet typically uses the same colour word *glas* to describe the mead, the Gododdin drink.[86] Gildas also calls Cuneglassus 'bear' and 'charioteer of the bear's stronghold'. This has raised interest as many scholars derive the name 'Arthur' from the British word for bear *arth*. One medieval version of *Historia Brittonum* gives a possible translation of 'Arthur' as 'horrible bear'. Maybe there is a connection between Cuneglass and Arthur, or 'Bear' might be a name or title in the area. Another option is that Cuneglassus might rule or come from a place called 'bear's stronghold' – there are two places with a name which means Din Arth or Din Eirth in modern Wales. We can be sure that Gildas does not think of Cuneglassus himself as having been a victorious war leader from the days before the siege of Badon Hill when kings and public officials kept to their stations because he has been wicked since his youth, not a feature of those leaders of the British resistance sparked by Ambrosius.

Whoever Cuneglassus was, he disappeared almost completely from subsequent Welsh historical or legendary material. He occurs only once outside Gildas, in the Harleian Genealogies, where he seems to appear as a cousin of the next tyrant, Maglocunus.[87]

'Last in my list but first in evil, mightier both in power and malice, more profuse in giving, more extravagant in sin, strong in arms but stronger still in that which destroys the soul.'[88] Maglocunus, Dragon of the Island. As with much of what Gildas writes, it is not entirely clear what he means by this epithet. Influenced by the ninth-century location of Maglocunus in Gwynedd,[89] many have taken it to mean he is located on the Island of Anglesey.[90] It is difficult, however, to think of a location for Gildas where the adjective 'insular' would automatically call to mind Anglesey. In reality, no sixth-century remains have been found at the Anglesey centre of the later kings of Gwynedd, with all the evidence suggesting the royal centre of the period was on the mainland, at Deganwy[91] or Caernarfon. When *Historia Brittonum* recalled the old proverb, that British kings ruled all of Britain with its three islands, the writer takes this to be Wight, Man and Orkney, not Anglesey, which he never mentions.

It is abundantly clear that Maglocunus is not a minor character skulking in an offshore island, 'The king of kings has made you higher than almost all the leaders of Britain, in your kingdom as much as your physique'. *Insula* (island) is never used by Gildas for any offshore landmass. Rather it is his preferred way of referring to Britain as a whole, beginning with the first words of his history, *Britannia Insula*[92] (Britain is an Island). Indeed, the last time he referred to Britain as a whole before this passage was 'the remembrance of so desperate a blow to the island'[93] – the Saxon Revolt.

The epithet '*Insularis Draco*'[94] should be taken as meaning 'Dragon of Britain'. This is most likely to refer to Maglocunus's pre-eminent position among the British tyrants, not to evoke a geographical location. In the northern extension to *Historia Brittonum*, likely to have been directed to the kings of Gwynedd of the ninth century, Maglocunus (Mailcunus, as his name is given there, in a modern form) is specifically located in the Gwynedd region, but described as 'Great King among the Britons'.[95] Gildas would have been aware of the hostile implications of the word 'dragon', used as a description of the devil in the Bible. He might, however, be drawing on an actual title used by Welsh warlords. In early Welsh it only ever appears as a description or title for a great warrior. A character called Uther Pendragon[96] (Chief Dragon/warlord) is mentioned in an early Arthurian poem, a character who was to become firmly established in legend as Arthur's father.[97]

That Maglocunus's power is widespread and encompasses more than his own kingdom is made clear by Gildas. He has 'deprived many of the aforementioned tyrants of their kingdoms and even of their lives'.[98] An obvious reading is that he means some of the aforementioned named tyrants, but this is hard to square with Gildas's attempts to convert them to a better life – if they are dead or powerless, this would be futile. Constantine, at least, is said to still be alive. Does Gildas just mean the tyrants he mentioned at the start of the section, or does he mean he has mentioned those deposed? The dead tyrants he has mentioned are the fathers and brothers of Aurelius Caninus. 'You are left like a solitary tree … remember the empty outward show of your fathers and brothers, their youthful and untimely deaths.'[99] Gildas calls Aurelius a lion's cub. Detailing the crimes of Maglocunus, he tells how he overthrew his uncle and his bravest soldiers, whose faces were not very different from those of lion cubs.[100] Is this an indication they are related to Aurelius and to Constantine? The war between Maglocunus and his uncle has been muddied by comparison with the Harleian Genealogies, which make Cuneglassus's father an uncle of Maglocunus. Latin, however, has a different word for maternal uncle – mother's brother – the relationship he gives to Maglocunus's adversary, and paternal uncle – father's brother, as Eugein Dantguin, Cuneglassus's father, is in the Genealogies.[101]

Gildas gives more biographical details about Maglocunus than about any of the other tyrants, and his denunciation of him is longer than that of all the other tyrants put together. Whether this represents some personal animosity (Gildas knows that Maglocunus is unusually tall, for instance)[102] or just because he is such a significant figure we do not know.

Maglocunus has changed tack previously. In the first years of his youth, when he was strong in arms, he began to dream of taking power by force. With sword, spear and fire he dispatched the king who was his mother's brother and his soldiers. But after his victory, he pondered the godly life and rule of monks (one of the few explicit mentions of them in Gildas's book)[103] and eventually decided to enter a monastery himself. Maglocunus had as his teacher the most refined master of all Britain. This 'refined master',[104] presumably a monastic teacher, probably an abbot, is yet another of the unnamed characters who fill Gildas's work. Aside from Ambrosius and the martyrs, it is the wicked whom Gildas thinks it necessary in many cases to name, Maglocunus did not remain a monk, and it may be this reversion to his old ways that evokes Gildas's special ire. Other works attributed to Gildas specifically detail the penances for monks who lapse in various ways. Gildas describes Maglocunus's return to his former life as 'not much against your will',[105] which may suggest some political machinations. He had a brother, who might have been ruling his former lands. Maglocunus married as soon as he left the monastery, but soon tired of the woman and murdered her. Next, he murdered his brother's son, so he could marry his wife. He was aided and encouraged by this latter woman, and married her publicly, to the acclaim of his supporters. Whether this related to the overthrow and death of other 'aforementioned tyrants' isn't clarified.

One last feature of Maglocunus's court we have briefly touched on is his chosen form of entertainment. 'Your excited ears hear not the praises of God from the sweet voices of the tuneful recruits of Christ, not the melodious music of the church but empty praises of yourself from the mouths of criminals who grate on the hearing like raving hucksters – mouths stuffed with lies and liable to bedew bystanders with their foaming phlegm'.[106] They may be the parasites whose lying tongues celebrate the king's new wedding. The 'northern history' at the end of the Harleian version of *Historia Brittonum*, as we have seen, gives the names of four men who were famous in British poetry during his time.[107] Maybe they were among these 'criminals'.

Our impression of Gildas's time is distorted at least to a degree by his emphasis on condemnation of the wicked rather than praise of the virtuous. He does make clear that a tiny number of rulers maintain 'controls of truth and justice'.[108] They support him by their prayers and all men admire them. Even mighty Maglocunus is only greater than 'almost all the leaders of Britain'.

Strangely enough, *Historia Brittonum* in its extended form, where it adds more information on Maglocunus and the later kings of Gwynedd, acknowledges that in Maglocunus's time it was another leader, Dutigern[109] (probably a scribal error for 'Outigern')[110] who is said to have been fighting against the Angles. In the main body of *Historia Brittonum*, the other two rulers with names ending in '-tigern' are associated with Buelt and Guorthigirniaun in central-eastern Wales and perhaps that connection is implied here.

The picture presented by Gildas more or less confirms, and expands, what we could see in *Historia Brittonum*. Britain has kings in his day. They clearly provide military manpower. They can carry out civil wars, and chase thieves all over the country. The men who feast at their tables are their 'fellow-soldiers'.[111] Now, though they turn their attentions on each other. This was not the case in the previous generation, when 'kings, public and private persons, priests and churchmen kept to their own stations'.[112] It is hard to see how a king could be kept in his station unless that means being subject to a controlling, perhaps higher authority, whether of divine or earthly nature. Once Ambrosius Aurelianus has kindled the fire of resistance, there must surely have been military leaders to coordinate their response. The kings are located in separate geographical areas, after all, but the victory at the siege of Badon Hill effectively stops the Saxon attacks across the country. What Gildas adds is that until that point, victory swings backwards and forwards between the Britons and the Saxons, explaining the picture of continuous British victories in *Historia Brittonum*, and unalloyed Saxon triumph in the *Anglo-Saxon Chronicle*.

No leader of the generation leading to the siege of Badon is named by Gildas. The resistance must have had a leader in the generation after Ambrosius. Whether it was a successor of Ambrosius of some kind (he had at least one child) or a public official occupying an established military role, *Magister Militum* or *Dux* or *Comes*, or one of the kings who came to dominate the others, as Maglocunus did or as the Anglo-Saxons reported some of their kings did at the time, what we can say is that as soon as any name was given to the leader of the victorious Britons at the siege of Badon Hill, it was Arthur.

Chapter 5

The Sources: Other Material

So far, the sources we have examined have given us a reasonably consistent picture of what was happening in Britain. Settlement and revolt by the Saxons in the early to mid-fifth century was followed by resistance by the Britons. Inspired initially by Ambrosius Aurelianus, the fight-back lasted into the next generation, with success oscillating between the two sides until the British victory at Badon. The British resistance was characterized by the rulers of regions of a fragmented diocese uniting for a common purpose and under a common leader. Initially this was Ambrosius, but latterly the only name given to the war leader who brought the campaigns to a conclusion is that of Arthur.

There is much in this story, however, which remains obscure. Arthur's campaigns are an enigmatic list of nine places, mostly unknown. Only a fraction of the kingdoms which existed are named, with their locations reasonably easy to ascertain. The situation in much of the country is simply not illuminated by the sources we have looked at. That includes a vast swathe of lowland Britain northwards from the Thames valley and eastwards of the Severn valley. There are simply no records of how it was settled by the Angles and how the British responded, until Bede records that in the seventh century its Angle ruler was a supporter of 'The king of the Britons'.

Something which is clear is that the lands involved in the British resistance to the Saxons are not confined to some small or remote enclave. The tyrants of Gildas's time chase thieves energetically across the country. Maglocunus has power much beyond his own land, having driven other tyrants from their kingdoms and their lives. Arthur can project power beyond just one area of resistance. Even a cursory identification of the battle locations suggests we must be dealing with at least some far-flung sites. That a significant part of Britain must have been involved in resistance is clear from *Historia Brittonum*'s pairing Arthur, Leader of Battles, with the *kings* of the Britons. It is clear too, from Gildas, where a British Proud Tyrant and Council, faced with threats from the Scots from the west and the Picts from the north, responds by settling Saxons from the east, who make their homes in the eastern part of the island. It is just as clear when the Saxon settlers, seeking redress for their grievances, burn the surface of the island from sea to sea.

This wide-raging context is often seen as a surprise. An Arthurian tourist industry, for example, emphasizes his connection with Cornwall. Cornwall, though, is but a small fraction of a kingdom, the *civitas* of Dumnonia, which existed at the time. It included, and indeed gave its name to, Devon. And Dumnonia was just one kingdom among many. Bede did not think it unbelievable that a king of the Northumbrian Angles should be fighting the Britons in Chester. Or that a British king, apparently from North Wales, intending 'to wipe out the whole of the English nation from the land of Britain',[1] should be fighting on the Northumbrian coast. The Romans, after all, had managed to fight Britons in Scotland and on Anglesey. The network of roads they built in the wake of their conquest continued to function as a means of traversing the country for centuries afterwards. In 1066, for instance, King Harold was fighting at Hastings just two weeks after his victory near York, having marched his army down the Roman road to London in just five days.

If we are now to shed more light on King Arthur's Country, we must turn to other sources of evidence beyond those we have considered already. The written sources up to the composition of the *Annales Cambriae* in the mid-tenth century are sparse. From the twelfth century onwards, however, there are very many sources which deal with Arthur. The vast majority are, to a greater or lesser extent, dependent on Geoffrey of Monmouth's 'History of the Kings of Britain', from 1135. He established the 'authorized version' of

Arthur's career.[2] Although he claimed an additional written source, it is apparent that what he wrote about Arthur's campaigns against the Saxons is largely derived from those sources we have already examined, embellished with large amounts of fictional material, circumstantial details and narrative tropes typical of historical writers of his time. As a comparison, for instance, one of the contemporary historians Geoffrey of Monmouth mentions by name Henry of Huntingdon, makes extensive and obvious use of Bede and the *Anglo-Saxon Chronicle* in his 'History of the English', sources we luckily possess and with which we can compare his work. He still, like Geoffrey, can give rousing speeches to leaders before they charge into battles clearly derived from twelfth-century practice and includes diverting incidents like King Canute trying to turn back the waves.[3]

There are, though, written sources referring to Arthur which are not obviously dependent on Geoffrey. Many of them derive from Wales and are found in manuscripts mainly from the fourteenth century. Some are closely or loosely modelled on continental romances and can be discounted as having any historical value for the study of the fifth and sixth centuries. What to make of the others is rather more difficult to say.

First, the dating of the manuscripts is easy to explain. Wales had a strong, flourishing culture of oral storytelling. This was maintained by the bards, professional speakers and lore keepers whose roles were protected by law. They were supported by the patronage of the Welsh nobility, especially by the paramount rulers of Wales, the Princes of Gwynedd. The Princes of Gwynedd claimed a lineage back to Maglocunus and beyond him to the rulers of the British North.[4] Their pedigrees included Cadwallon ap Cadfan, the seventh-century King of the Britons we will encounter later in this book. By the late thirteenth century, they were using the title 'Prince of Wales' to indicate their pre-eminent position. They were, however, up against the Kings of England, who claimed overlordship of the entire island. The Plantagenet English kings and their Anglo-Norman Lords simply had no interest in preserving the oral culture of the bards, aggrandizing their enemies in a tongue alien to them. So it is in the last era of the bards (the first example being in the poems of the late thirteenth-century *Black Book of Carmarthen*) that materials doubtless centuries old, genealogies, poems, snippets of lost tales and traditions, came to be written down lest they be lost forever.

Working out the ultimate age and origin of these preserved pieces of information is exceedingly difficult. Some may be no older than the wars of Llywellyn ap Gruffydd and Edward I, only separated by a generation from the manuscripts they are found in. Some may date back to the era they concern. We have already encountered a couple of these. The praise poem of Cadwallon, listing his battles, a possible analogue to the Arthurian battle list, comes from the fourteenth-century *Red Book of Hergest*, but could be from Cadwallon's lifetime or any stage in between (the same character features in the Northern history appended to the Harleian manuscript of the *Historia Brittonum*, in Bede and in Geoffrey of Monmouth, any of which could have inspired the original poet to compose his work). *The Gododdin*, the poem of the fateful expedition of the Britons to Catraeth, attributed to the sixth-century poet Aneirin, and already mentioned previously, is another.

The Gododdin exists in a fourteenth-century manuscript. Annotations show how it would be scored if delivered orally in a bardic competition held before one of the Welsh rulers. It would have wide appeal to them, involving the Men of the North, North Welsh heroes and a milieu, probably, of fighting against the English. But it also clearly contains features of real antiquity. The manuscript preserves two versions of the text, one 'cleaned up' with contemporary spelling and grammar, with the context and authorship clarified, one much older in its language and in its context. It does not include Bernicia as an English-held area (something Bede and *Historia Brittonum* say happened c. 540) and has no North Welsh participants. It is in this older text that the comparison of one of the Gododdin warriors, a paragon of generosity and warlike feats, is made to Arthur. This allows us to infer that the reputation of Arthur as, perhaps generous, perhaps a killer of more than 300 English in a battle, likely pre-existed the *Historia Brittonum*.

Along with the assault on the Welsh rulers of Wales, the Anglo-Normans were also determined to stamp their authority on the churches of Wales. Bishops were a key part of the government structure of the medieval state. The Norman Conquest of 1066 had seen Normans replace Anglo-Saxons throughout the hierarchy of the church. Something similar now happened in Wales. Cathedrals and abbeys were the record keepers of the time. As the Anglo-Norman Archbishops of Canterbury began to encroach on their ecclesiastical rights, as the Anglo-Norman kings and barons were encroaching on their lands, so the churches and abbeys of Wales found it expedient to write down the origins of those rights and privileges which had previously often been left unquestioned. Such ecclesiastical texts included charters in which sixth-century kings were alleged to have bestowed lands on the churches, and, often explicitly linked, *Lives* of the founding saints. Many of the saints' Lives which we still have are found in a single manuscript, compiled at Brecon Priory.

The Saints Lives occasionally include Arthur. The motif, from Gildas, that the tyrants chase thieves energetically all over the country, appears in *The Life of St. Cadoc* twice, once where Arthur and his men encounter a chase after absconding lovers. Arthur and the others are simply described as vigorous heroes, and Arthur is shown as lusting after the woman before being persuaded to rescue her. The lovers become the parents of St. Cadoc, and the father becomes a saint himself.[5] Later, the adult St. Cadoc encounters Arthur, who is now described as an illustrious king of Britain. Arthur has been pursuing a *dux* or leader of the Britons who has killed three of his men.[6] All the significant locations are in the south of Wales, though the Life includes encounters between the saint and characters from North Wales and the North. As an older man, the saint encounters King Maelgwn[7] (Maglocunus) and Gildas.[8] Although no wars against the Saxons are mentioned at all, the chronological framework is not far off what we would expect from the *Annales Cambriae*, that one man's life span could extend from the early career of Arthur to the time of Gildas.

The Life of St. Illtud presents that saint as a cousin of Arthur. He has previously served as a soldier in Britanny before being attracted to Arthur's court by his generosity to his soldiers. Arthur is described as a king and a great victor.[9] This is rather more in keeping with what we would expect. *Historia Brittonum* shows Arthur of course as a great victor, *The Gododdin* compares a generous warrior to him. The only other named character in the *Mirabilia* is Illtud,[10] and the wonder connected to him is fifty miles away from the two Arthurian ones. St. Illtud eventually becomes a revered cleric and goes on to teach Gildas.

The chronology of some of these Lives seems to work in terms of what else we know about the history of the period. With others it is more suspect.

The Life of Gildas written in the early twelfth century shows Arthur again in the mode of a 'King of all great Britain' and 'tyrant'.[11] He is pursuing a thief all over the place, in this instance a king, Meluas, who has abducted his wife. Meluas rules Somerset, from Glastonbury, and Arthur besieges him with the men of Devon and Cornwall. The situation is resolved by Gildas, even though Arthur has previously killed the saint's brother. This placing of Arthur at the time of Gildas seems perhaps at variance with the situation we have deduced, that the victor of Badon, fought in the year Gildas was born, is of the previous generation, and that Gildas's contemporaries have forgotten the lessons learned then. If *Historia Brittonum* correctly identifies Arthur as the victor of Badon, then the chronology presented in *The Life of Gildas*, if taken literally, is potentially problematic.

Another life, St. Paternus (Padarn), is set at the time of Maelgwn, king of the Northern Britons (Maglocunus in his role as overthrower of tyrants), who is at war with the southern Britons around the saint's native Dyfed.[12] The saint is subsequently threatened by Arthur, a rapacious tyrant who desires his seamless tunic. The saint chastises Arthur, who, suitably chastened, takes Paternus as his patron.[13] Here the chronology is again somewhat at variance from what we would expect. *Annales Cambriae* and the Northern History extension to *Historia Brittonum* are clear that Maglocunus is after Arthur, not a contemporary, as is also the plain inference from Gildas.

It is difficult to know what to make of this material. The whole milieu of warfare against the Saxons is largely missing, and the connections between the different types of material sometimes tangential. The general ambience is that of feuding British tyrants admonished by brave churchmen. Often Britain seems an almost pagan land, being evangelized by a few intrepid individuals.

An interesting example that somewhat extends the geography involved is the *Life of St. Carantoc* (Carannog in modern Welsh). Carantoc is older but has links to St. Cadoc, living thirty years before the birth of St. David. Although his miracles are fanciful, concerning a floating altar and a ferocious serpent, the circumstantial details are intriguing. Although Carantoc is a native of Ceredigion in west Wales, his travels take him, seemingly, across the Severn to where 'In those times Cato and Arthur were reigning in that country'.[14] They are also said to be 'living in Dindraithou'. Part of the country they rule over includes the 'fields of Carrum'. Arthur is a supporter of Carantoc and is blessed by him. Arthur is presented as the more active of the two, Cato stays in their citadel (*arx*) and in his hall there. Their status and how and why they rule with each other is not explained, but they are Christians, supportive of the saint.

These are not, though, the only materials which mention these figures and places. Cair Draithou is one of the twenty-eight *civitates* of Britain in *Historia Brittonum*.[15] One of the fourteenth-century Welsh genealogical manuscripts traces a medieval Welshman's pedigree back to a 'Cado'[16] (Cadwy in modern Welsh), himself the son of Gereint son of Erbin. Cato/Cado/Cadwy appears in other contexts, a Breton Saint's life,[17] the Triads[18] (pieces of bardic lore grouped in threes) and other genealogies. It is his supposed father Gereint son of Erbin, however, about whom more detail is preserved. He is the subject of a poem which bears his name in the earliest of the Welsh manuscripts, the late thirteenth-century *Black Book of Carmarthen*. Gereint is a warrior, a cavalryman, leading other cavalry, at the Battle of Llongborth. The poet gives more details of his feats then 'In Llongborth I saw to Arthur/brave warriors, they hewed with steel/Emperor, leader of battle/ In Llongborth was slain to Geraint/ brave warriors from the region of Dyfnaint (Devon/Dumnonia)/ and although they had been killed, they killed.'[19] The poem has several mistakes and seems to have been difficult for the copier to transcribe. Later versions of the poem survive, with differences, but which make it clear that Gereint himself has been slain, not just his men.

Who Arthur and Gereint are fighting is not explained in the oldest version, but in the later versions it is clarified that Geraint is 'an enemy to the English and a friend to the Christians'.[20] This is an important detail, as the hero in the poem is occasionally conflated with a 'Gereint king of the Britons' who fought the West Saxons in 710, according to the *Anglo-Saxon Chronicle*.[21] At that stage, both Britons and Saxons were Christians. It is also telling that Arthur is given the same title 'leader of battle' ('*llywiaudir llawur*')[22] as he is in *Historia Brittonum*. He is also given the Roman title 'Emperor' (a loan word) perhaps, like *dux* in *Historia Brittonum*, suggesting a different type of power to the British kings.

In this collection of materials, we do have what seems to be the same situation as we have seen in *Historia Brittonum* – kings of the Britons, with Arthur as the leader of battles, fighting against the Saxons. Cato as the sedentary ruler of a stronghold, ruling in partnership with an active Arthur seems the epitome of 'kings and public officials kept their status' as Gildas has it. The men of Dumnonia taking part in the fight-back would add additional poignancy to his disappointment in his contemporary Dumnonian Constantine.

The location of Gereint's battle, 'Llongborth' means 'Longship Port'. It could relate to any of the riverine locations of the *Historia* battle list – the mouth of the River Glein, the River Dubglas, the banks of the River Tribuit. All the sources, the saint's life, the genealogy, and the poem are independent, they are in different manuscripts and do not otherwise refer to each other, nor do they obviously derive from *Historia Brittonum*, however, they do seem to paint something of a consistent picture.

Chapter 6

The Arthur Brooch, Arthur's Alliance, Arthur's Battles and St. Cadoc

With its references to Carn Cabal, and the tomb of Arthur's son in Ercing, the *Mirabilia* establish that their author clearly saw Arthur as a figure operating in the southern or central part of the Welsh borders. Since it is the often-linked *Historia Brittonum* that today is the foundation of our idea of an historical Arthur, it perhaps seems reasonable that we should give some credence to this evidence.

Arthur also seems to be linked to southern Wales and the southern Welsh borderlands in *The Life of St. Cadoc*, a work we will return to later. In one part of the life he is linked to two sites north of Caerleon, Tredunnock and Rhyd Gwrthebau, in what is now Llanhennock,[1] with the implication from the text and other evidence that these are on the western borders of his territory. A place named Messur Pritguenn in the Llandaff Charters seems to be named after Arthur's ship *Prydwen* and seems to be located between the Wye and the Usk, in much the same area.

As also mentioned in the previous chapter *The Life of St. Carantoc* links Arthur to land on the other side of the Severn estuary in Somerset. Here he is linked to a ruler called Cado, presumably one of Arthur's allied kings, and locations such as Carrum or Carhampton. Cado himself could be the character after whom several Cadbury hillforts in the West Country, including South Cadbury, and Cadbury/Congresbury, both showing major reoccupation

Figure 24. Roman commander of Vandal heritage Stilicho as depicted on an ivory diptych. British leaders of the fifth and sixth centuries might have looked somewhat similar.

in the Arthurian period are named. It is not even impossible that Cado/ Cador is Arthur himself, since the *Mirabilia* twice refers in Latin to *Arthuri militis*, Arthur the Warrior, and the Welsh word *cadwr* means Warrior or Defender. We know that other Roman military terms were used as titles or names in the post-Roman period, so Arthur Miles/Cadwr could conceivably be something similar.[2]

Later tradition, of course, links Arthur to sites such as Caerleon, Glastonbury and South Cadbury. All in all, it is possible to suggest some kind of base area for Arthur centred around the Severn estuary and the River Avon and stretching from the Welsh border down into the English West Country. It is an area that has Dobunni territory at its centre. Is this King Arthur's Country?

It is hard to say anything much about the possible origins of Arthur himself. If Arthur existed, he may have originally come from a wealthy, perhaps royal, family, or he may have earned wealth and power, and the right to 'fight alongside the kings of the Britons' as the *Historia Brittonum* puts it, through his military successes. He may have come from a family of eastern Britons that fled the Saxons or he might have been a western Briton, perhaps from the powerful Dobunni. Or his family might not originally have been British all. Many commanders in the late Roman army came from families that originally were non-Roman. Arthur's family might, at some stage, have come from across the Channel or North Sea. It is impossible now to be sure.

If Arthur seems likely to have been originally a historical figure, however, we do need to consider whether the battle list seems practical and feasible as the victories of a single commander linked to this area. We now need to look at how Arthur might have fought his battles and where.

So what would Arthur's warriors have looked like? The Anglo-Saxons buried their warriors with their kit, so it is comparatively easy to get a sense of how they were armed and how they looked. Arthur's Christian warriors were buried without their kit so it is much harder to know what that included. However, there is a little evidence that can help us.

We have already mentioned the buckle from Longbridge Deverill that probably shows a British militia commander in scale armour and cloak.[3]

Brancaster rings are a type of late Roman ring found in Britain. Most show birds or animals on their bezels. However, one (found at Amesbury) shows four heads wearing crested helmets.[4] A fifth-century buckle from Newbury shows bearded heads that may also have crests.[5]

Some of the wheel or rosette designs on the buckle plates of Dobunni belt fittings resemble late Roman shield designs shown in the *Notitia Dignitatum*.[6] A soldier shown on a Roman fourth-century glass beaker from Germany has a shield design very like the cross-hatched diamond designs on Dobunni belt fittings.[7] One of the figures on the late Roman Piazza Armerina mosaics, with a yellow cloak, red shield and raised spear, has basically the same motif on his tunic as on his shield, and it is tempting to think that some Dobunni militiamen would have had these designs on their shields too.

The *Vergilius Romanus* is an extraordinary manuscript. It is now in the Vatican Library but was in the Abbey of St. Denis (now in the suburbs of Paris) prior to the fifteenth century. However, design elements and the manner of portrayal of figures in it suggest it was probably produced in Britain sometime in the fifth century.[8] *The Aeneid* seems to have been popular in late Roman Britain. A number of art items have been found that show reference to it.[9] The *Historia Brittonum* includes a legend that Aeneas was an ancestor of the Britons via Brutus[10] and it may well be that this story was already believed by some in Britain in the late Roman period.

The *Vergilius Romanus* contains several depictions of warriors which suggest, to some extent, what a fifth-century British militiaman would have looked like. The essentials for all militiamen would have been spear, shield and knife and belt. The particularly well-equipped are shown with scale armour and crested helmets. Tunics have embroidered patterns as seen on late Roman military outfits. Some have sun symbols on the shoulders that look like sun symbols found on some late Roman buckle plates linked to the Dobunni. A few carry bows and arrows.

However, there is another element to the kit, which is easy to miss when glancing at the beautiful illustrations, which is perhaps the most important of all for our understanding of what was happening in fifth- and sixth-century Britain and how Arthur may have operated in that period. The warriors of the *Vergilius Romanus* are mostly shown wearing cloaks, and on their right shoulders the cloaks of the Trojans (probably viewed by some fifth-century Britons as ancestors) are secured with small round brooches that seem intended to be annular or penannular with, in two or three instances, (for instance, the depiction of Ascanius shooting the stag with an arrow) the cloak colour clearly showing through the centre of the brooch.

By comparison, Turnus, the Italian enemy of Aeneas is shown wearing a much larger type of brooch, with what appears to be a broad, flat circular band or disc, and Trojan women are shown wearing flat disc brooches with no central hole. Coins from the end of the Roman period show the emperor's cloak secured by what appears to be a circular or rosette brooch, with probably a central stone, and with decorative strings of pears suspended from it. A similar brooch with a large red central stone surrounded by pearls and with pearls suspended from it is shown worn by the Emperor Justinian in the famous Ravenna mosaic.

We have already explored how in the decades around the end of Roman Britain, some British warriors seem to have been wearing traditional British penannular brooches instead of the Roman official and military crossbow brooch. The large Type F brooches with their zoomorphic terminals were in use in the early fifth century. However, by the late fifth century, by the time of Arthur, a new type of penannular brooch had come into use, the small, chunky Type G, pretty much the same size as the brooches shown being worn by warriors in the *Vergilius Romanus*.

They are smaller than Type F and some Type E. They are sometimes only two or three centimetres across. However, they are sturdier than the previous types. They are also, clearly, in design terms the successors to Types E and F. Some of them have the same distinctive ribbing on the hoops as some Es and Fs, and the terminals are, again, facetted, and they have picked up the almost diamond shape that appears on some Type F terminals and made that the main design element.

There are not huge numbers of Type Gs that have been found – perhaps less than a hundred.[11] However, they may have major significance.

In this period in Ireland high rank continues to be demonstrated by specific forms of penannular brooch and since these Type Gs are about the only British brooches being made at this time, and since they are clearly in design terms the successors to the Type E and F penannulars with their military/official links it is hard to see them as anything other than high status. They may be pretty much the only item of perhaps military/official kit, and indeed are one of the very few manufactured items of any description that we have from the British-controlled areas of this island during the time of Arthur.

You could maybe almost call them 'the Arthur brooch', not just because of their chronology (mainly dating about 500–600) but also because they may say a lot about where Arthur operated, and how he was able to exercise power and fight battles across the island.

We know that Britain fragmented into small kingdoms after the end of Roman control. Yet Arthur, according to *Historia Brittonum*, appears to fight battles spread across much of Britain. One of the question marks over Arthur has long been whether that was possible in such a fragmented world. The distribution of Type G brooches, showing an unexpected degree of design uniformity in this period, not only suggests that it was possible, but it gives clues as to how it was possible.[12]

Some elements of the distribution are not surprising. A lot of Type G brooches have been found in the areas where Arthur is most likely to have been based, in the territory on both sides of the Bristol Channel and north into the Welsh borderlands, and it has been suggested that this is where they were first developed. This is an area that was important militarily in the Roman period (see, for instance, the distribution of third-century military buckles), it is also an area that contains a lot of early post-Roman British activity, with cemeteries, for instance, at Cadbury Congresbury,[13] Camerton, Lamyatt Beacon, Portishead, Brean Down, Henley Wood, Cannington, Maiden Castle, Wint Hill, Caerwent, Nettleton, Glastonbury and possibly Bradley Hill and Barry Island etc.[14]

What is more surprising is the large cluster of Type G brooches found in the east of England, in Lincolnshire and north from there. And the Type Gs found in the east are very similar to the Type Gs in the west. There is a close link of some description here. The cluster around the Chester area and the examples from Cornwall are also very interesting. The Cornwall brooches are not only close to the traditionally Arthurian location, but also an area of definite sixth-century activity at Tintagel. They are also close the Saints Way which crosses Cornwall from Padstow in the north to the Fowey estuary in the south. This follows the route traditionally taken by Celtic saints from Wales and Ireland heading south to Brittany, another area with strong Arthurian connections. However, it is almost certainly a route also taken by many others in the centuries before that. Dobunni coins have been found in the area[15] and a Dobunni-type buckle plate from the end of the Roman period was found at Tywardreath, not far from Castle Dore and the Tristan stone.[16] As mentioned earlier, Glywys, founder of Glywysing, is said to have become religious later in life and to have travelled to southern Cornwall, where he founded the church named after him, the Church of St. Gluvias at Penryn.

There is another type of brooch which seems to sit alongside Type G as an indicator of post-Roman British activity. This is the so-called Type H, like Type G but with flared ends. Only a few examples have been found. The southern distribution is similar to Type G, including examples from Baginton and Amesbury (both interesting locations); however, there are also a few examples from central Scotland, which is intriguing.[17]

We should also probably briefly mention here so-called 'hand pins'. They have been given this name because of their distinctive decoration on the ring which looks a little like a closed hand. These are not military items but could be high-status items and we will include them here because they represent another of the extremely few British items from this period, and because they come from similar areas to some Type Gs. There are so-called proto-hand-pins from Gloucester and Oldcroft, Gloucestershire, and Welton le

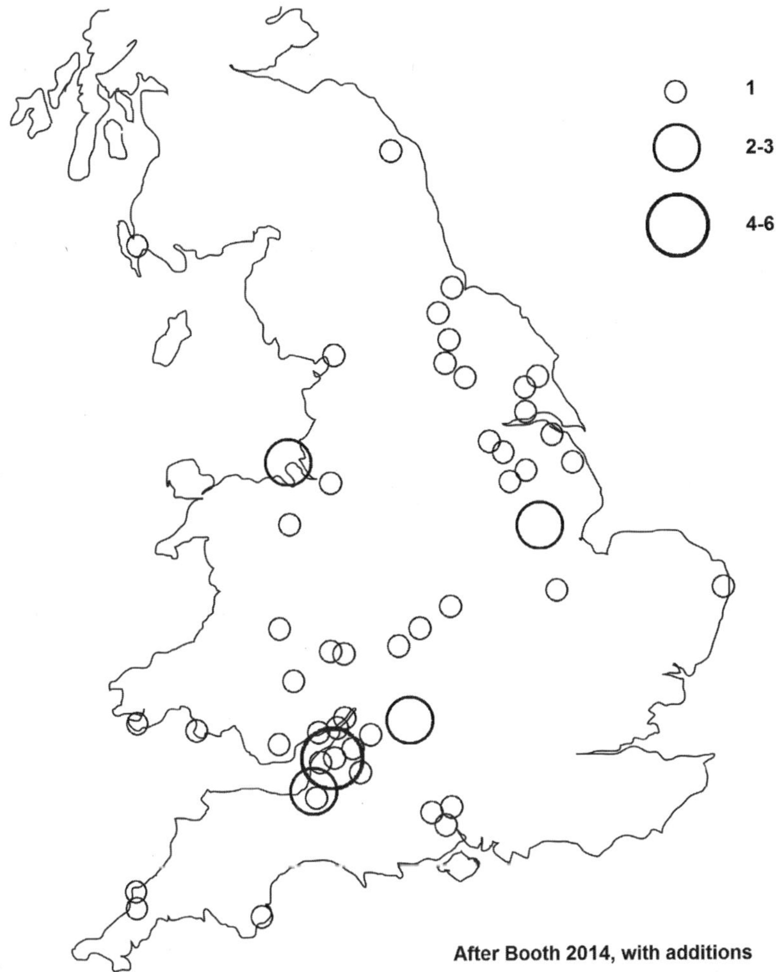

Figure 25. Distribution of Type G Penannular brooches. (After Booth, Reassessing the long chronology of the penannular brooch in Britain, 2014, with additions Laycock)

Wold, Lincolnshire. There are hand pins from Horsley, Gloucestershire, from Burghwallis, Doncaster, from Low Toynton, Lincolnshire, from Blidworth, Nottinghamshire, from Tripontium, Leicestershire, and from Chilton Trinity and Long Sutton, Somerset.[18]

So what is happening here?

In Chapter 1 we explored how an alliance between the Dobunni of Cirencester

Province, and the Corieltauvi of Lincoln Province seems to have developed around the time of the end of Roman Britain. An explanation of the Type G distribution could be that this alliance was renewed towards the end of the fifth century, with the arrival of the 'Arthurian' period. The political geography by then had slightly changed. There had been Anglo-Saxon settlement along the Lincolnshire coast and in the southern Corieltauvi region, around Leicester. However, the area around Lincoln was still under British control and would retain a distinct identity as the Kingdom of Lindsey.[19] If this alliance had been restored, then it would enable an Arthur based in the west to operate also in the east and north-east. The *Historia Brittonum* states that Arthur led an alliance against the Saxons. This could be solid evidence of a key element of that alliance.

However, the location of many Arthurian battles is somewhat uncertain so, in order to further to assess the meaning of the Type G distribution, we now need to consider in detail Arthur's battles (mainly those listed in *Historia Brittonum*,[20] plus a couple of others) and where they may have happened.

The first battle that *Historia Brittonum* attributes to Arthur is said to take place at the mouth of the River Glein. There are two rivers called Glen, which are usually suggested as the site of this battle. Glen and Glein both seem to come from the same British source which means 'clean'. The River Glen in Lincolnshire eventually now flows into the River Welland near Spalding. The River Glen in Northumberland passes Yeavering and then flows into the River Till.

Just to the north of the Lincolnshire Glen was an area of extensive salt production and salt works in pre-Roman, Roman and medieval times. In terms of there being an Anglo-Saxon presence accessible from areas of British control, both sites are feasible for an Arthurian battle. And both sites are close to a Type G presence as well. A Type G comes from Wooler, just a few miles from the hillfort on Yeavering Bell and the location of the Anglo-Saxon palace at Yeavering that was once in the kingdom of Bernicia.[21] It is hard to say which is the more likely of the two as an Arthurian battle site, as they both make sense in terms of the political geography of the period, and they both make sense in terms of Type G.

Another Glein option would be the River Sence near Leicester. The village names Glen Parva and Great Glen are thought by place name experts to suggest that an earlier name of the Sence was the Glen.[22] The mouth of the Sence is pretty much Atherstone, with the Roman town of Mancetter on Watling Street nearby, and the Roman pottery industry site of Mancetter/Hartshill. There is a hillfort at Hartshill, now hollowed out to contain a reservoir, and in the Domesday Book in 1086 Hartshill is recorded as Ardreshill.

There is perhaps a fourth Glein option. Variant readings on Glein in manuscripts of *Historia Brittonum* include Glem or Glemu. This would suit the River Glyme north of Oxford. This is said to be a Celtic river name[23] and when it appears in the place name, Glympton, some early forms do also have forms with 'n' (e.g. Glintone 1086, Clantona 1235–36). The mouth of this river seems a likely site for a battle. It is close to Ambrosden and where the main Roman road between St. Albans and Cirencester crosses the river, there are linear earthworks.[24] These are pre-Roman, but like several hillforts could have been reused in the post-Roman period.

After Glein, *Historia Brittonum* states that Arthur fought his next four battles at the River Dubglas in the region of Linnuis.

It has been persuasively and powerfully argued that Linnuis is the natural linguistic progression from late British Lindes (the territory of Lindum, the Roman name for Lincoln, and origin of the name of the Kingdom of Lindsey based on Lincoln) to early Welsh Linnes and then Old Welsh, Linnuis.[25] Clearly, it makes sense that a British area with Anglo-Saxon settlement on three sides of it could be the location of multiple battles in this period, and clearly, in terms of Type G, it makes sense that the location of many Type Gs, and one of the key elements of Arthur's possible alliance, would be the site of numerous battles.

Dubglas has sometimes been taken to mean black-blue. However, that is assuming that the second syllable of Dubglas is *glas*, and not *glais*. *Glais* means stream and is found paired with Dub in several place names. In Scotland, for instance, there is Douglas in South Lanarkshire (Duvelglas c. 1150). In Wales there is Dowlais (Dugleis c. 990–c. 1010). It is thought that two Welsh rivers now called Dulas may originally have been Duglais. Black is, of course, a common name for dark-watered rivers around the world, for obvious reasons. Blue is, by contrast, not a particularly common name for rivers. With our heads full of Mediterranean seaside photos and pictures of swimming pools we instinctively think of water as blue. However, rivers that actually usually look blue are very rare and Blue River is not a common name around the world.

In Wales there are a number of examples of Afon Ddu, Black River, and in England there are a number of rivers like the River Dove in North Yorkshire and the River Dove in Derbyshire where it is thought the original name was British Dub with a British word meaning river, and where the modern name has kept the British dub element, little changed, but the English word river has replaced the original British word for river.

There is no river Dubglas or Dubglais still in the Lindsey area. If, however, we assume the original name was Dub Glais, Black river (see, for instance, the Tain Bo Cuailnge which features rivers called Glais Cruind and Glas Gatlaig where Glais/Glas is separate) and that, perhaps, the author of *Historia Brittonum* was including both Latin and British words for river, just as later in the passage he includes both Latin and British words for forest (if the battle list was, as many think, originally a poem, perhaps the author needed Glas with Dub, in order to rhyme with Bassas), and that perhaps the Glais/Glas element has since been replaced by English words for stream or river then there are a number of just about possible candidates in or near Lindsey.

The first of these we will look at is the River Devon that runs north to Newark-on-Trent. It has been suggested by a place name expert that the earliest forms of the River Devon's name (e.g. Difune 1239, Dyven 1351) may indicate that it comes from British *dubno* (a similar word to *dub* with some similarities of sense, including deep, dark, mysterious).[26]

However, this word when used of watercourses seems often to be linked to mountain streams in deep valleys which is not hugely appropriate for the Devon, and there is another River Devon in Scotland which is known in Gaelic as the Duibhe, which is basically the same word as the *dub* in Dubglas and means black. Watson derives the Scottish Devon from British Dubone or Dobona 'black one'.[27] Similarly in France the Dheune (Duina 873) is thought to have been probably originally something like Dubis or Dubina, derived from *dub*, or black. The Irish surname Dubhain means black or dark, and has later forms that include Devane, Devin. Compare other early forms of the River Devon's name, Deuene and Devyn.

Another possible derivation for the River Devon would be Dub Afon, also meaning Black River (see suggested derivation of Scottish river Doon from *Dubh abhainn*, Black River).

Ultimately it is not possible to say that the Devon definitely is the Dubglas of *Historia Brittonum*, but etymologically it seems just about possible it could be the same river. There is no other modern river name in Lindsey that could be derived from Dubglas. And it would be make some sense if it the Devon is the Dubglas. The River Devon is not far from the Lincolnshire Glen, and it crosses under the major Roman road, the Fosse Way, near Newark-on-Trent. The probably pre-Viking estate of Kirton-in-Lindsey may once have included Newark, so this would also probably be in Lindsey.[28] There was a Roman settlement at East Stoke (called Ad Pontem) a few miles south-west of Newark, which was defended by a stone wall two and a half metres thick,[29] and presumably, judging by its name, was a strategic location with a bridge linking Fosse Way to the suspected Roman road up the Greet Valley on the west side of the River Trent. East Stoke was the site of a battle in 1487. Newark was an area of major Anglo-Saxon settlement in the late fifth and early sixth century (about the time of Arthur) on the western edge of an area that was then largely Anglo-Saxon culturally and, because of its strategic location at the junction of Fosse Way and the Great North Road, was the site of much fighting and three sieges separate during the English Civil War. Somewhere near where the River Devon meets the Fosse Way would seem a likely place for Arthurian battles. If there were four battles here then, logically, they could have been attempts by Arthur to keep control of the Fosse Way in this area and maintain the connection between his forces in the west and his British allies in the east. The next Roman settlement up the road from Ad Pontem is the defended site of Crococalana at Brough, five miles from Newark on the other side.[30] A Type G penannular was found at Norton Disney,[31] a couple of miles east of Crocoalana/ Brough, and another was found at Tuxford,[32] to the north-west of the area.

Another just about possible candidate for Dub Glais would be Dove Brook, in the outskirts of Leicester. It is suggested that Dove is derived from British *dub*, dark/black.[33] However, Dove Brook was only ever a minor feature, and Leicester, while being a major Roman city and major location for early Anglo-Saxon settlement, was probably a little beyond the borders of Lindsey.

There is also a River Dove in Yorkshire near Barnsley, but again that is some distance from Lindsey's borders.

Arthur's sixth battle, according to *Historia Brittonum* was at the River Bassas. This is a difficult one. Nobody has really come up with a totally convincing location for this battle. One possible location is Baschurch in Shropshire, which was probably a major site in the post-Roman kingdom of Pengwern and was described in an early poem as the churches of Bassa and said to be the site of the grave of Cynddylan (see Chapter 8), and another is Bassingham, a site in Lincolnshire and Lindsey. In terms of post-Roman geography and Type Gs, both are possible. If the Bassas battle was at Baschurch it might suggest Arthur was fighting somebody apart from the Saxons, but the distribution of Anglo-Saxon brooches in the sixth century does extend along the Roman road Watling Street almost as far as Wroxeter[34] so a battle against Anglo-Saxons at Baschurch is not impossible. There is also the River Biss in Wiltshire which joins the River Avon near Bradford-on-Avon with its possible Vortigern connection. However, there seems nothing to show that Bassas could change to Biss. Perhaps the closest is Ekwall's suggestion that Biss may derive from a British word like *bys*, *bes*, *bease*, meaning a finger.[35]

Next, we come to Cat Coit Celidon. Despite attempts to look for this elsewhere (e.g. Caludon Castle, Coventry) there is broad agreement that this battle should be located in the Caledonian Forest. Where in the Caledonian Forest exactly, is another question. References to the sixth-century Battle of Arfderydd[36] suggest Myrddin fled into the Caledonian Forest after the fighting and since the location of this battle is often said to be at Arthuret, just north of Carlisle and Hadrian's Wall, it is possible wooded areas in the vicinity were regarded by some as a part of the Caledonian Forest. A Type G has indeed been found at Luce Sands along the Scottish coast west of Carlisle,[37] and, interestingly enough, this is in an area that has other Arthurian connections. There is also a Type H from nearby in Galloway, as well as those Type Hs further north.[38]

One of the earliest people recorded carrying the name Arthur is a prince of Dalriada called Artur or Artuir, who lived sometime in the sixth century and was killed at the Battle of Miathi in the late sixth century. Dalriada was a kingdom that spanned the Irish Sea in the early medieval period from

Country Antrim to Argyll. Dalriada, on both sides of the sea was quite close to Luce Sands. And there is a Welsh Triad which mentions a northern court of Arthur at Pen Rhionydd. Etymologically, Rhionydd is thought to derive from the Roman period name Rerigonium and is thought to be the origin of the modern name Loch Ryan, not far from Luce Sands.[39] This area is a communications hub now, with the port of Cairnryan and its ferry crossing to Northern Ireland, and was a communications hub in the early post-Roman period. Luce Sands seems to have seen post-Roman activity. There was a major early Christian site at Whithorn[40] and post-Roman evidence, including penannular brooches, has been found at the Mote of Mark hillfort.[41] Some imported Mediterranean pottery of the period, like that found in England in the west country made it this far north. Arthur at some stage is said to have fought Caw of Strathclyde and some of Caw's children are said to have travelled to Wales. Did Arthur ever get to Caledonia? It is impossible to know, but it is certainly not inconceivable he had some connection with this area.

After the Battle of Coit Celidon, *Historia Brittonum* says that Arthur's next battle was at Guinnion, or Guinon Castle. There actually is a Villa Guinnonui listed in the Llandaff Charters,[42] however that was a *villa* (a word used in the charters to describe a farm or estate) rather than a castle and was located somewhere in Gwent and perhaps seems an unlikely Arthurian battle site.

The *Historia Brittonum* goes into more detail about this battle than any other battle, including the Battle of Badon Hill. It says that during the battle Arthur carried a depiction of the Virgin Mary on his shoulders and, after putting the Saxons to flight, pursued them the whole day, killing many of them. Halsall has argued persuasively that the author of the Arthurian battle list viewed Guinnion as perhaps Arthur's most important battle and deliberately arranged his description of the battles, and constructed the sentences describing them, so that Guinnion was literally, as well as metaphorically, at the centre of it.[43] It's an interesting observation by Halsall because two of the most plausible candidates for the site of Guinnion would have been both literally and metaphorically at the centre of Arthur's activities if those were based on a Type G alliance between east and west.

If you look at the distributions of pre-Roman coinage of the Dobunni, the Corieltauvi and the Catuvellauni to the south, they all meet roughly in the area where Watling Street (and now the M1) travels from Milton Keynes to Rugby. This area, in the early fifth century, was the bridge between the horsehead buckle Dobunni areas in the west and the horsehead buckle Corieltauvi areas in the west, and in the late fifth century, it was the bridge between King Arthur's Country and Arthur's possible allies in Lindsey and the east. Again, if you look at where, in the post-Roman period, the distribution of Anglian material meets the distribution of Saxon material and both meet the culturally British area to the west of that it is pretty much the same area.[44]

And if you look at Type G distribution, this is pretty much where the western group ends, with an example found at Bensford Bridge, Warwickshire.[45] A beautiful British late Roman or early post-Roman 'hand pin' was found at Tripontium, on Watling Street in this area.[46] And there is an unusual cluster of Type Fs in the area.[47] These brooches are generally reckoned to be a little earlier than Type Gs; however, they are reckoned to have an official or military function and the cluster here seems out of the ordinary and interesting.

The area is in the gap between rivers that drain into the North Sea and rivers that drain into the Bristol Channel, Irish Sea etc. It is on the watershed between Trent heading north and east and Avon heading south and west. It also controls access to the vital salt wells at Droitwich, then, perhaps, Britain's most major source of an indispensable product. It is likely that just as Ambrosius may have relied on the wealth of Droitwich for some of his finances, so Arthur may have done the same. At some stage, probably in the sixth century, ten new hearths, each about two metres long, on which salt brine could be boiled, were built from salvaged stones. The earliest of the radiocarbon dates associated with this activity is 340–540 and another hearth has a date of 440–625.[48]

Could the rare bear figurine found near there have some connection to Arthur, a name often derived from the Celtic word for bear?[49] Could even the name of Droitwich itself be connected to the castle of Arthur and Cador named as Dindraithou in *The Life of Carantoc* (which is probably the same as Cair Draitou/Droithan/Droitan/Druith in *Historia Brittonum*)? This would be Dun Draithou, the hill Draithou, or Cair Droitan, the fortress Droitan. Droitwich is the *wic* or settlement Droit or a similar name (Drihtwych 1347, Drethwyche 1503, Draytewiche 1533[49]). *The Life of Carantoc* does, admittedly, imply that Dindraithou is in the west of England, rather than the Midlands, but the name similarities are interesting.

The geographic centre of England is fairly close to all this today, and certainly you could argue that in terms of sixth-century strategy this was pretty much the centre of Britain then.

At the southern end of this centre zone, near Milton Keynes, was the Roman settlement of Magiovinium. About forty miles further up Watling Street was the Roman settlement of Venonis or Vennonis. It is situated on a strategic Roman crossroads where Fosse Way crossed Watling Street, and, for that reason, has sometime been called 'the centre of Roman Britain'.

To the west of this line is the Forest of Arden area. It is an interesting, wooded area that had Anglo-Saxon cultural areas on three sides but not within in. The area still has a Celtic name (probably meaning high area rather than the bear's wood, though it was sometimes written as Arthern or Arthden) and to the west is Brailes, a Roman-period centre and a name that is thought may incorporate the British word *lys* meaning 'royal court'.[50] Lys is a place name element found fairly frequently in Wales. It is extremely rare in England.

When an initial Roman V as in Magiovinium or Venonis was written in Welsh, it would naturally change to a Gu. So, we would have Magioguinium and Guenonis. The Magio element in Magiovinium probably means simply Great or Greater[51] and could be being used to distinguish the settlement near Milton Keynes from the settlement with a very similar name a short distance further up Watling Street. Magiovinium is, also incidentally, perhaps a Latin translation of Ehangwen, a name sometimes given as the name of one of Arthur's courts.[52] Without Magio (and the Ravenna Cosmography, for instance, splits some names into their constituent elements, with Camulo Dono, for instance for Camulodunum[53]) we have Guinium and Guenonis. This is very similar to the Guinnion or Guinon of the original *Historia Brittonum* texts.

The other main candidate for Guinnion is Vinovium at Binchester in Durham. There are Type Gs, not far from here. However, etymologically Vinovium would perhaps more naturally become something like Guinnwy, rather than Guinnion.

The *Historia Brittonum* states that Arthur's ninth battle was at the City of the Legion or Cair Lion.

There were three cities that could have been described in late Roman Britain as City of the Legion. There was Eboracum/York, home to Legio VI Victrix, Isca/Caerleon, home to Legio II Augusta, and Deva/Chester, home to Legio XX Valeria Victrix.

All three cities have Type Gs from nearby. However, Arthur's battle probably did not take place at York, because the name is York is derived ultimately from Eboracum, and the city has continuously been known with some name derived from Eboracum. For instance, in his list of the cities of Britain, the author of *Historia Brittonum* refers to Cair Ebrauc.[54]

Caerleon is still called that and has traditional Arthurian connections. However, in Welsh literature Caerleon was usually called Caerleon-on-Usk.

The other city that seems to have been called Cair Legion is Chester, with Bede, for instance, mentioning Carlegion as its British name. There is that interesting cluster of Type Gs in the Chester area[55] and an early post-Roman trading port at Meols,[56] there are strategic and valuable salt workings nearby at Middlewich, Nantwich and Northwich that were valued by the Romans and protected by forts, and Chester was the site of a major battle between Britons and Anglo-Saxons in the early seventh century. In addition, the traditional site of the so-called Alleluia victory in which St. Germanus is said to have won a victory in the 420s over Picts and Saxons by getting the local Britons to terrorize the invaders by sonic warfare (making a loud noise so they thought a huge army was approaching)[57] is at Maes Garmon (the Field of Germanus) at nearby Mold. There is an eighteenth-century monument to the battle there.

It is worth here, though, also briefly exploring the Lion question. There are some intriguing Leon and Lion connections in the early medieval world. We have already mentioned St. Paul Aurelian in Chapter 2, a man with possible family connections to Ambrosius Aurelianus. Having travelled from Wales to Cornwall, where the village of Paul is named after him, he travelled to Brittany where he founded a monastery in an abandoned Roman fort which became known as Castell Paol. Today it is known as St. Pol de Leon, because the region of Brittany where it is based is known, for unknown reasons, as Leon (French for lion). There is also an area in Herefordshire, that was once known as Leon or Lene, containing Leominster[58] (which has an early legend about a lion[59]) and which was once probably once part of Powys. The lion appears on some late Roman buckles in Britain[60] and was a symbol of medieval Powys.

There is also the legendary kingdom of Lyonesse, mentioned in Arthurian stories, and supposedly located off Cornwall. The early poem *Teyrnon's Prize Song* that has references to Arthur also includes the phrase 'breastplate of Lleon'.[61] There do seem to be quite a lot of lions around, though having said all that, Caerleon or Chester are still the most probable locations for Arthur's *Historia Brittonum* battle.

Arthur's next battle, his tenth battle, was on the River Tribuit, Tribruit or Trat Treuroit. The key early Arthurian text *Pa Gur*, which recounts the exploits of Arthur and some of his men, mentions Bedwyr fighting on the banks of the Trywruid or Tryfrwyd.[62] It is widely assumed that Tribuit, Treuroit and Tryfrwyd are all names for the same battle.

Many suggestions have been made for the possible location of this battle. However, there is a river on the maps that still has a very similar name. Little, if any attention has been paid to this in the search for Arthur's battles, perhaps because it is not in the most obvious region for an Arthurian battle. However, as we shall explore, it is actually very close to an alleged battle involving Arthur.

The River Triffrwd flows into the Dulas River near Talgarth in Wales. It is an old name. It is unclear what the earliest forms of the name were, but forms from the fourteenth century onwards include Treffroid and Tryfrwd.[63] Tryfrwd is clearly very close to Tryfrwyd.

'F' in Welsh is pronounced like an English 'V' whereas 'Ff' is pronounced like an English 'F'. However, there was plenty of scope for both flexibility and errors in earlier Welsh spelling. The early form Tryfrwd for the river near Talgarth suggests this, as does the fact that in some medieval Welsh manuscripts an 'f' could sometimes stand for an English 'f' and sometimes for an English 'v'.[64] *Ffrwd* is a Welsh word that means 'swift brook' or 'torrent'. It is, however, written *frut* in the early medieval Llandaff Charters. If Tribruit/Treuroit/Tryfrwyd is the original name, then getting to Trifrut/Tryfrwd and then by assimilation to the word *Ffrwd*, to Treffroid/Triffrwd is far from impossible. Tryfrwyd would mean something like 'the speckled river' which might seem appropriate for the Triffrwd dappled, as much of it is, by the shade of trees over it.

And there are other reasons for thinking that the Talgarth Triffrwd may indeed be the Arthurian Tryfrwyd.

The *Historia Brittonum* does not specify who Arthur's opponent was in the tenth battle, though it does make a blanket assertion that Arthur's opponents in all his battles were Saxons. The *Pa Gur* says Bedwyr was fighting Garwlwyd at Tryfrwyd. *Garwlwyd* means 'rough grey'. Cwm Garw Llwyd, for instance, is a place name in Carmarthenshire.

The Garwlwyd of the *Pa Gur* may or may not be the same as a Gwrgi Garwlwyd mentioned in the Welsh Triads, who is a figure from Welsh legend about whom very little is known. It has been suggested that originally Gwrgi Garwlwyd may have been some kind of a werewolf (*Gwrgi* means 'man-hound') perhaps linked to a figure in Irish stories with a somewhat similar name, German Garbglas.[65]

Garwlwyd does not seem to be a Saxon. And, as we shall explore over the Battle of Camlann, Arthur did not only fight against Saxons. Considering how many times Gildas mentions British civil wars in his work on the fifth and sixth centuries, it would be surprising if Arthur did not also fight British opponents on several occasions.

In fact, *The Life of St. Cadoc*[66] gives details of a battle between Arthur and Brychan, born in Ireland, but a ruler of Brycheiniog in Wales, who had his capital at Talgarth, a couple of miles from the River Triffrwd.

Cadoc is a major early Welsh saint and, as discussed in Chapter 5, the Life written about him, and the mention made of Arthur in it, is one of the key early sources on Arthur that come from before the time of Geoffrey of Monmouth.

In *The Life of St. Cadoc* it is said that Cadoc's father was Gwynllyw a late fifth-century ruler of a small kingdom named after him in South Wales near Caerleon. St. Woolos Cathedral in Newport is named after him. Gwynllyw is said to have been a son of Glywys of Glywysing, another kingdom in South Wales. As explored in Chapter 2, the names Glywys and Glywysing may have some kind of connection to Gloucester and the Dobunni.

In *The Life of St. Cadoc* it says that Gwynllyw wanted to marry Gwladys, the daughter of Brychan, and when Brychan refused, Gwynllyw took 300 men and abducted her from Brychan's capital at Talgarth. Furious, Brychan gathered his own forces and those of his friends and allies and pursued Gwynllyw and his men. Gwynllyw unwisely decided to fight rather than flee. Brychan's forces killed 200 of Gwynllyw's men and then Gwynllyw fled. Arthur, Bedwyr and Cei, the same figures who appear in *Pa Gur*, were sitting on a hill, called

Brochriwcarn (Bochriw cairn) playing a game. Arthur took a fancy to Gwladys and decided to seize her for himself but was talked out of it by Bedwyr and Cei, and, in the end, Arthur decided to take pity on Gwynllyw, and Arthur with his men attacked Brychan's forces and put them to flight. Gwynllyw consequently escaped with Gwladys, married her, and soon after St. Cadoc was born.

The situation seems broadly plausible. The church at Talgarth is dedicated to St. Gwendoline, another daughter (or granddaughter) of Brychan and she is reputedly buried there.[67] There is some evidence of links between Dobunni areas and Gwynllywg, for instance, in the Dobunni-type belt buckle found at Caerwent.[68] Many post-Roman kingdoms were based on existing tribal territories, whereas Brychan's kingdom was perhaps not. The origins of the small kingdom of Brycheiniog (from which we get Brecon and the Brecon Beacons) are somewhat obscure but seem to involve some combination of a local ruler and Irish allies.[69] Such a process of formation could have led to border disputes with neighbours like the Dobunni. One of Brychan's sons was called Arthen (see Llanarthen near Newport and Cefn Arthen in Brycheiniog).

A place called Fochriw, over twenty miles south of Talgarth, is thought by some to be the site of the Bochriw cairn mentioned by the author of the Life, writing at the monastery of Llancarfan even further south. However, the Life does indicate that the place name derives from the Welsh word for 'cheek' which is still *boch*. 'Boch-' names are very rare in Wales, so it is worth noting that on the high ground just to the north of Talgarth is a place called Boughrood in English, Bochrwyd in Welsh. Early forms include Bochred, from 1250, not that long after the Life was written, and Bochryd.[70] Could this be the site of the Bochriw cairn?

There is a hill there and the mound of a castle. Standing on the high ground at Boughrood you can look across the Wye valley and see the hill above Talgarth church (dedicated to St. Gwendoline, Brychan's daughter or granddaughter) on the other side a few miles distant. Since the location of Brychan's fort/palace at Talgarth is not known, it is even possible that it could once have been visible from the hill at Boughrood. And wherever Arthur, Bedwyr and Cei might have been sitting, it seems plausible to connect Bedwyr's Battle of Tryfrwyd and the *Historia Brittonum* battle with the Arthur, Bedwyr, Cei battle after the abduction from

Talgarth, and with the River Triffrwd which is pretty much at Talgarth.

The whole area is just to the west of the western borders of the Dobunni. The nearest Dobunni coin was found at Llanthony Priory a few miles east and there are some from about ten miles north as well.[71] There is easy access to the area from the possible stronghold of Ambrosius at Sutton Walls (about forty miles along the Roman roads) and areas strongly associated with Arthur, including what is said to be the location of the tomb of his son are nearby. St. Maelog, thought by some to have been one of Arthur's warriors, founded a monastery at Llowes nearby, where he is said to be buried and the church at Llandefalle almost on the River Triffrwd is thought by some to have originally been dedicated to him. There is even a field called Dinas Arthur, 'the fort of Arthur', mentioned in a document about sales of land in the Llanthony area about 200 years ago.[72] Type Gs are not too far distant.[73]

We might even be able to find the actual battlefield itself. There are several hillforts in the area which could have been connected to the battle, including one above the town of Llyswen. The name Llyswen means 'white court' suggesting early royal connections and the church there is also dedicated to St. Gwendoline. There are also intriguing linear earthworks around the Norman-era castle of Bronllys (another royal court) which have prompted some to suggest earlier occupation, perhaps Roman or post-Roman.[74]

However, ancient battles were often fought where a road crosses a river. It is widely assumed a Roman road runs along the Dulas valley on the route from the Roman fort of Y Gaer to the Roman town at Kenchester and is reckoned to cross the Triffrwd at one of two points.[75] It probably crossed the river where the A438 now crosses it, but may have crossed where the A470 does. One of those crossing areas may represent Arthur's Tryfrwyd battlefield. There is a place name next to the Triffrwd, just south of the A470 crossing and next to a smaller crossing which, on old maps, is called Gwern-y-bedd, or 'the marsh of the grave' – '*y-bedd*' is a place name element sometimes associated elsewhere with ancient burials.[76]

It would definitely be interesting to explore archaeologically the possible locations of the Tryfrwyd battlefield to see what may remain. However, it is notoriously difficult to find actual archaeological evidence of ancient battles, particularly where, as in the sixth century, numbers of fighters involved would mostly have been small. Armies would probably usually have consisted of hundreds of fighters (like Gwynllyw's 300 men), and if there were thousands they would have been in the low thousands. If Arthur (and his forces) really did kill 940 at the Battle of Badon, as *Historia Brittonum* claims, there probably was not much left of the enemy force afterwards. Corpses abandoned on the battlefield would have rotted or been removed by wild animals. Iron weapons would have been either removed by locals or would have rusted away.

Perhaps the only potentially relevant finds in the area so far are a Roman military buckle that may be too early to have anything to do with Arthur,[77] though Roman troops in Wales do seem to have been wearing third-century kit into the late fourth century,[78] and a Celtic scabbard chape or pommel.[79] This again may be too early; however, no real parallels have been found for it so far. The faces on it do look somewhat similar to those on the Sutton Hoo whetstone sceptre and with Brychan's Irish connection added to the existing cultural mix in the area, it is difficult to know what weapons might have been carried at the time. A few miles south of the Triffrwd, an area is marked on old maps as Cwm Gelanedd, the valley of slaughter, or of heaps of corpses. It is some distance from the Triffrwd, but there again, the account of the fighting in *The Life of St. Cadoc* might suggest a running battle moving over some distance.

It is even possible that we could come up with a date for the Battle of Tryfrwyd. It is reasonable to guess that St. Cadoc could have been born a year or two after the abduction of his mother, so if we know the date of St. Cadoc's birth we could get at least some idea of the date of the battle. The prestigious *Dictionary of Irish Biography* gives his birth date as c. 497, which would make the battle possibly around 495. So far, we have unfortunately not been able to find the basis on which the *Dictionary of Irish Biography* entry quotes 497; however, a date of around 495 for the Battle of Tryfrwyd is consistent with the probable general chronology of Arthur.

Brycheiniog, Brychan's kingdom, would eventually become the Lordship of Brecknock under Anglo-Norman marcher lords. Brecknock produced the name Brecon. In 2023, it was decided to change the main name of the Brecon Beacons National Park to the Welsh version Bannau Brycheiniog (meaning the Peaks of Brycheiniog) bringing Brychan's kingdom into the news once again.

So we reach the eleventh battle. Two entirely different names are given for this: Mount Agned and Bregomion/Breguoin/Bregion. Textually Bregomion/ Breguoin/Bregion seems preferable to Mount Agned, so we will go with that. There is no real agreement on where either place name might be located.

One suggestion for this battle site is Bremenium, the Roman site at High Rochester in Northumberland. Theoretically this may be linguistically possible (though in Wales Roman Bremia, with the same root as Bremenium, became Brevi in the Latin *The Life of St. Cadoc* and then Welsh Brefi, as it is still is). However, another option with perhaps as much, or more, going for it is the Roman site of Branogenium, at Leintwardine in Herefordshire.

Defences were built around the Roman site there in the second century. A mile or two to the south is Brandon Camp, a hillfort containing a Roman fort and with some intriguing linear cropmarks nearby. Leintwardine is also a little north of Sutton Walls (see Chapter 2) and a Type G has been found at Wellington, Herefordshire, which is also the site of a Roman villa. A name like Branogenium could conceivably produce something like Bregomion/ Bregion.

In the *Antonine Itinerary*, Branogenium's name seems to be given as Bravonium, perhaps a variant.[80] This is interesting, as a connection is often drawn between the battle mentioned in *Historia Brittonum*, and another battle, the Battle at the Cells of Brewyn mentioned in an early poem attributed to the great British poet Taliesin, and praising late sixth century ruler Urien of Rheged.[81] It has been suggested that the author of *Historia Brittonum* 'borrowed' this battle from Urien for Arthur.

This is not impossible. Equally, it is not impossible that one location was the site of two battles. There are plenty of instances of this in British history partly because the same geographic and strategic factors that dictate the location of a battle in one era can still apply in another era, and since the author of *Historia Brittonum* mentions Urien, it might seem strange to shift a battle from one character to another within his brief work.

Bravonium could produce Breguoin and Brewyn.

Interestingly there is a more modern example of how these place name changes could have occurred. Bryngwyn, meaning 'white hill' is a name attached to a few places in Wales. Bryngwyn about twenty-five miles south-west of Leintwardine is recorded as Brewen in 1231, and as Bringwyn in 1291.[82]

Could Urien's battle be linked with Leintwardine? There are some suggestions of sixth-century post-Roman ecclesiastical activity at Leintwardine and certainly there is an Anglo-Saxon foundation there by about 800, at the latest, which might account for the reference to the (presumably monastic) Cells of Brewyn.

Some have suggested Leintwardine to be too far from Rheged for Urien to be fighting there. However, this argument does not necessarily seem convincing. The kingdom of Rheged seems to have been situated mainly somewhere in the region of what is now Cumbria, but it is very unclear where Rheged's borders were and how far south it stretched. It is also unclear who Urien's enemy at the Cells of Breywn was, but the same poem that mentions the Cells of Brewyn also mentions Urien's involvement with Powys and Leintwardine may have been part of Powys at one stage. It was certainly on the borders of Powys. The poem also mentions a place called Pencoed, meaning 'end of the wood'. There are several places with this name, or versions of it, in Britain, and one of these is Pencoyd in Herefordshire.

The last battle in the *Historia Brittonum* list is the battle mentioned by Gildas, the Battle of Badon Hill.[83] Gildas refers to it as a siege. It is not clear in either account who might be besieging whom, but the *Historia Brittonum* account perhaps seems to indicate that Arthur was doing the attacking. He is said personally to have killed 940 men, so it would have been a busy day for him.

Gildas unfortunately gives no indication of which Saxons were being fought at Badon and he gives no indication of where the battle took place. However, most of what he writes about in the period around his lifetime concerns the west of Britain, what is now Cornwall, Devon and Wales, so his Badon is unlikely to be very far from there.

Gildas also, of course, does not indicate who led the Britons at Badon. This does not mean it was not Arthur.

Various Lives of the Saints, including one of the Lives of Gildas suggest the Church did not really approve of Arthur. Indeed, Arthur is said to have killed one of the brothers of Gildas, which, if true, would not have endeared him to Gildas. The reference by Gildas to unnamed offspring of Ambrosius Aurelianus whom Gildas reckoned not equal to Ambrosius demonstrates that he did not always name those of whom he disapproved. In addition, Arthur may well have been dead by the time Gildas was writing. The usually given *Annales Cambriae* date for Camlann is 537. Gildas was almost certainly writing in the 530s or 540s.

As discussed in Chapter 2, the *Annales Cambriae* date for Badon is somewhere around 516, and there could also be several other dates early in the sixth century depending on how the date is calculated. This unfortunately does not help much in trying to decide who Arthur's opponent would have been, and where the battle might have been fought.

With some Arthurian battles, a problem is that there are too few candidates as the possible battle site. With Badon, the opposite is the problem.

The combination of Badon being a hill, and Gildas mentioning a siege has led many to assume that the battle took place at a hillfort. More specifically, many have assumed that the battle must have taken place at one of the places called Badbury. Etymologically Badbury used to be interpreted as meaning 'the fort of Badda'. However, recently there has been more acceptance that one or more of the Badburys could really mean Baddan fort, with Baddan being Celtic in origin.[84] The trouble is that there are several Badburys.

There is Badbury Rings in Dorset (Baddan byrig 901), where a small fire has been dated to the fifth century and where an early post-Roman ditch cuts the Roman road past the hillfort.[85]

There is Badbury (Baddeburi 955) in Wiltshire, close to the Roman town at Wanborough, and the hillfort of Liddington Castle. It also happens to be close to Barbury Castle, site of a battle between Saxons and Britons in 556 and with a name that was originally Beran byrg, the fort of Bera (a rare Anglo-Saxon name) or the fort of the bear, which in a region where bears were already extinct does raise at least the possibility of an Arthurian connection.

There is Badbury Hill (Badbery 1539) in Berkshire.

There is Badby (Baddan byrig 944) in Northamptonshire.

There is Baumber in Lincolnshire (Badeburg 1986).

And this is before we even get on to names that could conceivably be linked to the Battle of Badon Hill, like, for instance, Baydon (Beidona 1086) in Wiltshire or Budbury (Bodeberie 1086) the hillfort at Bradford-on-Avon with its possible Vortigern connections. Or Bath. This is identified in later Welsh legend as the site of Badon, and a beautiful enamelled penannular Type F brooch was found in the baths, suggesting fifth-century activity there, but the identification of Bath as Badon may be simply due to the similarities between Badon and the Anglo-Saxon name of the city (Bathum in its early form in 796).

Interestingly almost all these possible locations are situated close to, or in, Type G zones. Badbury Rings has perhaps the most evidence of early post-Roman activity.

It is worth mentioning here one further candidate which has been mostly overlooked. There are some suggestions in Welsh legend that Badon was near the Severn. For instance, in *The Dream of Rhonabwy*, Arthur is shown on an island in the Severn before he marches to Badon. In Somerset, near Tytherington, a few miles from the Severn estuary, is a place called simply Baden Hill. The place name was first recorded in 1592, is Badowne Hill in 1680, Battle Hill in 1683 and Badden Hill in 1839 and the English Place Name Society suggests that it includes the Saxon name Bada or Badda. There is no hillfort on Baden Hill itself, but the fact that Gildas mentions siege does not automatically indicate a fort, since hills too can be besieged and if there was a fort or settlement at Badon, Gildas is perfectly capable of saying so. He could use the word *castellum* or he could refer to turf walls, as he does in his description of a Roman wall from sea to sea. If we do need to look for a hillfort here, then Little Abbey Camp is a hillfort about a mile from Baden Hill (about the same distance that Liddington Castle is from Badbury) and it had extensive occupation in the late Roman period. Bloody Acre hillfort is about a mile off in another direction. A late Roman spur, a late Roman buckle, a late Roman strap end of militia type and a Type G brooch have all been found very close.[86]

The site is pretty much on a key Roman crossroads where the north–south road meets the east–west road heading to the Roman period ferry crossing point to Caerleon in South Wales. If we are looking for islands in the Severn where Arthur might have been prior to Badon, there is Chapel Rock, at the end of Beachley peninsula, where there are ruins of an old chapel, traditionally founded in the fourth century and next to the Roman ferry crossing point on the west side of the Severn. On the other side of the Severn is Aust (Augusta 1105, Augst 1375) sometimes thought to derive from the name of the Legio

II Augusta which would regularly have used this crossing, and there is even an Arthureslands field listed there in 1501, though the name is probably much too late to be at all relevant. Not far off (about ten miles) is Ozleworth, a place name that includes the very rare Anglo-Saxon name Osla, which is also the name of Osla Big Knife said to have fought at Badon. Baden Hill is quite close to Bath. Baden Hill is also not a huge distance from Dyrham. The Dobunni lost a decisive battle there against the Saxons in 577. Could Arthur have won a decisive victory nearby, about sixty years earlier?

We have considered the twelve battles that *Historia Brittonum* attributes to Arthur, so now we must look at Camlann. The name Camelot is very similar, so we will also look at that name here as well. For how could we look at King Arthur without mentioning Camelot?

Camelot is not mentioned in early Arthurian texts. Some think that Camelot is merely a name derived from the Roman name for Colchester, Camulodunum. That may be true. However, the first reference to Camelot has Arthur leaving Caerleon one Ascension Day and holding court at 'Camaalot'.[87] Getting to Colchester from Caerleon and holding court there would be quite a task even these days with the M4. Some have suggested that the name Camelot is derived from Camlann. Camelot could easily be entirely mythical; however, when looking for possible sites for Camlann, it seems at least worth being aware of possible Camelot locations in the vicinity.

A prime candidate for Camlann is Camboglanna, the Roman fort of Housesteads on Hadrian's Wall. Etymologically, this is probably fine. However, as with Badon, etymologically there are quite a number of options for Camlann. There are, a Gamlan and two Camlans in north-west Wales. Then there are names associated with rivers called Cam or something similar. There is a Cam Beck next to Housesteads, but there are Cam River names elsewhere. There is a Cam next to South Cadbury hillfort which is the origin of the nearby place name Queen Camel, and presumably one reason South Cadbury was identified in local tradition as Camelot. There is a Camelford in Cornwall, with Slaughterbridge often suggested as the site of Camlann. There is the mysterious Camel Hundred, a region of north-west Worcestershire which was located next door to Droitwich and is called Kamel in a document of 1150.

The first mention of Camlann is in the *Annales Cambriae* where it is mentioned that both Arthur and Medraut died there. That text does not state whether Medraut was Arthur's opponent, but in later tradition that it is what Medraut/Mordred became. Medraut does not help us locate Camlann. However, the next earliest reference to Camlann, after the *Annales Cambriae*, is in the Welsh poem *Culhwch and Olwen*[88] and it is interesting. It states that Gwyn Hywar, overseer of Cornwall and Devon, was involved in plotting Camlann. If there is any truth in this tradition it perhaps suggests a west country location for Camlann, or at least somewhere closer to there than Hadrian's Wall or north-west Wales.

It seems fair to say that, at this stage, finding an agreed location for Camlann (and Camelot) is not possible. However, in the spirit of exploring a possible link between Camlann and Camelot and taking into account the activities of Gwyn Hywar in Cornwall and Devon, it is worth considering three locations which have not had much interest taken in them in this respect previously.

The first of these we will look at is the River Camlad, just to the west of Shrewsbury and Wroxeter. Near where it flows into the Severn, there is a strategic ford that became a meeting place for English and Welsh royalty in the Middle Ages. The ford was also on the Roman route west from Wroxeter and is guarded by a Roman fort (occupied until at least the late fourth century) and settlement at Forden Gaer. There are also two hillforts along the length of the Camlad. This river is worth mentioning because it is in the same area as two other possible Arthurian battle sites, Baschurch (Bassas) and Leintwardine/Branogenium (Breguion), and because the river's name is basically Camelot. The name is recorded as Kemelet (1227) and Camalet (1577).

Incidentally, in the Roman and post-Roman period this area would have been part of the territory of the Cornovii, the Dobunni's northern neighbours, and probably at some stage allies (the Roman town at Wanborough, Wiltshire, in Dobunni territory was, for instance called Durocornovium, fort of the Cornovii). Arthur's palace at Celliwig is in Cernyw.[89] This is the British name for Cornwall and, for that reason, Celliwig is normally assumed to have been in Cornwall. However, Cernyw or something similar would also have been the British word for the *civitas* of the Cornovii. There is an Upper Chilwick Meadow on the River Camlad near Pentre which may or may not be relevant.

The second is probably a slightly more likely candidate for a Camlan/Camelot location. Camerton in Somerset was originally Camelartone (954), the farm on the Camelar or Cameler (now Cam) river. However, there is more to Camerton than just this. Eminent Iron Age archaeologist Barry Cunliffe suggests the Dobunni had more than one capital and suggests Camerton may have been their southern capital.[90] There is a lot of early Roman military material from Camerton and at least one late belt fitting,[91] and Camerton continued to be a major settlement into the late Roman period and beyond. A Type G brooch was found there.[92] Late Roman or post-Roman modifications were made to buildings in the town and outside the town is a cemetery probably dating from the fifth to seventh centuries.[93] It is a strong candidate for being the site of an Arthurian court (close to numerous sites of Arthurian interest and also with easy access from Caerleon just across the Severn estuary) and, being easily reached from Cornwall and Devon where Gwyn Hywar was allegedly plotting, it is a strong candidate for being Camlann or close to Camlann.

Now to a third candidate. In Chapter 2 we looked at the Roman palace at Woodchester with its possible connection to Ambrosius Aurelianus. As mentioned, nearby is the Dobunni's hillfort at Uley with a Roman period temple and a probable Christian basilica or monastic site at the time of Arthur.[94] The name Uley is Saxon. However, the river next to the hillfort and the little town next to that have a very British name, another Cam. The location obviously seems to make some sense, however, there is no Camlann name there now. Camlann could potentially be derived from something like the bank of the Cam, or the enclosure on the Cam, or land by the Cam. Or Camlann could perhaps have changed into a less recognizable format. The hill next to Uley and Cam is, for instance, called Cam Long Down. Down in this name means simply 'hill'.

If you were searching for the grave of Arthur, and if he was not buried at Glastonbury (which he may have been) Camerton's fifth-to-seventh-century graveyard, or the area around the Christian site at Uley would be reasonable places to look.

If we were looking somewhere grander, but still in the area, how about the late Roman or post-Roman mausoleum that is thought to be located under Wells Cathedral?[95] Wells is a few miles from Glastonbury, a few miles from the Roman and post-Roman site at Shepton Mallet and about ten miles from

Camerton. Or how about the mausoleum and high-status burials under St. Mary de Lode in Gloucester or the burial with a gold braid round its head under Worcester Cathedral already discussed in Chapter 2?

Another place to look would be the early post-Roman cemetery at Henley Wood, where some of the dead from the Cadbury-Congresbury hillfort seem to have been buried. The cemetery seems to have been organized so that the most important burials were near an old religious site, Temple 3, so one of the burials closest to the temple would probably be the most likely for Arthur.

Or if we were looking further west, another place worth considering is Merlin's Cave, Symonds Yat, where somebody took the trouble to create a small early medieval cemetery in a cave, including burials dating from the sixth or seventh centuries, very close to the cave called King Arthur's Cave.[96] In the old legend Arthur is asleep in a cave waiting to wake and rescue Britain. Could the cave at Symonds Yat be where Arthur was laid to rest?

Before we conclude our look at Arthurian battles, we must now explore the Battle of Llongborth.

The poem describing this battle is one of the early sources for Arthur.[97] The hero of the poem is Geraint son of Erbin, but mention is also made of Arthur's brave men fighting ferociously. Arthur is described as an emperor. The poem makes mention of cavalry and states that Geraint is from Duvneint/Dumnonia/Devon. Beyond that, it is far from clear what is happening in the poem.

Geraint is a name known in Dumnonian genealogies, though it is not certain which Geraint this is, and it seems reasonable to assume that the battle would have taken place somewhere accessible both to Dumnonia and Arthur's forces.

Llongborth could perhaps just be a word meaning port, but usually the name of a battle is regarded as one of the key elements in any account of a battle. Few accounts of battles just say it was 'at a port' and in the battle list of *Historia Brittonum*, the name of the battle is usually the only information given. The most likely location for Llongborth is the one usually accepted, that is Langport in Somerset. It is close to Dumnonia and close to numerous sites of Arthurian interest, including Glastonbury, South Cadbury and the Roman town at Ilchester. There is plenty of evidence of Roman occupation in and around Langport, including the Roman villla at Low Ham with its spectacular mosaic depicting passages from *The Aeneid*. It is not very far from the main cluster of Type Gs. If you go to Langport you will find that part of the town is on a key strategic hill overlooking much of the surrounding area, and it was the site of a battle during the English Civil War during which cavalry also played a significant role. There are mysterious linear earthworks defending the hill at Langport, which are generally assumed to be either Anglo-Saxon or from the Civil War but could be earlier. And Langport actually IS a port, situated on the River Parrett.

All in all, there seems little reason to look elsewhere for the site of the Battle of Llongborth. It is not clear who Geraint's opponent at Llongborth was, but, at the time, the nearest Saxon settlements were probably only about twenty to thirty miles east of Langport, so it is quite possible that Geraint and Arthur's men were fighting the Saxons there.

On the other hand, one of two versions of *The Life of Gildas* also mentions Arthur being involved in an armed dispute not far from Langport.[98] In the Life, a local ruler, Melwas, abducts Guinevere and takes her to Glastonbury. Arthur summons all the forces of Cornubia and Dibneria (Cornwall and Devon) and gets ready to attack the castle where his wife is held. Gildas then intervenes and negotiates a peaceful end to the situation, with Guinevere's return to Arthur. Langport is about ten miles from Glastonbury, and the forces of Cornubia and Dibneria reference would match Geraint's Dumnnonian connections. If there is any truth to the Melwas story in *The Life of Gildas*, perhaps there actually was a battle before the situation was concluded.

Some people have attempted to make coherent campaigns out of the list of Arthur's battles. This is probably trying too hard. History is often not that neat. We should expect a British military leader of Arthur's period to be fighting a variety of enemies in a variety of campaigns at a variety of different times. And this is probably what we have with Arthur. What is coherent though is that pretty much all the likely battle sites fit into the areas covered by the distribution of Type G brooches suggesting that perhaps it can be termed 'the Arthur brooch', and most of the likely battle sites are consistent with the idea of basing his activities on a personal power base in and around the territory of the Dobunni, and basing his long-distance power on an alliance with the *civitas* of the Corieltauvi or its successor, the Kingdom of Lindes/Lindsey.

We will return, later in this book, to the question of what Arthur's battles may have achieved. However, it is worth noting here, as has been noted by others, that the culturally Anglo-Saxon area of Britain, that area where culturally Anglo-Saxon cemeteries and culturally Anglo-Saxon settlements are found, hardly expanded at all between about 500 and 580. That could be due to Arthur's victories.

Chapter 7

Cadell, Caninus, Penda and a New Dynasty in King Arthur's Country

No early sources suggest that Arthur created a dynasty. The *Mirabilia* states that in the region called Ercing, at a spring called Licat Amr, there is the tomb of Amr, the son of Arthur, and the text states, without further explanation that Arthur killed him and buried him there.[1]

In the Llandaff Charters the stream now called Gamber is recorded as Amyr, and Licat Amr, meaning the source of Amr is probably therefore the source of the Gamber, or Gamber Head. However, there is also in the Domesday Book, a place called Lagademar, which seems likely to be derived from Licat Amr and this seems to be associated with Garway.[2] The two places are, however, very much in the same area, so that at least is something.

Another son of Arthur, Gwydre, is said in *Culhwch and Olwen* to have died hunting the boar Twrch Trwyth, while Duran, son of Arthur, is said to have died at Camlann. Perhaps the best-known figure said to have been a son of Arthur is Llacheu/Loholt, but he too is said to have died a violent death. If these characters ever existed, they seem to have left little hard evidence behind them.

It has been suggested that Llacheu/Loholt could be linked to the mysterious Mais Mail Lochou mentioned in *The Life of Dyfrig* (St. Dubricius), in Ergyng. Some would interpret this as the Field of Prince Lochou. However, it is perhaps more likely that this is Mais Maillochou, the Field of Mailloch, or

St. Maelog, said to be buried at nearby Llowes. A reference in the Llandaff Charters to 'campo malochu' probably supports this interpretation.[3]

Could Llacheu/Loholt be linked to the man referenced in the name Ager Louhai, the Field of Louhai, near Tintern Parva in the Llandaff Charters?[4] Could Duran be somehow linked to the Roman site at Dorne on Fosse Way, which has early forms Dorene and Doron and which Ekwall suggests may derive from Duronum? It is just possible, but neither connection can be proved.

Various other figures are said to have been children of Arthur. In some traditions Medraut/Mordred is said to have been a son of Arthur. A daughter called Archfedd gets one mention. Her name sounds a little like Archenfield, a town that preserves the name of Ergyng, though supposedly the name Archfedd is derived from her appearance.

If there was an Arthur whose power base was the Dobunni, that base seems to have fragmented somewhat after his death. The 577 reference in the *Anglo-Saxon Chronicle* to the killing in battle of three British kings Conmail, Condidan and Farinmail and the capture of Gloucester, Cirencester and Bath, seems to suggest that the Dobunni were still sufficiently united to be able to send a united army into battle in emergencies, but were, by then, sufficiently disunited as to have separate leadership for their three main cities.

It is worth, at least briefly, considering here whether any royal treasures that the forces of Wessex may have captured at Deorham or shortly afterwards is still with us today, because it's not entirely impossible.

The Sutton Hoo treasure is generally regarded as the finest Anglo-Saxon treasure ever found. Some of the pieces found definitely are Anglo-Saxon, though some of the pieces are, or may be, British. There is the British hanging bowl, already old and patched when it was buried in the early seventh century. There is a unique long-handled iron war axe-hammer, the head of which has some similarities to a Roman military pickaxe. It evokes the intriguing explanation of the name Arthur added to one version of the *Historia Brittonum*, where the text says Arthur means either a fearsome bear (the conventional etymology), or an iron hammer that smashes the jaws of lions (presumably a weapon of a type particularly associated by the writer with Arthur). The mysterious lamp stand or standard also seems to have some possibly British or Roman design elements, like the classical volutes and spike on the base, which would have allowed it to be forced into the ground, like the foot rest and spike on Roman standards. A cauldron chain was made in a distinctively British fashion.[5] The great plate is stamped to show it is an official piece made during the reign of eastern Roman emperor Anastasius 491–518 and could have come to the west of Britain (during the time of Arthur) with the Byzantine trade ships that visited there. It has been persuasively argued that the great whetstone sceptre was probably originally a Celtic symbol of British royalty.[6] Whetstones with mysterious powers are found in Celtic legend (for instance, the whetstone of Tudwal Tudglyd), the Greywacke stone from which it is made is not found in south-east England,[7] and the faces on the Sutton Hoo sceptre seem much more Celtic than Anglo-Saxon. In particular, with their long, expressionless, slightly triangular faces, they are close to some (particularly Priam with his bearded but moustacheless face) of the faces in the *Vergilius Romanus* (thought by many to have been made in fifth-century Britain) and to an early medieval bronze head found on Glastonbury Tor.[8] The Glastonbury head could potentially link the sceptre to the west country and perhaps to Dobunni territory. Perhaps the faces on the sceptre represent Dobunni royal figures. Perhaps Vortigern, Ambrosius Aurelianus and Arthur are in there somewhere. Perhaps.

How could these pieces have conceivably got from Dobunni territory to Sutton Hoo? It is impossible to say. However, the person buried at Sutton Hoo seems to have been Rædwald, king of East Anglia, and a so-called Bretwaldas (a sort of semi-official position as pre-eminent king of his day). Usually, it is reckoned that the Bretwalda concept is a solely Anglo-Saxon concept; however, it might have been British as well. Some have suggested the term means ruler of Britain; Bede describes the concept as having 'imperium' a Roman term that is the origin of the word 'imperator', 'emperor' and such overkings were known to the Britons – Cassivellaunus, for instance, united a number of tribes against Rome and Arthur is described in the poem about the Battle of Llongborth as emperor. Ceawlin, victor of Deorham, was Bretwalda in his time. When Ceawlin lost power, Æthelbert of Kent became Bretwalda, and then Rædwald took the position. Could some royal treasures also have passed from hand to hand? Or perhaps marriage links were involved somehow, or diplomatic royal gift-giving. Obviously, all this is very speculative, but it is

Figure 26. Some of the main kingdoms and territories of early medieval Britain.

interesting to consider.

We shall return to the Dobunni later, but right now we need to have a look at some of what was happening in the territories around them.

The main source for what was happening in the British territories near the Dobunni in the early sixth century is, of course, Gildas. He spends a lot more time discussing the individual morality (or, as he saw it, lack of morality) of local rulers than discussing the politics of it all, but from him, we know that in his time, Dumnonia had a ruler called Constantine, there was Vortiporius in Dyfed, and Maglocunus (or Maelgwn) in Gwynedd. A ruler named Cuneglasus, also mentioned by Gildas, seems to have been in Rhos.[9]

This leaves Aurelius Caninus, as the other one of the five rulers named by Gildas. Some have attempted to link him to Ambrosius Aurelianus. However, Aurelius and Aurelianus are different names, and one is a first name and the other a second name. As discussed in Chapter 2 it is not possible to be certain of a connection between the two.

There may, however, be some kind of link between Aurelius Caninus and one Aurelius Cervianus. Both have Aurelius as a *nomen*, both have an animal-based second name, starting with a 'C'. Caninus is derived from the Latin for dog, while Cervianus comes from the Latin for stag.

The name Aurelius Cervianus is found inscribed on a little copper alloy disc which shows troops of Legio XX Valeria Victrix and Legio II Augusta alongside animals, including a stag for Cervianus. Some have suggested, from the kit of the troops depicted that it is third century. However, the kit is similar to formal attire of soldiers shown on some late-fourth-century coins, and the peacocks shown on the disc, and how they are depicted, links the disc to British horsehead buckles plate from the end of the Roman period.

The disc is now in Paris,[10] but seems to have been found in Italy originally. It seems reasonable therefore to link the disc to the only time we know that units of Legio XX Valeria Victrix and Legio II Augusta were probably with each other in Italy in the late fourth century and this is during the reign of Magnus Maximus 383–388.[11] The line of cross-hatched triangles around the rim also link it to a Celtic shield mount from Tal-y-Llyn in northern Wales.[12] Cervianus is not a known Roman *cognomen*, so could Aurelius Cervianus have been a British officer, perhaps from a powerful British family? The stag on the disc is reminiscent of the bronze stag on the Sutton Hoo whetstone sceptre, which itself has been attributed to west or north Britain.

There seems to be a rough geographical order in how Gildas lists the five rulers. He starts in Cornwall and Devon, then includes Aurelius Caninus, then moves to Dyfed in south-west Wales, then up to Cuneglasus and Maglocunus in northern Wales. If this is true, then we need to be looking for Aurelius Caninus somewhere in the centre. With this in mind, some have suggested that Caninus is either a pun on a British name or a Latin

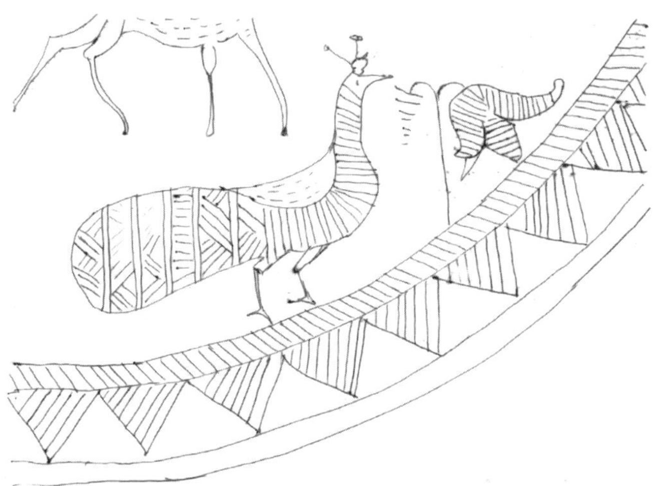

Figure 27. Detail of the Cervianus disc, showing a peacock and tree of life similar to those on Peacock Plate Horsehead Buckles.

approximation of it, and have suggested that Aurelius Caninus is, in fact, Cynan Garwyn, the ruler of Powys at the time of Gildas. Some versions of the Gildas text do actually have Conanus instead of Caninus and it seems likely that there is a pun in Gildas that confirms this identification.

A poem, supposedly by the great Welsh poet Taliesin but perhaps later, praises Cynan Garwyn mentioning his many conquests.[13] The poem describes him as 'descended from Cadell', and indeed the Powys dynasty of the period is often referred to as the Cadell dynasty. Cadell seems to have been acknowledged as the founder of the dynasty of which Cynan Garwyn was a part. This figure is also mentioned in the *Historia Brittonum*.[14] There St. Germanus encounters a bad ruler, Benlli, at a city (probably Foel Fenlli in northern Wales) and after fire from the skies burns the city, St. Germanus appoints a friendly local man as king and founder of the dynasty. This was Cadell, or Catellus, the Latin spelling of Cadell. In his attack on Aurelius Caninus, Gildas calls him a lion's whelp. The word he uses for whelp is the Latin *catulus*, surely a pun on 'Catellus'.

There may even be a double pun here. As mentioned in the previous chapter, there is an area of what is now Herefordshire but was probably part of Powys in the sixth century which was known as Leon or Lene, and a legend about a lion connected with Leominster presumably reflects that. Often, Gildas seems to select the animals he incorporates into his sermon because of their biblical connections, however, if Cynan Garwyn had some particular connection to the Leon/Lene area, then this might be an added reason for Gildas calling him 'a lion's whelp'.

There is then the question of what 'Garwyn' means. There has been some confusion over this. Some have suggested it means 'white thigh' or 'white chariot.' Either is possible. It is at least worth asking whether there is some link to Cervianus. If Cynan became Caninus, could Carwyn be linked to Cervianus?

The prime source for what was happening with the Anglo-Saxon neighbours of the Dobunni in the early sixth century is the *Anglo-Saxon Chronicle.*

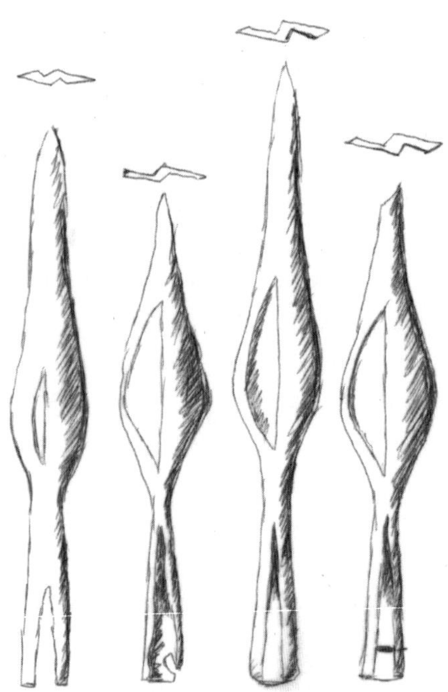

Figure 28. Spearheads possibly showing a mixture of British and Anglo-Saxon design influences. Swanton type I1. (After Swanton, *The Spearheads of the Anglo-Saxon Settlements*, 1973)

The Anglo-Saxon kingdom that would come to dominate western England and eventually the whole of England is Wessex. The *Anglo-Saxon Chronicle* accounts for the origins of Wessex by stating that Cerdic and Cynric arrived in 495 with five ships in what is now Hampshire, fought various battles against the Britons and established a kingdom. One of these battles was at Cerdicesford. Cerdicesford became North Charford and, like Triffrwd, because the place name locates the potential battlefield in quite a small area, with specific features from the time, it is one of the few places where one can get a sense of how a battle of these period in Britain might have gone. All of this does not appear implausible except that Cerdic,

Cynric and Ceawlin, probably the first three kings of the West Saxons all seem to have British names.

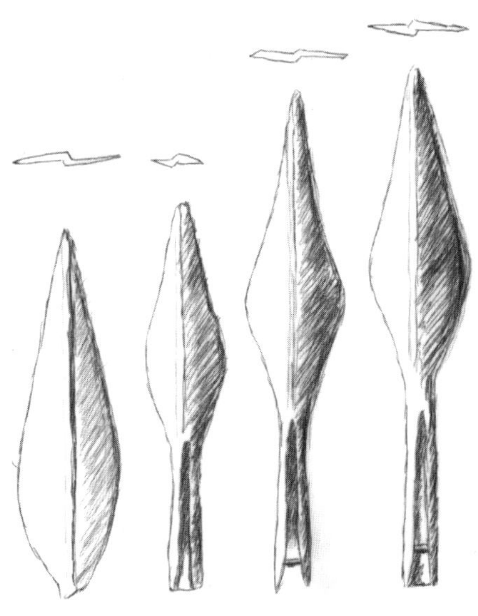

Figure 29. Spearheads possibly showing a mixture of British and Anglo-Saxon design influences. Swanton type K1. (After Swanton, *The Spearheads of the Anglo-Saxon Settlements*, 1973)

Cerdic is Caradoc, one of the most famous of British names, and better known to some in its Latin form, Caratacus. There are a few genuinely Anglo-Saxon names that start with the letters Cyn; however, Cyn- or the original British version Cuno- meaning hound is a hugely popular name element in British names and the Celtic name Cunorix, which would be the British version of Cynric, is found on a post-Roman inscription.[15] The father of Cunorix, also mentioned on the same stone, is Coline or Colinus which is, yes, the British version of Ceawlin and, of course, is still a popular name today.

It seems impossible to avoid the conclusion that the so-called West Saxons were, originally, a combination of local Britons and Saxon immigrants, with the royal family having in its early years a major British element. The story of Cerdic and Cynric arriving in five boats was probably fabricated later, with the intention of giving a more Anglo-Saxon origin to the royal house of Wessex.

A seventh-century burial at Lowbury Hill, in Berkshire may have something to say about all this. The date and location of the burial would normally suggest this was a culturally Anglo-Saxon burial, however, his spearhead carried a design in enamel (normally reckoned to be a sign of British involvement) and analysis of the man's teeth showed that he had grown up in either Cornwall or Ireland.[16]

Other types of spears from the period and region also seem to show mixes of British and Anglo-Saxon influences.[17]

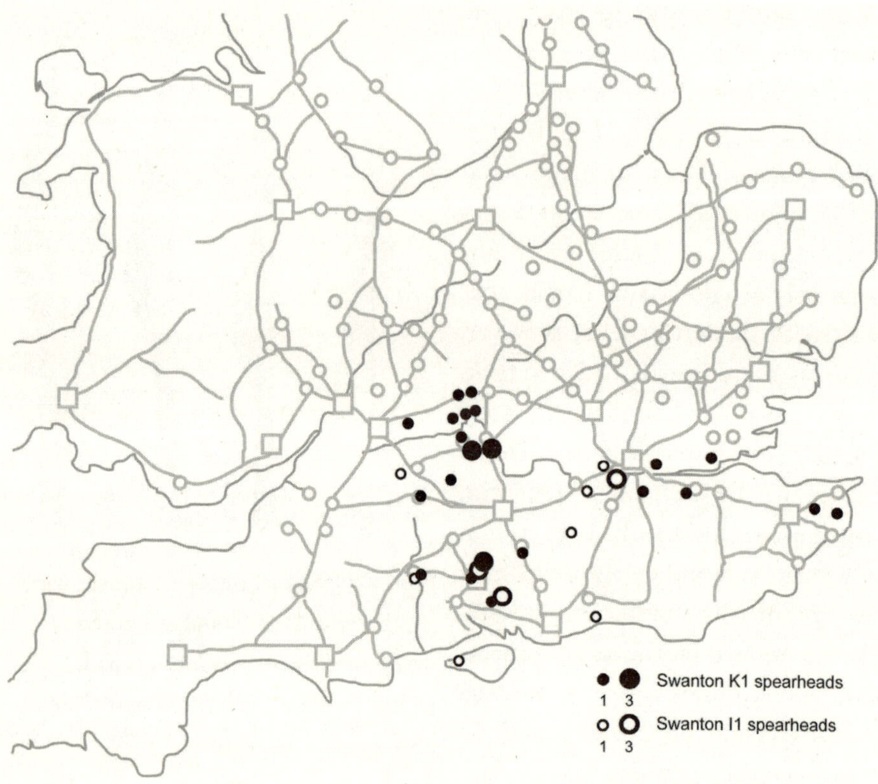

Figure 30. Distribution of Swanton I1 and K1 spearheads. (After Swanton, *The Spearheads of the Anglo-Saxon Settlements*, 1973)

Meanwhile events were happening elsewhere that would transform the Welsh borders, the Midlands and eventually the whole of England. A medieval text, the *Flores Historiarum*,[18] records that in 527, invaders from Germany occupied East Anglia and then some of them invaded Mercia and fought the British there. About the same time, a figure called Icel appears in Britain, and will be later known as the founder of the Iclingas, the royal family of Mercia that would include such figures as Penda, and Offa who would exercise power over other Anglo-Saxon kingdoms and declare himself King of the English.

Icel was later said to be descended from a royal dynasty in the continental Anglian homelands. However, we do not know whether this is true, just as we do not know whether Icel arrived on a boat from Germany, or whether, as probably

Figure 31. Distribution of fifth-century Anglo-Saxon cemeteries. (Various sources)

with Cerdic and Cynric, his family had been here for a long time already.

We do know that there are some interesting place names in eastern and central England which contain the name Icel.[19] The Prosopography of Anglo-Saxon England database[20] only contains the one Icel, so it is likely these places do have some genuine connection to the Icel of the Iclingas. There is Ickleton in Cambridgeshire, Ickleford in Hertfordshire and probably Icklingham in Cambridgeshire. Icklingham is Ecclingaham in 1086 and place name experts

Figure 32. Location of main group of Creoda, Pybba and Penda place names.

claim the personal name involved is Ycel, but since the Prosopography of Anglo-Saxon England database contains no examples whatsoever of this as a name, it seems reasonable to think Icklingham is also linked to Icel.

Apart from the name, the places themselves are interesting. Icklingham, in Iceni territory, and close to the western borders of the tribe/*civitas*, was a major late Roman settlement, and, judging by coin and treasure finds in the area, perhaps one of the wealthiest places in late Roman Britain. Icklingham is also at the start of the ancient ridge route that leads across central England via the Chilterns. Ickleton is a little further west along the route and is immediately next to the Roman city of Great Chesterford which had a hugely strong wall built round it late in the Roman period. Ickleford is further west along the ridge route still and is near Pirton where early post-Roman activity has been suggested.

And what about the name? It does not really seem to be an Anglo-Saxon name, which begs the question: what else might it be? In Chapter 1 we looked at the possibility that Bottisham (on the ridge route between Icklingham and

Ickleton) retains the name of Boudica, Queen of the Iceni, in it. It seems worth at least asking whether Icel could also be linked to the Iceni? Could Icel, for instance, be Iceni with a diminutive, something like Icellus perhaps – the little bloke from the Iceni? It's impossible to say; however, the place names do at least suggest that at about the time the *Flores Historiarum* suggest somebody was invading Mercia from East Anglia, Icel may indeed have been moving west from East Anglia into central England.

This suggestion seems to be confirmed by Knebworth. Knebworth is a few miles south of Ickleford and it contains the name Cnebba who, in Mercian royal genealogies is the successor to Icel. Again, Cnebba is an unusual name, with no other examples listed on the Prosopography of Anglo-Saxon England database.

Cnebba's successor was said to be Cynewald. There are three Cynewalds and four Cynewealds on the Prosopography of Anglo-Saxon England database, so this is an actual Anglo-Saxon name. On the other hand, as mentioned when looking at Cynric, Cyn/Cuno is also a hugely popular element in British names of the period. Cynwal and Cynwalan are both British names of the period. A St. Cynwal was a disciple of St. Dubricius, and two Cynwals are listed among the warriors of Arthur mentioned in early texts. Cuno names were popular with the Dobunni. The temple at Nettleton was dedicated to Apollo Cunomaglus and one of the Dobunni kings at Deorham is named in the *Anglo-Saxon Chronicle* as Conmail, the same name as Cunomaglus. And looking more broadly at British Cyn-names, if, for instance, we look at a royal genealogy connected with Pengwern, a mysterious British kingdom in the early medieval period in the west Midland and Welsh borders, we find Cyndrwyn, Cynddylan, Cynan, Cynwraith.[21]

In terms of Cynewald place names, we get Kinwalsey in Warwickshire, Kinvaston in Staffordshire, Killamarsh in Derbyshire and Killingwoldgraves in East Yorkshire. As you would expect from a name with a few other examples in the Prosopography of Anglo-Saxon England database, the spread is wider; however, Kinwalsey and Kinvaston (site of a Roman fort) are in an area of England that was part of early Mercia.

Cynewald's successor was said to be Creoda. There is a Creoda who may have ruled Wessex in the early sixth century (some think he did not actually exist), but there is no other example of this name in the Prosopography of Anglo-

Saxon England database. Again, there are possible British Celtic parallels. St. Crida, of Creed in Cornwall, is, for instance, a Celtic saint.

Creoda is the grandfather of Penda, the king who established Mercia as a major kingdom, and Creoda is usually reckoned to have been around sometime in the late sixth century. The timing is interesting. It means that Creoda was around in the years after a Dobunni army was smashed and three of their kings killed in the Battle of Deorham in 577. The forces of Wessex are said to have captured Bath, Cirencester and Gloucester after the battle, but no mention is made of the rest of Dobunni territory.

This is where a bunch of Creoda place names are found and, which is particularly fascinating, they are appearing in a part of Britain that was not culturally Anglo-Saxon in the late sixth and early seventh centuries. (There are also a small number of Creoda names further south, but those may be connected to a Wessex Creoda.) There is Kersoe, Worcestershire and an ancient site referred to as Creodan ac, also in Worcestershire. There is Curdworth in Warwickshire. In Herefordshire we have Cradley, a site in the Golden Valley referred to in the Llandaff Charters as Petra Crita, and a very interesting Credenhill. Credenhill is a hillfort next to Kenchester, the largest Roman town in the north-west of Dobunni territory. If you were establishing yourself in control of the northern part of Dobunni territory in the post-Roman era, you would want to be at Credenhill.

Next we come to Pybba, the father of Penda. Again, there are no other examples of this name in the Prosopography of Anglo-Saxon England database. Again, there are possible British parallels. There is the king of nearby Ergyng called Peibio, or Rhuvawn Pebyr, from *The Dream of Rhonabwy*. Again, there are a bunch of place names connected to this figure in, or near Dobunni territory. In Worcestershire we have Pedmore, Pepper Wood, Pepwell and possibly Peopleton. In Shropshire there is Peplow, in Gloucestershire Pebworth, and in Somerset Publow. A small group of eastern names, including Pebmarsh and Pebehale in Essex seem unlikely to be connected to the Mercian Pybba, so either there was another Pybba, or the name in the place names was something else originally.

And now we reach Penda, the man whose military campaigns made Mercia a military power, who ruled in the early seventh century and who was killed in

655. Again, there are no other occurrences of this name in the Prosopography of Anglo-Saxon England database. *Pen* is a Celtic word meaning head or chief, and possible British parallels include a ninth-century Northumbrian monk. There is also Bede's reference to Penta or Panta as an old (presumably British) name of the River Blackwater in Essex.

Once again, we have a bunch of Penda place names in and around Dobunni territory. As you would expect from such a major figure who expanded Mercian territory hugely, the spread is a little further with Penda. There is Peddimore in Warwickshire, Pendeford in Wolverhampton, Pinvin and Pendiford both in Worcestershire, Pinbury and Pimbury Park both in Gloucestershire, Pensworth Farm in Wiltshire, and Pendley Manor in the Chilterns. Pendean Farm in Sussex is probably not connected to the Mercian Penda. However, Penda's name was often written as Panta in Welsh and Pauntley in Gloucesterhsire near the Welsh border, and Pontesford and Pontesbury, both in Shropshire contain the name Pant. The Prosopography of Anglo-Saxon England database only gives one example of this name and suggests it may be linked to the Welsh name for Penda.

Penda's brother was Eowa (no other examples in the Prosopography of Anglo-Saxon England database). The only place name in England containing Eowa is Evenlode, in Gloucesterhire.

The *Historia Brittonum* states that Penda had twelve sons, but, if so, it is not entirely clear who they all were. Two of Penda's sons, Wulfhere and Æthelred, had conventional Anglo-Saxon names. His two daughters, Cyneburh and Cyneswith, had names that could be conventional Anglo-Saxon names but both start with Cyn-. A man called Merewalh also seems to have been his son, or perhaps son-in-law. The name is an Anglo-Saxon name probably meaning 'Famous Briton or Welshman'. Incidentally, this is the Merewalh who is the ruler involved in the lion of Leominster legend, in which St. Eadfrith interpreted a vision of a lion for the king and subsequently the minster of Leominster was built to mark the event.

And another of Penda's son was called Peada. There are no other examples of the name in the Prosopography of Anglo-Saxon England database. British possible parallels include Welsh versions of Peter, like Pedr (as in Artuir ap Pedr) Pedyr and Peder, and Peada did help found the Abbey at Peterborough dedicated to St. Peter. In about 653 Penda made Peada king of the Middle Angles and after Penda's death, Peada was king of parts of Mercia for a few months before he was murdered. Of four Peada place names, three seem linked to his time as King of the Middle Angles. They are Padworth, in Berkshire, Padnell's Wood, Rotherfield Greys, Oxfordshire, and Pednor Fms, Chesham in Buckinghamshire.

So, what is going on here? It is, of course, impossible to be entirely sure when these place names linked to early members of the Mercian royal family appear in culturally non-Anglo-Saxon areas. They could theoretically have appeared long after the time of the early Iclingas, as a kingdom of Mercia originating elsewhere, expanded west. However, the apparent progress of these names across the country does seem to match the probable advance of each generation of the royal family, even as far as the Peada place names, which seems to suggest a strong possibility that the early Mercian family did, in fact, make its original base in a culturally non-Anglo-Saxon area.

Figure 33. Some key locations in early Mercia.

Penda was pagan and Bede disliked him because of that. Penda did not persecute Christians and allowed his son Peada to become a Christian, but clearly there was an Anglo-Saxon element in the identity of the early Mercian royal family. However, just as Christianity had been the religion of the political leadership during the late Roman period, so, by the sixth century, paganism had become the religion of the political leadership in the centre and east of England. Penda's family, even if British or part British, might have adopted paganism as a means of adopting the culture of the politically powerful. They would probably not be the only ones. Cenwalh, with a name suggesting partly British origins, was a king of Wessex in the seventh century but was pagan initially. Cædwalla was another king of Wessex later in the seventh century and still had a totally British name, yet he seems to have been pagan for much of his life and was only baptized soon before his death.

The Anglo-Saxon names of some of his children indicate that Penda in his lifetime made use of some Anglo-Saxon cultural elements. Similarly, Cerdic, Cynric and Ceawlin seem to have had British names, but they also adopted Anglo-Saxon culture.

However, from a full analysis of the personal name and place name evidence, it seems hard to escape the conclusion that the supposedly 'Anglo-Saxon' kingdom of Mercia originated as a kingdom in the northern part of Dobunni territory, in a culturally British region, still almost entirely populated by Britons, and led by a royal family that, in its origins, was largely, or entirely British.

The 'takeover' of this area by the incoming Iclingas might have taken place completely peacefully. There is no claim in any of the sources that the Iclingas established their original kingdom by violence, and it is an interesting aspect of British tribal life that British tribes seem to have been comparatively flexible when it came to accepting talented newcomers to their area as war leaders.

In the pre-Roman era, for instance, a Gallic leader called Commius, who at one stage served with Caesar, seems to have ended up fleeing to Britain and becoming the leader of the Atrebates tribe here.[22] After Claudius sent his troops into Britain in the invasion and defeated the Catuvellauni/Trinovantes alliance, its leader Caratacus seems to have escaped to Wales and there led the Silures tribe against the invaders. And judging by the geography of the battles they fought, which seem to progress along the western *civitas* borders of the Belgae, there is a possibility that Cerdic and Cynric conducted some similar kind of 'takeover'.

There is also the possibility of some traditional leadership link between the Dobunni, the Iceni and the Corieltauvi. One of the rulers named on Dobunni coins is EISV. Some people think this is an abbreviation and that EISV of the Dobunni is the AESV and ESVPRASTO of the Iceni, and that he is the IISVPRASV of the Corieltauvi. Equally the ANTED of Dobunni coins could be the ANTED and ANTEDIO of Iceni coins.[23]

It is even possible to wonder whether the name of the kingdom itself is actually Anglo-Saxon. Usually, Mercia is interpreted as meaning the kingdom of the border, from the Anglo-Saxon word *mearc* meaning 'border' or from *mierce* meaning 'border people'. This may be true, but it has caused a lot of debate since nobody is particularly sure to what border it might refer. Some have suggested it meant the border between Northumbria and the kingdoms further south, while others, taking a view which perhaps seems based on later realities rather more strongly than on those applying during the birth of Mercia, have seen it as the border between Anglo-Saxon kingdoms and Welsh kingdoms.

It seems, therefore, at least worth asking whether somehow the origin of the word might also be linked to the Welsh word *march* meaning horse, plural *meirchion*, horses. As we have already seen, the horse was a traditional symbol of political and military power in Celtic Britain. The Dobunni decorated their buckles with horseheads. There are several examples of burials of all or part of horses' skeletons (particularly skulls) on Dobunni sites of the pre-Roman and Roman period that suggest ritual significance. The Ravenna Cosmography mentions an unidentified location somewhere in the southern Welsh borderlands called Eposessa, which means something like 'place of the horses'. It also mentions a Marcotaxon somewhere in the north where British *march* (horse) seems to be a place name element. There are several place names mentioned in the Llandaff Charters that contain *march* or *meirchion*, horse or horses, as a place name element. There is a Taliesin poem *Can y Meirch*, Song of the Horses, and still a place on Offa's Dyke called Rhos y Meirch, Moor of the Horses. Meirchion was also a personal name that appears in early Welsh royal genealogies.

The question of early Mercia's Britishness is not a matter of minor significance. It is hugely significant in terms of our understanding of the origins of England, and in terms of what England became. It is also hugely significant in terms of our understanding of the possible similarities between Arthur and Penda. If Penda was largely or almost entirely British, operating within a largely or almost entirely British context, with a base in much the same area as both Ambrosius Aurelianus and Arthur, then it perhaps allows us to understand Penda in terms of Arthur and, in looking at Penda, about whom we know rather more historically, get more of a sense of some aspects of how Arthur might have operated a century and a half earlier. Both Arthur and Penda are said to have led alliances of British kingdoms against the Anglo-Saxons but we know more about how Penda did it and what he achieved. Between them, Arthur and Penda may have changed the future of Britain and England forever.

Chapter 8

Britons, Anglo-Saxons, Old Alliances Renewed and the Victory of Mercia

Our main source for the history of seventh-century Britain is Bede's *Ecclesiastical History of the English People*.[1] However, it has long been acknowledged that actually Bede may have had comparatively little contact with Mercian sources and may have had comparatively little knowledge about what was actually going on in Mercia. He was firmly based in Northumbria and mainly experienced the Mercians as enemies of the territory where he was based. Other sources also give little information about early Mercia. However, from what is available in Bede and sources such as the *Anglo-Saxon Chronicle* it is possible to get a broad sense of how and where Penda operated.

Penda's Mercia seems to have its origins in the northern territory of the Dobunni, however, Penda was soon to expand the territory he controlled.

It seems to be very telling that the first campaign he conducted appears to have been to free the southern Dobunni from the West Saxons. The *Anglo-Saxon Chronicle* records West Saxon forces capturing the region in 577 after the Battle of Deorham. In the *Chronicle* entry for 628 it records that Penda fought the West Saxon kings at Cirencester, previously *civitas* capital of the Dobunni and possible capital of the Roman province of Britannia Prima, and that afterwards Penda came to an agreement with the West Saxons. It is generally thought that this meant the West Saxons withdrew from the area, because soon it becomes part of the Mercian province or sub-kingdom of the

Hwicce. In fact, soon the majority of what had been Dobunni territory would be reorganized into two such regions, the Hwicce in the east, eventually based around the old Diocese of Worcester, and the Magonsæte in the west.

The extent of the territory of the Hwicce is reflected in place names like Wychwood in Oxfordshire, Whichford in Warwickshire, Wichenford and Wychbury Hill in Worcestershire. The Magonsæte probably took their name from the Roman-period Dobunni town of Magnis/Kenchester that was the main Dobunni settlement in the west.

Different sources give different dates for the start of Penda's reign. The *Anglo-Saxon Chronicle* reckons he became king in 626, while Bede indicates he started ruling around 633. The *Historia Brittonum* suggests an even later date. Obviously, some of the sources may be inaccurate, however, it may equally be that there were different views on what constituted being a king and ruling. Certainly, at the time, military and political might would probably have been more important than the niceties of any kind of coronation ceremony.

The *Mirabilia* records that the salt wells at Droitwich were in the province of the Hwicce. These salt wells continued to be a major source of income for Mercia, as they may have been for Ambrosius Aurelianus and Arthur. It is even possible they were decisive in the origins of Mercia since pottery with some design similarities to pottery from the east appears at Droitwich in the late sixth century, in a phenomenon very unusual in Worcestershire.[2]

The most important of the salt wells was known as the 'Great Upwic Pit' and it formed part of the royal Mercian estate of Wychbold. Work has been done analysing the salt distribution networks from Droitwich and the salt routes that led from it. There were several salt routes leading through Oxfordshire, often identified as Saltstrete or Saltway, and connecting to river routes across England. Droitwich salt was sold more widely from London. It has been suggested that a cluster of high-value coinage found at Bidford-on-Avon is connected to the use of this location in salt transport.[3] All this is in the later Anglo-Saxon period; however, the need for salt, for food flavouring and preservation was a constant from pre-Roman times onwards, and these later Anglo-Saxon salt routes probably show much continuity from earlier times. A major early Mercian minster was established at Hanbury near Droitwich as early as 660.

In addition to reuniting the Dobunni lands, Penda was also moving east.

In Chapter 6 we considered the centrality of the area around Venonis that may have been the location for Arthur's Battle of Guinnion Castle. Penda and his successors would make the area around there the core of the Mercian kingdom. From 669 at the latest, Lichfield, named after the nearby Roman settlement of Letocetum on Watling Street, would become the site of the Mercian bishopric, and nearby Tamworth, also close to the Roman town of Mancetter on Watling Street, would become the political capital of Mercia.

Place name evidence suggests that the Iclinga dynasty may have already had some links to the area around Tamworth prior to Penda. Kinwalsey, named for Cynewald is nearby. However, it may be also that Penda had to fight for the area initially. Some of this area was culturally Anglo-Saxon.

Something that would mostly define Penda's rule and would make him closer to the Arthur of the *Historia Brittonum* than to Anglo-Saxon kings is that he relied for much of his military power on alliances with British kings and led the combined forces against the Saxons. We have evidence that suggests Mercians used such an alliance either to capture Litchfield in the first place, or to defend it.

Figure 34. Coin of Byzantine Emperor Justinian. Both British and Anglo-Saxon rulers of the early medieval period took some inspiration from the ruler culture of the Byzantine empire.

Poetry about a Welsh prince called Cynddylan, who is linked to Pengwern, a kingdom in what is now the Welsh borders area, describes him answering Penda's call, and it describes a major battle outside Lichfield.[4] Fascinatingly, there is a part of the text which in its original form does not seem to make sense, and an amendment accepted by many, but rejected by some, would interpret one word as the name Arthur and, therefore, refers to the Britons from Cynddylan's kingdom as 'young whelps of great Arthur'.[5] If the word should be interpreted as Arthur, then it would firmly establish that Penda was, in some sense, operating in some kind of Arthurian context, and that Penda was almost certainly aware of Arthur and his campaigns. Some have even suggested that at some stage Penda married Heledd, sister of Cynddylan, which, if true, and if the poem does refer to 'whelps of Arthur' might almost make Penda one himself.

A less explicit, but similar sort of deduction can be made from the text of the *Historia Brittonum*. The *Historia Brittonum* with its battle list is, of course, our main early source for Arthur. Intriguingly, the author also chose to make Penda a major subject in his work.[6] It is an interesting association of the two figures. Depending on the date of the assembly of the Arthurian material within the *Historia Brittonum* it is not impossible Penda was aware of it, particularly since it seems to have been assembled in Wales.

Bede describes Penda as a very energetic man.[7] Penda was about to show just how energetic he was.

Edwin of Northumbria had been pursuing one of the regular activities of conventional Anglo-Saxon monarchs: he had been attacking the Britons. Specifically, he had been attacking Cadwallon of Gwynedd in Anglesey and North Wales. Cadwallon had managed to fight off the Northumbrian attack but now he wanted revenge and Penda was ready to assist.

There may even be place name evidence for this alliance. Chadbury in Norton and Lenchwick, Worcestershire, was originally Ceadweallanbyrig in 860, which became Chedeslburie and eventually the present name. It is not clear precisely which figure is involved here, but this area is in Dobunni territory and is probably far too far north for Cædwalla of Wessex, so Cadwallon of Gwynedd seems at least a possibility.

The combined forces of Mercia and Gwynedd advanced east and probably in October 633 met the forces of Northumbria at the Battle of Heathfield, traditionally at Hatfield Chase near Doncaster. The location is an interesting one. Doncaster is a strong Type G area with several examples of the brooch coming from around Doncaster. It is also on the edge of what had been Corieltauvi territory and was now on the edge, or probably within the boundaries, of the partly British kingdom of Lindsey. It cannot be too far from the location of Arthur's four battles in the region of Linnuis.

There are a couple of other possible locations for the battle. There is a Hatfield

Grange (Hethfeld 1232) near Cuckney which would also be on the edge of Lindsey. And there is actually a Hatfield (Hathfeld 1275) in the parish of Norton-juxta-Kempsey, in Worcestershire not that far from Ceadweallanbyrig, though this might be too far west for the battle.

The allied forces of Penda and Cadwallon smashed the Northumbrian army, killing Edwin and his son Osfrith and capturing his other son Eadfrith. As the Northumbrians struggled to recover from this massive defeat, Cadwallon continued with his war, advancing into Northumbria and attacking settlements. Bede reckoned Cadwallon intended to 'cut off the entire English nation' and describes Cadwallon reigning over Northumbria for a year.

The extended campaign, however, was not to end well for Cadwallon. Oswald eventually managed to gather an army and met Cadwallon's army at the Battle of Heavenfield near Hexham. The location of the battle is now marked by a large cross and a church of, yes, St. Oswald, located on the hill where Oswald is said to have raised his battle standard.[8] This time Cadwallon's forces were defeated and Cadwallon himself was killed at a place called Denisesburna.

Penda was not at the battle, probably because his priorities lay elsewhere. He was attempting to extend his area of influence across the centre of England, in some senses, deliberately or otherwise, replicating what Arthur may have achieved in terms of political and military geography. It is interesting to note that, just as he seems to have taken a particular interest in retaking southern Dobunni land, early in his career, so Penda and his successors seem to have taken a particular interest in taking and holding Lindsey. Lindsey became an area of contention between Northumbria and Mercia and there was almost certainly more fighting there. For much of his reign, it seems likely that Penda controlled Lindsey.[9]

To the south Penda expanded into Middle Anglia. This essentially consisted of much of the area that had had horsehead buckles that was not in Dobunni territory (see Chapter 1) and included the part of the former Coreiltauvi *civitas*/tribal area that was south of Lindsey. Place names connected with Penda's family reflect the importance of the area to Penda. And there are some Hwicce names here too which seem to indicate a link now between the west and east of Penda's kingdom. There is Whiston in Northamptonshire (Hwiccingtune 974) and Whissendine (Wichingedene 1086) and Witchley

Warren (Hwicceslea 1075) both in Rutland.[10] The Rutland two are very close to Peada's great Middle Anglian foundation at Peterborough Cathedral.

At some stage in this period, about 635, Penda found himself with a battle, probably on the eastern border of Middle Anglia, with the forces of the East Angles under their king Egric and former king Sigebert. Sigebert had sometime before all this retired to a monastery. However, he had previously been a talented military leader and the East Angles decided they needed him at the battle to inspire the troops. Sigebert refused the invitation, whereupon the East Angles forced him out of the monastery and carried him to the battlefield. When they got him there Sigebert still refused to carry a weapon. Penda's forces defeated the East Angles, killing or scattering them, and both Egric and Sigebert died.

By this stage, Penda had pretty much recreated the old alliance of Dobunni and Corieltauvi that probably emerged in the last years of Roman rule and may have re-emerged under Arthur. It is, therefore, worth pausing before looking at the rest of Penda's battles to consider a little what kind of kingdom Penda was building.

It seems clear that Penda was building a territory with both significant ethnic and cultural diversity. It was not a British or Anglo-Saxon kingdom; it was both British and Anglo-Saxon.

We have already considered some of the evidence for British elements within the Mercian royal family, and there is more evidence of this in *The Life of St. Guthlac of Crowland*.[11] Living in the late seventh and early eighth century, Guthlac was born into a family connected to the Mercian royal family. His father was called Penwalh which probably indicates some British links, and Guthlac himself is said to have led a multi-ethnic warband in his youth and is said to have understood the British language after spending time in exile among Britons.

Penda himself was pagan, but all his children would become Christian, and he allowed Christian clergy to operate and preach in his territory. There were clearly already many British Celtic Christians in Penda's territory. The appearance of the place name element Eccles, derived from the Latin Ecclesia, is generally reckoned to indicate a location where a church has existed since before the arrival of the Anglo-Saxons. In the area we are considering there is Eccles, near Manchester, Exhall near Alcester and Exhall north of Coventry,

Eccleswall in Satffordshire, Eccleston south of Chester and perhaps Eccleswall in Herefordshire. Missionaries from the Anglo-Saxon kingdoms were also operating in Mercia at the time. Bede states that Penda did not obstruct the preaching of Christianity and that the king had respect for Christians who followed the teachings of Christianity but he had no respect for those who claimed to be Christians but did not follow the teachings of their religion. Mercia itself would become Christian after Penda's death. The interestingly named Sexwulf was bishop of Mercia, at Lichfield, around 675, and about the same time, the magnificent All Saints Church was built at Brixworth, Northamptonshire

In archaeological terms, Mercia was part Anglo-Saxon at this time and part British. The Staffordshire hoard dating probably from Penda's time and found in the core of Penda's Mercia, not too far from his capital at Tamworth, contains outstanding examples of Anglo-Saxon work of the period, but then this is war booty.

One aspect of the culture of this time that we should explore here is Celtic hanging bowls.[12] These bowls carried escutcheons richly decorated with Celtic patterns picked out in coloured enamel. Some, like the great bowl from Sutton Hoo have been found whole. In many instances it is just the escutcheons that have been found, often by metal detectorists. They are clearly products of Celtic craftsmanship and design, yet they are rarely found in Wales or Cornwall. Instead, some of them seem to have been made in Scotland and Ireland and one unfinished example of a hanging bowl escutcheon was found at Seagry, about fifteen miles south of the Dobunni capital at Cirencester.[13] These hanging bowls are mainly found in England, often in otherwise culturally Anglo-Saxon areas. They seem almost all to date from the period 550–700, with most being seventh century.

There has been much debate about how and why these very distinctively Celtic items are suddenly found across England in the seventh century. It seems worth considering whether, in fact, this phenomenon may, in part, represent the Celtic cultural influence across England of Mercia's part-British royal family, at a time when it was establishing political dominance over much of the country as well.[14]

There were others who would dispute that dominance, the Northumbrians in particular. Oswald led an army south into Mercia. Sometime probably around August 642 Penda and British allies (including Cynddylan) met the Northumbrian army in battle at a place called Maserfelth or Maserfield. The Northumbrians were thoroughly defeated, and Oswald lost his life. Eowa, Penda's brother was also killed.

The exact location of Maserfield is unknown. Traditionally the battle is said to have taken place at Oswestry. There is a major hillfort there, and the place name Oswestry was Oswaldestroe in 1191 and does originally mean 'Oswald's tree'. One expert suggests the battle actually took place further into Wales at Forden, a place we have already mentioned because it is a strategic ford and close to the Camlad river.[15] Maserfield probably means 'field field' in the sense that it seems to be a combination of the Welsh word *maes* for field and the Anglo-Saxon word. For that reason, it is worth considering Maisermore, just outside Gloucester. This is derived from Maes mawr, Welsh for great field, and it is a very rare example of an English place name including *maes*. Whatever the exact location of Maserfield is, there is general agreement that it was somewhere near the Welsh borders, and when we consider the location of Arthur's battles it shows that he could have been fighting the Saxons in this area. Baschurch, possible location of Arthur's Bassas River battle, and Branogenium/Leintwardine, possible location of Breguoin, are both very much in the same part of England as Oswestry.

As the dominant power in central England, Penda and Mercia were now able to project power across the island, in something like the same manner that the *Historia Brittonum* battle list suggests Arthur could. It seems likely that if Penda had been a Christian, then he would have made it into Bede's list of rulers who wielded *imperium* over the English and he would have been listed as a Bretwalda.

The king of the West Saxons, Cenwealh, was married to Penda's sister. Cenwealh made the mistake of dumping Penda's sister for another wife, and, in 645, Penda kicked him out of Wessex. Cenwealh took refuge with Anna, king of the East Angles. Anna was subsequently killed, and Æthelhere who took over from Anna, got the hint, and served under Penda in a subsequent campaign.

At some stage probably in the late 640s, Penda led an army into the land of the

Northumbrians and besieged Bamburgh. This location is only just over ten miles from Yeavering and the mouth of the River Glen, one of the possible locations for Arthur's battle at the mouth of the river Glein. The Mercians attempted to set Bamburgh ablaze. According to Bede they gathered a huge quantity of wood, wattle and thatch, piled it all up on the land side of the fortress and set light to it. However, apparently the wind turned their own fire on the attackers, injuring some and forcing others to retreat. This was all due, in Bede's view, to divine intervention and the prayers of Bishop Aidan. Penda would conduct further raids into the north after this. Bede records Penda returning at some stage after the death of Bishop Aidan, and burning down the church and village that had been his home. However, Bede does claim that the post the bishop had been leaning against when he died, refused to be burned.[16]

Finally, in 655, Penda gathered a large army from his own forces and those of his allies and set off. The army contained contingents led by thirty royal commanders (kings or more minor rulers) under Penda. Among Penda's allies on this campaign was Cadafael ap Cynfeddw of Gwynedd. However, it seems clear that there were other British kings accompanying Penda on his campaign. The *Historia Brittonum* mentions the kings of the Britons, *reges Brittonum*, joining Penda's expedition. Interestingly this is the same phrase that the *Historia Brittonum* uses in its description of Arthur, stating that he fought alongside the kings of the Britons '*cum regibus Brittonum*'. It is perhaps another sign that the author of *Historia Brittonum* saw significant parallels between Arthur and Penda.

Northumbria had, prior to this, fragmented along tribal lines. Deira, previously the *civitas* of the Parisi in east Yorkshire, had been separated from the old territory of the Brigantes and Votadini to the north, now known as Bernicia. It is worth noting here that both Deira and Bernicia are originally British names. Deira is linked to the British river name Derwent and, ultimately, like the name Derry, is linked to the word for an oak tree. Bernicia, or Bryneich as it sometimes appears in Old Welsh poetry, means something like 'the land of mountain passes'.[17] The kings of Northumbria, Deira and Bernicia may have had Anglo-Saxon names, but there was still a large British element in their kingdoms.

According to the *Historia Brittonum*, at some stage Penda besieged Oswiu of Bernicia at Iudeu and forced Oswiu to return treasures he had stolen from the Britons. The location of Iudeu is far from certain. It is said to have been on the Firth of Forth and Bede mentions it as Urbs Giudi. Some have suggested Stirling as a possible location, but this is probably too far north. King Oswald seems to have besieged Edinburgh in around 638 and the southern shore of the Firth of Forth seems a more plausible location for Iudeu.[18] Again, when we consider Arthur's battle in the Caledonian Forest, the siege of Iudeu demonstrates how an army based in central Britain could and did operate this far north.

Whatever happened at Iudeu and whenever and wherever it happened, Penda's forces eventually met Oswiu's army in a massive battle near the River Winwæd in November 655. Again, the exact location of this battle is debated. However, Oswiu's campaign after the battle concluded in the area of Loidis (from which Leeds takes its name) so it is usually assumed that the actual battle took place not that far from there. There is a location near Leeds called Whinmoor and Cock Beck with a place now called Penda's Fields has been suggested as a possible location, but there is great uncertainty.

What does seem certain is that some of Penda's allies abandoned him before the actual battle. The *Historia Brittonum* states that Cadafael ap Cynfeddw of Gwynedd withdrew along with his troops under cover of darkness before the battle and subsequently acquired the nickname Cadomedd, battle-shirker, because of what he did.[19] Bede states that Æthelwald of Deira also decided to give the battle a miss. Penda's forces were defeated and Penda himself was killed. The slaughter took place in poor weather and Bede records that many died in the swollen River Winwæd.

The man who had created Mercia was dead, but Mercia itself was not. After a brief period of Northumbrian occupation, a Mercian rebellion put Wulfhere, son of Penda, on the Mercian throne and Wulfhere did much to restore Mercian dominance of central and southern England. In the eighth century the efforts of Æthelbald of Mercia and Offa, who both claimed Eowa, Penda's brother, as their ancestor, made Mercia the dominant power in England. It is the period of the full Mercian supremacy and Offa probably claimed the title Rex Anglorum, King of the English.

Penda, a partly or almost wholly British leader with an original power base in an almost entirely British part of the island, working alongside British allies had halted the Anglo-Saxon advance westwards and changed the course of Britain and England forever. Arthur, or a figure like Arthur, may have attempted something similar in the early sixth century and probably had success in it for a time but was not able to consolidate his gains for generations after his death and was not able to establish a ruling dynasty. Penda did manage to consolidate his gains for generations after his death and his family did manage to establish a ruling dynasty.

The famous Repton stone carries a carving of a mounted warrior, his shield raised in the air as he rides out. It is an eighth-century Mercian carving often thought to show a Mercian king, perhaps Æthelbald of Mercia, grandson of Penda's brother. However, with his scale armour and pleated tunic he looks (apart from the moustache) very like the portrayal of Aeneas fighting Turnus in the *Vergilius Romanus* and you think that this is pretty much how the British militia leader probably portrayed on the Longbridge Deverill buckle would have looked and pretty much how Arthur himself would have looked as he led the 'kings of the Britons' to battle.

The most widely known king of Mercia today is, of course, Offa, of, yes, Offa's Dyke fame. He, again, was a descendant of Eowa, Penda's brother. Eowa was Offa's great-great-grandfather. Offa was perhaps the most powerful monarch in England prior to Alfred the Great and his reputation extended across Europe as well. The emperor Charlemagne proposed that his son should marry one of Offa's daughters and in 796 Charlemagne sent Offa a letter that we still have, about pilgrims and trade. Offa minted beautiful silver coins bearing his name and portrait and, taking some ideas from Charlemagne's coinage, he created English silver pennies that would be the forerunners of much later English coinage.[20] By the time of Offa, Mercia was bigger and more English than it had been in the time of Penda and, unlike Penda, Offa fought campaigns against Welsh kings. His forces fought a Welsh army at Hereford in 760 and the *Annales Cambriae* records three campaigns conducted by Offa against the Welsh. The dyke that now carries his name was probably mostly constructed on Offa's orders to delineate Mercia's border with Wales. Nevertheless, there was to be no big English advance into Wales under Offa. The Normans would make some advances into southern Wales; however, it would not be until the time of Edward I in the thirteenth century, 800 years after Arthur and some 650 years after Penda, that England would seize control of Wales. The long delay between the arrival of the Anglo-Saxons in eastern England and English political control of Wales meant that Wales would never be English, even when English kings were ruling it.

Offa died in 796. The first Viking raid on England had already occurred in 789 and more would follow even before Offa's death. In 793 the Vikings sacked the monastery at Lindisfarne. However, Offa could probably not have guessed the extent of the devastation that the Vikings would bring to Mercia.

Mercia would suffer hugely from Viking attacks and would eventually be annexed by the kingdom of Wessex as it finally united England. However, coins found recently featuring both Alfred ('the Great') of Wessex and Ceolwulf II of Mercia indicate a firm alliance between them at some stage and suggest Mercia may have played a more prominent role in this period than previously thought.

The idea of Mercia and the Midlands as separate, unique regions has also lived on. Mercia has, for instance, appeared in the names of various military and police units. And what became the flag of Mercia, a yellow saltire on a blue field, is still flown over the town of St. Albans because of Mercian royal involvement in the abbey there.

Mercian culture continued to inspire, long after the days of Penda, and long after the days when it was a separate kingdom. J.R.R. Tolkein, though born in South Africa, grew up in the lands of Mercia. He spent time as a child living in Sarehole and then Birmingham and visited a lot of the surrounding places and areas, like Alcester, Alvechurch and the Malverns. The world Tolkein would later construct in his books, with all its Arthurian influences, also owed a lot to Mercia. For instance, the land of The Mark (Tolkein's version of the name Mercia) or Rohan has a strong Mercian influence on its language.

Chapter 9

A Britain Changed Forever

For Gildas, writing probably sometime in the 540s it seemed like the worst had passed.

He was writing not long after the era of Arthur's victories over the Saxons and he wrote that the Britons' war with foreigners was at an end, and that it was only civil wars that were then the problem. He wrote that that war generation, what would be Arthur's generation, were mostly dead and had been replaced by a generation who knew nothing about the courage, dignity and self-discipline needed in time of war, by a generation who had known only prosperity and had given themselves over to vice and pleasure. If you looked through conservative newspapers from the 1970s and 1980s you would probably find many articles claiming pretty much the same.

As mentioned earlier, one of the great mysteries about Gildas has always been where he was writing. It tends to be assumed that he was not writing within the realms of one of the rulers he criticized so vehemently in his text. Judging by the description Gildas gives of them, they do not seem like the kind of people who would take kindly to being openly criticized in such a vigorous fashion. There are two lives of St. Gildas. One states he ended up in Brittany at the Abbey of St. Gildas de Rhuys there.[1] The other Life claims him for the church at Street near Glastonbury. The two claims are not necessarily mutually exclusive, in that Gildas, as so many other Celtic saints of the period seem to have done, could have spent time on both sides of the Channel. The claims of St. Gildas de Rhuys have perhaps been taken a little more seriously, perhaps because the Abbey is an old and impressive institution holding in its treasury reliquaries of St. Gildas, and because of suspicion over Glastonbury Abbey's medieval attempts to claim King Arthur and those connected with him for their own. However, it is worth noting here that the churchyard at Street is of the rounded type usually associated with Celtic foundations, and careful observation has found a bank surrounding part of the churchyard, again a possible indication of a Celtic churchyard.[2]

If Gildas was writing in Street and thought the worst of the Britons' woes in that region were over, he was very wrong. Whether it was due to Arthur or some other cause, the Anglo-Saxons had advanced little for most of the sixth century. However, by the late sixth century they were on the move again, advancing into British areas.

In 556 West Saxon forces defeated the Britons at Beran Byrig, which is probably Barbury Castle near Swindon. Then, in 571 the West Saxons advanced into the upper Thames region and advanced into the Chilterns, taking Eynsham, Benson, Aylesbury and Limbury. In 577, as already discussed, at the Battle of Deorham, the West Saxons defeated a Dobunni army and then seized the southern part of Dobunni territory. By 584 the West Saxons had reached Fethanleag, north of Oxford. They seem to have been defeated there, but still, this is deep inside central Britain. In 614 the West Saxons defeated a British army at Beandun. The exact location is unclear; however, the most likely option is Bindon near Axmouth in Devon (Benedon 1311, possibly from *bean dun*, a hill where beans grow). Just as Fethanleag is far into the centre, Bindon is getting far west. Meanwhile in the north Deira and Bernicia had been united to form a powerful Northumbrian kingdom and sometime in the early seventh century a Northumbrian army under Æthelfrith had advanced westwards as far as Chester, where it smashed a Welsh army, and probably killed several Welsh kings. Soon after that the forces of Northumbria and the East Angles met at the Battle of the River Idle fighting for control of the territory between them, including the largely British Kingdom of Lindsey, the northern part of what had been Corieltauvi territory.

Then all these huge Anglo-Saxon advances pretty much stopped. Why?

Because of Penda. Just as Arthur, or a king like Arthur, probably stopped the Anglo-Saxon advances around the end of the fifth century, the victories that Penda, with his partly British forces and totally British allies won over various Anglo-Saxon kingdoms almost totally halted their advances for decades. And when, after Penda's death the Anglo-Saxon advances continued, they were at a slower pace and in much more limited areas, because the might of the Mercian supremacy dominated so much of England and so much of English history in the late seventh century and in the eighth century. If you go to Dorset and visit Lady St. Mary Church in Wareham, you can see inside there British inscriptions dating from the seventh or eighth centuries. It is fascinating that there was a specifically Celtic local British culture as far east as this, as late as this.

If you want to see the evidence of that in the ethnic and regional make-up of England today, then, in some sense, you can. In 2015 a pioneering analysis of British ancestry was published. Over twenty years the researchers analysed the DNA of people whose grandparents were all born within fifty miles or eighty kilometres of each other, effectively producing a DNA picture of local communities at the beginning of the twentieth century.[3]

The research shows a fascinating picture of the effect of Anglo-Saxon immigration on the genetic make-up of Britain. In the east, centre and south of England, representing the areas where Anglo-Saxons settled early and in quantity, there is 10–40 per cent Anglo-Saxon genetic component and much genetic homogeneity produced, presumably, by the process of immigration and integration across that zone.

In Wales and Scotland, where Anglo-Saxon immigration was never extensive you can, unsurprisingly, see separate, defined, ancient genetic groups. In the west of England too, however, there are separate, defined genetic groups that may well have been there since the Iron Age. There is a Cornwall group, a Devon group, a southern Welsh borders and west Midlands group in the old northern region of the Dobunni where the Iclingas first established Mercia, a northern Welsh borders group around Liverpool, Chester and Manchester, a West Yorkshire group, a Cumbria group and a Northumbria group.

Obviously, these are all local areas with a proudly distinct culture and heritage, and some of that is down to the fact they have each had a distinct culture and heritage probably since before the Romans. If the west of England had been as extensively settled as the east, England would have been a different place to what it is, with a different history to what it has had. England has never been totally Anglo-Saxon. It was from the start a combination of Anglo-Saxon alongside various Celtic tribes, First Nations in a sense, to use a terminology from Canada and Australia. On that genetic map you can see the Cornovii of Cornwall, the Dumnonii, the Dobunni, perhaps the Welsh borders Cornovii, the Brigantes, the Carvetii and the Votadini. The fact that you can still see them on the map probably owes a lot to Arthur and Penda.

Now, of course, we have new communities in England from across the world, adding to the exciting cultural mix that is in England. And when you look at the culture of Anglo-Saxon England in the eighth century and beyond you can easily see the influence of the Britons of Mercia, Bernicia and elsewhere on it.

We have already looked at how the spread of Celtic enamelled escutcheons from hanging bowls across England may reflect the spread of Mercian power. Some identical motifs soon appear in artwork found in 'Anglo-Saxon' kingdoms and became part of what is termed 'insular' art, so-called because it reflects the unique combination of Celtic and Anglo-Saxon art found in these islands (*insula* being the Latin for island) and nowhere else. There is even a particular category of art design called Mercian which includes beautiful interwoven patterns and animals. It is also worth repeating here another point we have already mentioned – that, alongside Mercia with its British origins, the other two main 'Anglo-Saxon' kingdoms competing for power after the death of Rædwald, king of East Anglia, were Northumbria and Wessex, both of which seem to have had major British involvement in their creation.

Taking the long view of England, the nation's history has also been a unique blend of various cultures and peoples, and the more Celtic areas of England have played a huge part in that. The legend of Arthur too has made a huge contribution to making Britain and England what it is, giving both a founding hero to inspire and unite.

This is not the place to explore all the massive contributions that the more Celtic areas have made to England, but to take one example, we should perhaps mention here the Industrial Revolution. Much of this phenomenon that made Britain the global superpower of the age and which still contributes so much to our place in the world today happened in the north and west of England and in the Celtic countries bordering those areas, and the Industrial Revolution owed a lot, not just to the mineral resources of those areas, but also to the hard work and talents of the people living there.

And today's politicians talking about 'levelling up' so much, could probably learn a bit from Mercia. A kingdom born in the West Midlands took over London and made itself the richest place in Great Britain.

Notes

Generally, unless otherwise stated, information on the place names of Roman Britain is from Rivet & Smith 1979; earlier forms of English names are sourced from searches on the English Place Name Society website or Mills 1999, and information on Welsh names comes from searches on the Historic Place Names of Wales website. Abbreviations for original sources are found on page 184.

Chapter 1

[1] See, for instance, John Everett Millais *The Romans Leaving Britain*

[2] Russell & Laycock 2010

[3] DEB 6

[4] For earlier forms of English place names, see English Place Name Society epns.nottingham.ac.uk and/or Mills 1999

[5] See photo 1 and Portable Antiquities Scheme for brooches and distribution finds.org.uk. See Rivet & Smith 1979 for all Roman place names in Britain.

[6] See photos 2,3

[7] Gagnol, Feugere, Zaaraoui 2020

[8] Ammianus Marcellinus, *Roman History* 27, 8

[9] For distribution and discussion of door-knob spear butts see Portable Antiquities Scheme and Hunter 2010

[10] Hawkes & Dunning 1961, Appels & Laycock 2007 and Henry 2022

[11] See Laycock 2008, Chapter 6 for fuller discussion

[12] See photo 6, Portable Antiquities Scheme ref. HAMP-34EBF6

[13] E.g. edition.cnn.com/travel/article/uk-roman-villa-wiltshire/index.html

[14] See fig. 8 and Buora

[15] See fig. 10 and Aurrecoechea Fernandez 1999. See Laycock 2009 Chapter 1 for discussion.

[16] Gagnol, Feugere, Zaaraoui 2020

[17] Laycock 2008, Chapter 6

[18] Henry 2022

[19] See, for instance, Portable Antiquities Scheme ref. NMS-6B34F7

[20] See, for instance, Portable Antiquities Scheme ref. LEIC-AE8085

[21] See, for instance, example from Richborough in Hawkes & Dunning 1961

[22] See photo 8. For typology see Booth 2014. For similarities between crossbow brooch and penannular E terminals compare, for instance, Bayley & Butcher 2004 figs. 317, 318, 319 with figs. 419, 421, 423, 424 with For discussion of use by soldiers see Collins 2010. For example, see Gerrard 2013 199–200 for an early fifth century warrior buried at Mucking with Roman-type belt set, spear and penannular brooch

and reconstruction drawing of the warrior. And see Suzuki 2000 151–52 for a similar fifth century quoit brooch found with a sword and silver-inlaid buckle at Benouville, Normandy. Also see Portable Antiquities ref. CAM-8F56A2 which appears to be a Type F terminal decorated with birds of a type normally found on military/militia/official buckles.

[23] DEB 14

[24] Zosimus 6. 10. 2.

[25] Zosimus 6. 5. 2–3

[26] See, for instance, coin distributions of Reece periods 19-21 in Bland 2018

[27] In my map, I have attempted to group culturally similar tribes/*civitates* into provinces, which seems the most logical approach

[28] See Chapter 4 for a detailed discussion of Gildas

[29] See, for example, Colchester buckle and buckle plate in Hawkes & Dunning 1961

[30] Henry 2022 fig. 6.29

[31] For Dobunni Geometric design examples, see Portable Antiquities Scheme BERK-6D6584, WAW-6AD751, BUC-E114D2, HAMP-5F68B3. For Corieltauvi Peacock design examples see Portable Antiquities Scheme NLM-ED23EA, NARC-F83FC9, NLM-72E927, Hawkes & Dunning 1961 Tripontium. See, for example, a strap end from Kenchester which has both a peacock and tree of life motif but also a wheel motif and cross-hatched triangle

[32] See Hobbs 1997 for this phenomenon, Faulkner 2000, fig. 2.20 and for coins specifically see Bland 2018 Reece Periods 21–22

[33] Walton and Moorhead 2016, Chapter 4 figs. 1 and 2

[34] Henry forthcoming

[35] See Laycock 2008 and Russell & Laycock 2010 for more discussion of militias and civil wars

Chapter 2

[1] See Chapter 3 for a full discussion of HB

[2] DEB 23

[3] See photo 10 for examples of Supporting Arm Brooches

[4] See Portable Antiquities Scheme for more examples of Supporting Arm Brooches. For distribution, see Portable Antiquities Scheme, county heritage records etc. and James Gerrard forthcoming

[5] See, for instance, www.theguardian.com/uk/2003/aug/11/artsandhumanities.arts1

[6] See photos 11,12

[7] See Pearson 2002 for a general discussion of the Saxon Shore forts and discussion of Richborough

[8] Bland 2018 Maps 25–27 and Richard Henry forthcoming

[9] See, for instance, Portable Antiquities Scheme ref. KENT-AB6B72 and Lyne figs. 77 and 81
[10] See Suzuki 2000 for a general exploration of QBS with many of the main examples
[11] See Suzuki 2000, 111–20 for a discussion of Hengest and QBS. See Swift 2019 for recent distribution maps
[12] DEB 25
[13] See index of names in Mommsen
[14] Coe 2001
[15] HB 66
[16] Portable Antiquities Scheme refs. HAMP-E4D0B5, HAMP-722FA3, HAMP-BCF8D0, HAMP-E7D6E3, HAMP-F7A764, WILT-F77983, WILT-169D92, SUR-0B883B
[17] Heighway 2012
[18] Clarke 1979
[19] See, for example, Portable Antiquities Scheme ref. GLOE5FE4D and HAMP-BAE647
[20] Gerrard & Henig 2017, catalogue 5–7
[21] Russell 2017, 251
[22] See, for instance, the English Place Name Society website entry on Cadbury Manor which accepts that the personal name Cada that it contains is 'probably of British origin'. Congresbury (see Mills 1998) contains the Celtic personal name Congar
[23] Dark 2000, 116 etc. and see Barber & Pykitt 1997, 47 for possible link to Ambrosius
[24] Dark 2000, 123–24
[25] Bannister 1916
[26] Portable Antiquities Scheme ref. HESH-465F26
[27] htt.herefordshire.gov.uk/herefordshieres-past/the-anglo-saxon-period/herefordshire-sites/marden-cemetery
[28] Breeze, p. 7
[29] There is also a rare post-Roman fragment of Type G penannular brooch from Wellington Portable Antiquities Scheme ref. WAW-5ACBD8
[30] Hurst 2006
[31] Portable Antiquities Scheme ref. WAW-537B43, WMID-513546, WMID-6A099C
[32] Hurst 1997, 24
[33] The *Mirabilia* refers to salt springs in the country of the Hwicce as the fourth *miraculum* and it says salt can be boiled from them to salt various foods, and they are

not near the sea, but they come from the ground
[34] Portable Antiquities Scheme ref. WAW-5B1E48, WAW-0FABC1, WAW-A8E117, WAW-D54FA4
[35] Anglo-Saxon Droitwich, Archaeology Section, Hereford and Worcester County Council
[36] Historic England list entry for Droitwich
[37] Maddicott 2005
[38] Rivet & Smith 1981
[39] Thomas 1994, 265–67
[40] Hathaway, SJE, 468
[41] DEB 3
[42] See White 2007 for a general discussion of the area in Roman times and after
[43] See, for example, Photo 16
[44] See, for example, Portable Antiquities Scheme ref. BERK-6D6584, WAW-6AD751
[45] WILT-169D92
[46] Bennett, Riddler & Sparey-Green 2010, fig. 71
[47] Reece 1997, 10
[48] Faulkner 2000, fig. 2.20 and for coins specifically see Bland 2018 Reece Periods 21–22
[49] Bryant & Heighway 2003
[50] Dark 2000, 120
[51] White 2007, fig. 24.7
[52] Photos are available online or look at *Archaeologia Cambrensis, 1900* Journal of the Cambrian Archaeological Association
[53] Coe 2001, 212-213
[54] Lyne, fig. 79
[55] Suzuki 2000, 144, fig. 20
[56] Portable Antiquities Scheme ref. DOR-DF5E7A

Chapter 3
[1] HB 56
[2] HB 56
[3] HB 48
[4] HB 62
[5] E.g. HB 28
[6] DEB 10.2
[7] HE BkII, 2, 84
[8] HB 56

[9] HB 65
[10] HE bkV, 24
[11] HB 56
[12] HE bkV 24
[13] HB 56
[14] ASC 508
[15] ASC 833
[16] DEB 23.1
[17] DEB 24.3
[18] DEB 25.2
[19] HB 40
[20] DEB 28–36
[21] DEB 31.2
[22] DEB 28.1
[23] HB 62
[24] DEB 26.2
[25] Dumville 1985, para 26
[26] HB 49
[27] HB 47
[28] HB 35
[29] Epistola 2
[30] Vita 29
[31] Anderson 1936, 3.9
[32] Snyder 1998, 82
[33] DEB 25.1
[34] DEB 26.1
[35] HB 42
[36] HB 48
[37] DEB 25.3
[38] E.g.Higham 2002, 58
[39] Higham 2018, 193–94
[40] Green 2007, 145
[41] Higham 2018, 186
[42] DEB 31.1
[43] HB 42
[44] HE BkI 16, 3
[45] Huyshe trans 1908, 9
[46] White 2007, 199
[47] Fulford 2021, 190

[48] HB 56
[49] HB 16
[50] Morris 1980, 50
[51] AC CCCLXV
[52] HB 31
[53] HB 20
[54] HB 16
[55] HB 66
[56] HB 46
[57] Morris 1980, 9
[58] DEB 34.6
[59] Barber 1972, 98–99
[60] Higham 2018, 187
[61] Higham 2018, 188
[62] Barber 1972, 98–99
[63] HB 62
[64] Gidlow 2004, 8
[65] Koch 1997, B2.38
[66] Koch 1997, B2.28
[67] Dumville, 1985, para 26
[68] Bartrum 1966, 10
[69] HB 66a
[70] HB 73
[71] HB 73
[72] E.g. silently in Morris 1980, 83
[73] HE bkIII.9, 146
[74] HE bkIV.11, 227
[75] HB 54
[76] HB 71
[77] AC LVI
[78] HB 63
[79] HE bkV.24, 353
[80] DEB 20.1
[81] Snyder 1998, 39
[82] Snyder 1998, 35–37
[83] HB 66
[84] Gidlow 2010, 213
[85] HB 66
[86] AC IX

[87] AC LXXII
[88] AC XCIII
[89] AC CLXVIII

Chapter 4

[1] DEB 65
[2] Winterbottom 1978, 80–86
[3] DEB 26.1
[4] DEB 1.2
[5] DEB 26.1
[6] DEB 24.2
[7] HE bkI.22, 42
[8] DEB 5.1
[9] DEB 7
[10] DEB 13.1
[11] DEB 3.1
[12] DEB 20.3
[13] DEB 2
[14] DEB 3.2
[15] DEB 25.1
[16] DEB 3.2
[17] DEB 3.2
[18] DEB 4.2
[19] DEB 19.2
[20] DEB 18.3
[21] DEB 13.2
[22] DEB 74.1
[23] HE bkII.2, 84
[24] DEB 18.2
[25] DEB 24.3
[26] DEB 10.2
[27] DEB 32.1
[28] DEB 3.2-3
[29] DEB 1.14
[30] White 2007, 50
[31] DEB 23.4
[32] DEB 10.2
[33] White 2007, 85
[34] Koch 1997, 18

[35] DEB 66.5
[36] DEB 67.5
[37] HE BkII.2, 82
[38] DEB 27
[39] Gidlow 2010, 20
[40] Bromwich 2014, 161
[41] Bromwich 2014, 5
[42] Koch 1997, 23
[43] Schaffner 1984, 153
[44] Koch 1997, 13
[45] HB 8
[46] Epistola 2
[47] White 2007, 34
[48] DEB 18.1
[49] DEB 6.2
[50] DEB 28.2
[51] DEB 33.4
[52] DEB 17.2
[53] DEB 32.1
[54] DEB 33.4
[55] DEB 26.1
[56] E.g. DEB 33.4
[57] DEB 4.4
[58] DEB 25.1
[59] Williams 1899, 43
[60] DEB 4.4
[61] DEB 24.3
[62] DEB 28.1
[63] E.g. Dark 1994, 102–3
[64] DEB 26.3
[65] DEB 33.2
[66] Williams 1899, 13
[67] Williams 1899, 85
[68] DEB 19.1
[69] Williams 1899, 99
[70] DEB 28.1
[71] DEB 23.4
[72] DEB 25.3
[73] DEB 24.3

[74] DEB 25.3
[75] Snyder 1998, 19
[76] DEB 28.1
[77] DEB 30.2
[78] DEB 31.1
[79] ASC p19
[80] DEB 24.1
[81] Dark 2000, 157
[82] Sims-Williams, 2003, 32
[83] DEB 31.1
[84] Bartrum 1966, 10
[85] DEB 32.1
[86] Koch 1997, 58
[87] Bartrum 1966, 10
[88] DEB 33.1
[89] HB 62
[90] E.g. Dark 1994, 78
[91] White 2007, 168
[92] DEB 3.1
[93] DEB 26.2
[94] DEB 33.1
[95] HB 62
[96] Jones 2019, 33
[97] E.g. MD, 5
[98] DEB 33.1
[99] DEB 30.2
[100] DEB 33.4
[101] Bartrum 1966, 9–10
[102] DEB 33.2
[103] DEB 34.1
[104] DEB 36.1
[105] DEB 34.3
[106] DEB 34.6
[107] HB 62
[108] DEB 26.3
[109] HB 62
[110] Bartrum 1993, 258
[111] DEB 27
[112] DEB 26.2

Chapter 5

[1] HE BkII.20
[2] Gidlow 2004, 230
[3] Gidlow 2004, 189
[4] Bartrum 1966, 9
[5] Wade-Evans and Lloyd 2013, 27
[6] Wade-Evans and Lloyd 2013, 69
[7] Wade-Evans and Lloyd 2013, 73
[8] Wade-Evans and Lloyd 2013, 85
[9] Wade-Evans and Lloyd 2013, 197
[10] HB 71
[11] Williams 1899, 99
[12] Wade-Evans and Lloyd 2013, 257
[13] Wade-Evans and Lloyd 2013, 261
[14] Wade-Evans and Lloyd 2013, 145
[15] HB 66a
[16] Bartrum 1966, 45
[17] Bartrum 1966, 23
[18] Bromwich 2014 Triad 75
[19] Jones 2019, 22
[20] Jones 2019, 21
[21] ASC 710
[22] Jones 2019, 22

Chapter 6

[1] See Lloyd 2017 for St. Cadoc locations, see Coe 2001 597-598 for Messur Pritquenn
[2] For Carantoc, see Chapter 5 and Gidlow 2004, 274, for use of terms *Protictor* and *Tribunus* see Thomas 1994 80–83 and 268–70. Cedwyr the pural of cadwr appears in *Pa Gur.*
[3] Photo 6
[4] Gerrard & Henig 2017, cat. 6
[5] Appels & Laycock 2007, fig. SL 12.2
[6] See, for instance, shield designs for Prima Flavia Pacis or Equites Constantiani Feroces
[7] Dixon & Southern 2014, fig. 21
[8] Dark 1994, 185–91. Also see Portable Antiquities Scheme OXOn-B0F2DE for very late fourth century, or fifth century British copy of a *siliqua* of Honorius showing very similar depiction of the human face to that in the *Vergilius Romanus*

[9] See, for instance, the Low Ham mosaic, and the recently found Rutland Roman villa mosaic, and also see the appearance on some coins of Carausius of the phrase '*Expectate Veni*' believed to reflect a line of the *Aeneid*.
[10] HB 10
[11] Photo 19. For more examples and discussion see Dickinson 1982, Booth 2014 and Portable Antiquities Scheme
[12] See fig. 25
[13] See photo 20
[14] Dark 2000, 105–25
[15] See Portable Antiquities Scheme
[16] Photo 16 top centre, Appels & Laycock 2007, fig, SL 8.21
[17] Booth 2014 191–94
[18] See Young 2005 for examples and discussion and Portable Antiquities Scheme for additional examples
[19] Green 2020 has extensive discussion of Lindsey
[20] HB 50
[21] Dickinson 1982, cat. 30
[22] See, for example, English Place Name Society entry for Glen Parva
[23] Mills 1998 on Glympton
[24] Grimsdyke section at Glympton
[25] Green 2020, 89–93, 95–99
[26] Cox 1971, 93–94
[27] See River Devon entry in Fife Place-Name Data at Glasgow.ac.uk
[28] See Leahy 2007, 54–56 and Green 2020, 231 etc.
[29] Nottinghamshire Monument Record M3012
[30] Nottinghamshire Monument Record M3625
[31] Portable Antiquities Scheme ref. DENO-DD5FA4
[32] Laycock
[33] Cox 1971, 487
[34] See Portable Antiquities Scheme
[35] See EPNS, The Place Names of Wiltshire
[36] A rare 'cocked hat' sword pommel has been found near Arthuret which could be of the right date for the battle see Portable Antiquites Scheme ref. LANCUM-4466DE
[37] Dickinson 1982, cat. 19
[38] Booth 2014, 192
[39] Rivet & Smith 1979, 447
[40] Dark 2000, 207–8 etc.
[41] Dickinson 1982

[42] Coe 2001, 874–75
[43] Halsall 2013, 169–71
[44] Based on maps generated from Portable Antiquities Scheme website
[45] Dickinson 1982, cat. 1
[46] Young 2005, fig. 4
[47] Booth 2014, 181
[48] Hurst 1997, 17–27
[49] Portable Antiquities Scheme ref. WAW-D54FA4
[50] See Milles 1998 and English Place Name Society website on Brailles
[51] Rivet & Smith 1979, 406
[52] Ehang = wide or large, Gwyn = white
[53] Rivet & Smith 1979, 204–15
[54] HB 7
[55] See fig. 25
[56] Dark 2000, 130–32
[57] As detailed in the *Life of St. Germanus* by Constantius
[58] See Mills 1998 on Kingsland, Monkland, Leominster and Lyonshall
[59] See the story of Merewalh, Edfrith and the lion, and the carving of the lion on Leominster priory
[60] See for example Portable Antiquities Scheme ref. HAMP-E01F55 and Appels & Laycock 2007 Section 2, Chapter 9
[61] Lewis & Williams, poem 21
[62] See Bromwich 1991, 39–42 for discussion of this battle in *Pa Gur*
[63] Morgan 2016 149–50
[64] In the Landaff Charters for instance, a single f is often used where modern Welsh would have a double ff, so the modern word ffynon is simply written finhaun, finnaun, fynnaun. However, in the Llandaff Charters the f can also stand for a b/u/v/w sound as in the variants Craf/Crawnon Cyfylchi/Ciuilchi, Cyfair/Ciuerdied, Cynfran/Cinbran etc. The name Llandaff itself is translated into Latin as Landavensis with a v.
[65] Bromwich 2006, 385
[66] See Chapter 5, Gidlow 2004 172–73, Wade-Evans & Lloyd 2013
[67] See photo 26
[68] White 2007, fig. 24.7
[69] See Thomas 1994 Chapter 9 for a discussion of the Irish origins of Brycheiniog
[70] See Historic Place Names of Wales website both for rarity of Boch- names and early versions of Boughood
[71] See Portable Antiquities Scheme
[72] See Lloyd, S. 2017

[73] For instance, Portable Antiquities Scheme ref. NMGW-FF0EE5
[74] The 1887 Ordnance Survey map shows these earthworks quite clearly
[75] See, for example, the road maps in Roman Conquest, Occupation and Settlement of Wales AD 47–410, Cadw 2011, no nonsense-interpretation ltd.
[76] Also see *Englynion y Beddau*, the Verses of the Graves, a Middle Welsh poem that tells of the graves of famous heroes and warriors
[77] Portable Antiquities Scheme ref. NMGW-E718C4
[78] The sort of buckles and belt fittings being worn by soldiers and some officials in much of Britain and mainland Europe in the fourth century are largely absent from Wales and northern England, so it seems reasonable to assume earlier types continued in use there
[79] Portable Antiquities Scheme ref. NMGW-E6F3B0
[80] Rivet & Smith 1979, 275. Rivet & Smith also discuss 276–77 the possibility of deriving Brewyn from Bremenium via Welsh Bref- but do not clarify how to get from Bref/Brev/Brew to Breg- or Bregu-. On the contrary, under the entry for Bremia, they indicate that this led to the modern Welsh river name Afon Brefi, not to a river name containing any 'g'.
[81] Lewis & Williams, poem 7
[82] See Historic Place Names of Wales website
[83] DEB 26
[84] See, for instance, the English Place Names Society website entry for Badbury Rings
[85] Blog National Trust
[86] Early place names from Baddeley 1990/1994. Finds nearby, Portable Antiquities Scheme ref. GLO-C94D8E, GLO-DFA063, GLO-952CA5, GLO-7D6DF4
[87] In Chretien de Troyes, *Lancelot, The Knight of the Cart*. Spellings of the name of Camelot vary in different manuscripts of the poem
[88] Bartrum 1993
[89] Bromwich 1991, 234–38
[90] Cunliffe 2005, 191
[91] See British Museum website
[92] Dickinson 1982, cat. 8
[93] Dark 2000, 111
[94] Dark 2000 has much on Uley
[95] White 2007, 92 discusses this site
[96] Hoverd 2015
[97] See Chapter 5
[98] See Chapter 5

Chapter 7

[1] Gidlow 2004, 15

[2] Coe 2001, 297–98

[3] Coe 2001, 570–71

[4] Coe 2001, 65

[5] For iron hammer reference see Mommsen text of Gildas '*malleum ferreum quo confringuntur mole leonum*'. For discussion of the cauldron and chain see Bruce-Mitford 1983, 511–53

[6] Enright 2006

[7] Enright 1983

[8] Rahtz 1970

[9] See DEB 28-36 for his attacks on rulers

[10] In the collection of the Bibliotheque Nationale

[11] Magnus Maximus took an army from Britain to mainland Europe and would presumably have taken with him most of the best troops in Britain

[12] Savory 1964

[13] Lewis & Williams, poem 1

[14] HB 32–35

[15] Ref. WRXTR/1 in the Celtic Inscribed Stones Project database

[16] D'Amato, R. & Salimbeti, A. 2023, 22

[17] See figs. 28–30

[18] *Flores Historiarum*, Roger of Wendover. *Flores Historiarum*, Matthew Paris.

[19] For discussion of these possible place name links see Pretty 1989 and Jones.

[20] pase.ac.uk

[21] See Bartrum 1993 and see Brady 2017 for a general discussion of British links and elements in the early Mercian royal family.

[22] Commius appears in Caesar's accounts of his campaigns in Gaul as a leader of the Gallic Atrebates before fleeing to Britain. The appearance of the name COMMIOS on coins of the British Atrebates is widely thought to be linked to this figure and possibly a son of his. See Cunliffe 2005, 142–43

[23] See Talbot 2017 for a discussion of this possibility

Chapter 8

[1] Colgrave & Mynors 1969

[2] Hurst 1997 75–78

[3] See, for instance, Maddicott, J.R 2005, Richards & Naylor 2010

[4] Marwnad Cynddylan states that Cynddylan answered the call of 'the son of Pyd' and records a battle at Caer Lwytgoed, the old Roman site of Letocetum Wall near Lichfield and from which Lichfield took its name.

[5] Bromwich 1991 5 and note 10. The suggested amendment is from 'ar tir' to 'Artur' where it is argued the text needed a personal name to make clear sense
[6] HB 60 and 64–65
[7] HE 2. 20
[8] See photos 31, 32
[9] Green 2020 150–53
[10] See Caitlin Green on *The Hwicce of Rutland*
[11] Colgrave & Bertram 1956
[12] See Portable Antiquities Scheme for numerous examples
[13] Draper 2006, 49 for a discussion of the Seagry find
[14] See Bruce-Mitford & Raven 2005, and Portable Antiquities Scheme for distribution of hanging bowls and hanging bowl mounts. The distributions do not seem incompatible with the possibility that these items represent Mercian cultural and political influence.
[15] Andrew Breeze
[16] HE 3.17
[17] Jackson 1971, 701–5
[18] See, for instance, Fraser 2008
[19] HB 65
[20] See Portable Antiquities Scheme for numerous examples

Chapter 9

[1] See photo 18
[2] Calder 2003
[3] For summary of the fascinating findings see, for instance, ox.ac.uk/news/2025-03-19-who-do-you-think-you-really-are-genetic-map-british-isles, or www.theguardian.com/science/2015/mar/18/genetic-study-30-percent-white-british-dna-german-ancestry

Bibliography

Original Sources

AC: *Annales Cambriae*, Edition: Faral, E. (1929) *La Légende arthurienne: Etudes et documents, les plus anciens textes, vol 3*, Librarie Ancienne Honoré Champion

ASC: The *Anglo-Saxon Chronicle*, translation: Garmondsway, G.N. ed. and trans. (1953) *The Anglo-Saxon Chronicle*, Everyman

DEB: Gildas *De Excidio Britanniae*, Edition: Winterbottom, M. (1978) *Gildas: The Ruin of Britain and other documents*, Phillimore

HB: *Historia Brittonum*, Edition: Faral, E. (1929) *La Légende arthurienne: Etudes et documents, les plus anciens textes, vol 3*, Librarie Ancienne Honoré Champion

HE: Bede, *Historia Ecclesiastica*, Edition Colgrave, B. and Mynors, R.A.B. eds. And trans. (1969) *Bede's Ecclesiastical History of the English People*, Oxford University Press

MD. Malory, *Morte Darthur*, Edition: Vinaver, E. (1971) *Malory: Works*, Oxford University Press

Confessio: St. Patrick, *Confessio*, Edition: Hood, A.B.E. ed. (1978) *St. Patrick, His Writings and Muirchu's Life*, Phillimore

Epistola: St. Patrick, *Epistola*, Edition: Hood, A.B.E. ed. (1978) *St. Patrick, His Writings and Muirchu's Life*, Phillimore

Vita: Muirchu, *Vita Patricii*, Edition: Hood, A.B.E. ed. (1978) *St. Patrick, His Writings and Muirchu's Life*, Phillimore

Secondary Sources

Adams, J. dQ. (1993) 'Sidonius and Riothamus' in *Arthurian Literature 12*

Alcock, L. (1988) 'The activities of potentates in Celtic Britain AD 500–800: a positive approach' in Driscoll, S.T. & Nieke, M.R. eds. (1988*) Power and Politics in early medieval Britain and Ireland*, Edinburgh University Press

Aldhouse-Green, M. & Howell, R. eds. (2004) *The Gwent County History: volume I Gwent in prehistory and early history*, Cardiff

Anderson, W.B. ed. and trans. (1936) *Sidonius Apollinaris: Poems and Letters*, Loeb Classical Library

Appels, A. & Laycock, S. (2007) *Roman Buckles & Military Fittings*, Greenlight

Archibald, E. & Putter, A. eds. (2009) *The Cambridge Companion to the Arthurian Legend*, Cambridge University Press

Arnold, C.J. (1984) *Roman Britain to Saxon England*, Routledge

Ashe, G. (2003) *The Discovery of King Arthur*, The History Press

Aurrecoechea Fernandez, J. (1999) 'Late Roman Belts in Hispania' in *Journal of Roman Military Equipment Studies 10*, 55–62

Aurrecoechea Fernandez, J. (2001) *Los cinturonesromanosen la Hispania del Bajo Imperio*, Monographies instrumentum 19

Baddeley, A. (1990, 1994) *Tytherington in the Past*, The Trout Press

Bannister, A. (1916) *The Place Names of Herefordshire*, self published and printed by Cambridge University Press

Barber, C. & Pykitt, D. (1997) *Journey to Avalon*, Samuel Weiser
Barber, R. (1972) *The Figure of Arthur*, Longman
Barron, W.R.J. ed. (2001) *The Arthur of the English*, University of Wales Press
Bartrum, P.C. ed. (1966) *Early Welsh Genealogical Tracts*, University of Wales Press
Bartrum, P.C. (1993) *A Welsh Classical Dictionary*, The National Library of Wales
Bassett, S. (1989) *The Origins of Anglo-Saxon Kingdoms*, Leicester University Press
Bayley, J. & Butcher, S. (2004) *Roman Brooches in Britain*, Society of Antiquaries
Bland, R. (2018) *Coin Hoards and Hoarding in Roman Britain*, Spink
Böhme, H.W. (1986) 'Das Ende der Römerherrschaft in Britannien und die Angelsachsische Besiedlung Englandsim 5. Jahrhundert' *Jahrbuch des Römisch-Germanischen Zentralmuseum Mainz 33* 469-574
Booth, A.L. (2014) *Reassessing the long chronology of the penannular brooch in Britain*
Bosworth & Toller (1972) *An Anglo-Saxon Dictionary*, Oxford
Brady, L. (2017) *Writing the Welsh Borderlands in Anglo-Saxon England*, Manchester University Press
Breeze, A., *Historia Brittonum* and Britain's Twenty-Eight Cities, University of Navarre, Pamplona
Bromwich, R. ed. (2008) *The Arthur of the Welsh*, University of Wales Press
Bromwich, R. (2014) *Trioedd Ynys Prydein: The Triads of the Island of Britain Fourth Edition*, University of Wales Press
Brooks, D.A (1984) 'Gildas' De Excidio: Its revolutionary meaning and purpose' in *Studia Celtica* 18, 1983–84
Bruce-Mitford, R. (1983) *The Sutton Hoo Ship-Burial, Vol. 3, Late Roman and Byzantine silver, hanging-bowls, drinking vessels, cauldrons and other containers, textiles, the lyre, pottery bottle and other items*, British Museum Publications
Bruce-Mitford, R. & Raven, S. (2005) *The Corpus of Late Celtic Hanging-Bowls*, Oxford University Press
Bryant, R. & Heighway, C. (2003) 'Excavations at St. Mary de Lode Church, Gloucester 1978–9' in *Transactions of the Bristol and Gloucestershire Archaeological Society*, 121
Brycheiniog (2016), Cyfnodolyn Cymdeithas Brycheiniog, *The Journal of the Brecknock Society*, Cyfrol/Volume XLVII
Buora, M., *Militari e Militaria as Aquileia e nell'Attuale Friuli*
Calder, M. (2003) 'Early Ecclesiastical Sites in Somerset' in *Proceedings of the Somerset Archaeology and Natural History Society* 2003
Campbell, J. (1991) *The Anglo-Saxons*, Penguin
Casey, P.J. & Jones, M.J. (1990) 'The date of the Letter of the Britons to Aetius' in *Bulletin of the Board of Celtic Studies* 37
Charles-Edwards, T.M. (2006) *The Chronicle of Ireland*, Liverpool University Press
Clarke, G. (1979) *The Roman Cemetery at Lankhills*, Winchester Studies 3, Oxford
Coates, R. (2007) 'Invisible Britons: Linguistics' in *Britons in Anglo-Saxon England*, ed. N. J. Higham, The Boydell Press

Coe, J.B. (2001) *The Place-Names of the Book of Llandaff*
Coe, J.B. & Young, S. *The Celtic Sources for the Arthurian Legend*, Llanerch
Colgrave & Bertram (1956) *Felix's Life of Saint Guthlac*, Cambridge University Press
Colgrave, B. & Mynors, R.A.B. eds. and trans. (1969) *Bede's Ecclesiastical History of the English People*, Oxford University Press
Collingwood, W.G. (1929) 'Arthur's Battles', in *Antiquity* 3
Collins, R. & Allason-Jones, L. (2010) *Finds from the Frontier*, Council for British Archaeology
Collins, R. (2010) 'Brooch use in the fourth- to 5th-century' in *Finds from the Frontier*, Council for British Archaeology
Collins, R. & Gerrard, J. eds. *Debating Late Antiquity in Britain AD 300–700, BAR British series 365*, Archaeopress
Cox, B, (1971) The Place Names of Leicestershire and Rutland
Creighton, J. (2000) *Coins and Power in Late Iron Age Britain*, Cambridge University Press
Cunliffe, B. (2004) *Iron Age Britain*, English Heritage
Cunliffe, B. (2005) *Iron Age Communities in Britain*, Routledge
D'Amato, R. & Salimbeti, A. (2023) *Post-Roman Kingdoms: 'Dark Ages' Gaul and Britain, AD 450–800*, Osprey
Dark, K. (1994) *Civitas to Kingdom, British Political Continuity 300–800*, Studies in the Early History of Britain, Leicester
Dark, K. ed. (1996) *External contacts and the economy of Late Roman and Post Roman Britain*, Boydell
Dark, K. (2000) *Britain and the End of the Roman Empire*, Tempus
Dickinson, T.M. (1982) 'Fowler's Type G Penannular Brooches Reconsidered', in *Medieval Archaeology*
Dixon, K.R. & Southern, P. (2014) *The Late Roman Army*, Routledge
Draper, S. (2006) *Landscape, Settlement and Society in Roman and Early Medieval Wiltshire*, British Archaeological Reports, British Series 419
Driscoll, S.T. & Nieke, M.R. eds. (1988) *Power and Politics in early medieval Britain and Ireland*, Edinburgh University Press
Dumville, D.N. (1990) *Histories and Pseudo-histories in the Insular Middle Ages*, Variorum
Dumville, D.N. (1985) *The Historia Brittonum: The Vatican Recension*, Brewer
Ekwall, E. (1928) *English River Names*, Oxford
The English Place Name Society, EPNS, epns.nottingham.ac.uk
Enright, M.J. (1983) 'The Sutton Hoo Whetstone sceptre: a study in iconography and cultural milieu' in *Anglo-Saxon England* Vol. 11, Cambridge University Press
Enright, M.J. (2006) *The Sutton Hoo Sceptre and the Roots of Celtic Kingship*, Four Courts Press
Esmonde Cleary, A.S. (1989) *The Ending of Roman Britain*, Routledge
Evans, S.S. (1997) *The Lords of Battle: Image and reality of the Comitatus in Dark-Age Britain*, Boydell

Faral, E. (1929) *La Légende arthurienne: Etudes et documents, les plus anciens textes, vol 3*, Librarie Ancienne Honoré Champion
Faulkner, N. (2000) *The Decline and Fall of Roman Britain*, Tempus
Field, P.J.C. (1996) 'Nennius and his History' in *Studia Celtica* 30
Field, P.J.C. (1999) 'Gildas and the City of the Legions' in *The Heroic Age issue 1*
Fitzpatrick-Matthews, K.J. (2015) 'The xxuiii ciuitates brittannie of the Historia Brittonum: Antiquarian speculation in Early Medieval Medieval Wales' in *Journal of Literary Onomastics Vol 4, issue 1*
Fitzpatrick-Matthews, KJ (2018) *The 'Arthurian Battle List' of the Historia Brittonum*
Fitzpatrick-Matthews, K.J. (2020) 'Genealogioa Brittonum: revisiting the textual tradition of the Historia Brittonum' in *Studia Celtica LIV*
Fleuriot, L. (1999) *Les origines de la Bretagne*, Payot
Fraser, J.E. (2008) 'Bede, the Firth of Forth and the Location of Urbs Iudeu' in *The Scottish Historical Review* 87
Frere, S. (1967)*Britannia: A History of Roman Britain*, Routledge
Gagnol, M., Feugere, M. & Zaaraoui, Y. (2020) 'Boucle de type Viminacium a Sauvian' in *Instrumentum 19*
Garmondsway, G.N. ed. and trans. (1953) *The Anglo-Saxon Chronicle*, Everyman
Gerrard, J. & Henig, M. (2017) *Brancaster Type Signet Rings*
Gidlow, C. (2004) *The Reign of Arthur, From History to Legend*, Sutton
Gidlow, C. (2010) *Revealing King Arthur*, The History Press
Gidlow, C. (2014) 'Romans, Britons and Saxons: defending Britain in Gildas's *de Excidio Britanniae*' in *Lucius Artorius Castus and the King Arthur Legend*, Knjizevni Krug Split
Gil, E., Filloy, I. & Iriarte A. (2000) 'Late Roman Military Equipment from the City of Iruña/Veleia (Alava/Spain)' in *Journal of Roman Military Equipment Studies 11*, 25–35
Giot, P., Guigon, P. & Merdrignac, B. (2003) *The British Settlement of Brittany*, Tempus
Green, C. (2020) Britons and Saxons, Lincolnshire AD 400–650, History of Lincolnshire Committee
Green, T. (2008) *Concepts of Arthur*, Tempus
Halsall, G. (2007) *Barbarian Migrations and the Roman West 376–568*, Cambridge
Halsall, G. (2013) *Worlds of Arthur: Facts and Fictions of the Dark Ages*, Oxford University Press,
Härke, H. (2007) 'Invisible Britons: Culture Change' in *Britons in Anglo-Saxon England*, ed. N. J. Higham, The Boydell Press
Harris, A. (2003) *Byzantium, Britain and the West*, Tempus
Hathaway, S.J.E. (2013) *British Coastal Salt-Production in Southern Britain*, Bournemouth University
Hawkes, S.C. & Dunning, G.C. (1961) 'Soldiers and settlers in Britain, fourth to fifth century' in *Medieval Archaeology 5*, 1–70

Heighway, C. (2012) 'Goths and Saxons? The Late Roman Cemetery at Kingsholm, Gloucester' in *Transactions of the Bristol & Gloucestershire Archaeological Society 130*

Henry, R. (2022) *Roman Buckles and Brooches, Understanding the End of Roman Britain*, Greenlight

Henson, D. (2006) The *Origins of the Anglo-Saxons*, Anglo-Saxon Books

Herren, M.W. & Brown, S.A. (2002) *Christ in Celtic Christianity*, Boydell

Higham, N. (1992) *Rome, Britain and the Anglo-Saxons*, Routledge

Higham, N.J. (1994) *The English Conquest: Gildas and Britain in the Fifth Century*, Manchester University Press

Higham, N. J (2002) *King Arthur, Myth-Making and History*, Routledge

Higham, N.J. ed. (2007) *Britons in Anglo-Saxon England*, The Boydell Press

Higham, N.J. (2018) *King Arthur: the making of the legend*, Yale University Press

Historic Place Names of Wales www.historicplacenames.rcahmw.gov.uk

Hobbs, R, (1997) *Late Roman Precious Metal Deposits*

Hood, A.B.E. ed. (1978) *St. Patrick, His Writings and Muirchu's Life*, Phillimore

Hoverd, T. (2015) A report upon a Post-Roman cemetery at Merlin's Cave, Symond's Yat West, Herefordshire, Herefordshire Archaeology

Hughes, K. (1973) 'The Welsh Latin Chronicles: *Annales Cambriae* and related texts' in *Proceedings of the British Academy* 59

Hughes, K. (1980) *Celtic Britain in the Early Middle Ages: studies in the Scottish and Welsh Sources*, Boydell

Hunter, F. (2010) 'Beyond the Frontier: interpreting late Roman Iron Age indigenous and imported material culture' in *Finds from the Frontier*, Council for British Archaeology Research Report 162

Hurst, D. ed. (2006) *Roman Droitwich: Dodderhill fort, Bays Meadow villa and roadside settlement*, CBA Research Report 146, Council for British Archaeology

Hurst, J.D. (1997) *A Multi-Period Salt Production Site at Droitwich*, Council for British Archaeology

Jackson, K.H. (1945) 'Once again Arthur's battles' in *Modern Philology* 43

Jackson, K.H. (1949) 'Arthur's Battle of Breguoin' in *Antiquity* 23

Jackson, K.H. (1971) *Language and History in Early Britain*, Edinburgh University Press

Jarman, A.O.H. (1990) 'The Arthurian allusions in the Book of Aneirin' in *Studia Celtica* 24–25

Jones, G, 'Penda's Footprint? Place-Names Containing Personal Names Associated with those of Early Mercian Kings' in *Nomina*

Jones, B. & Mattingly, D. (1990) *An Atlas of Roman Britain*, Blackwell

Jones, M.E. (1988) 'The appeal to Aetius in Gildas' in *Nottingham Medieval Studies* 32

Jones, M. (1996) *The End of Roman Britain*, Cornell University Press

Jones, N.A. ed. (2019) *Arthur in Early Welsh Poetry*, Modern Humanities Research Association

Jones, T. & Jones, W. (1949) *The Mabinogion*, Dent & Dutton
Kilbride-Jones, H.E. (1980) *Celtic Craftsmanship in Bronze*, St. Martin's Press
Knight, J. (1996), 'Late Roman and Post-Roman Caerwent, Some Evidence from metalwork' in *Archaeologia Cambrensis*, vol. 145, 35–65
Knight, J. (2007) *The End of Antiquity*, Tempus
Koch, J.T. (1997) *The Gododdin of Aneirin, Text and Context from Dark-Age Northern Britain*, University of Wales Press
Konstan, A. (2008), *British Forts in the Age of Arthur*, Osprey
Lacy, N.J. Ed. (1996) *The New Arthurian Encyclopedia*, Garland Publishing
Lapidge, M. & Dumville, D.N. eds. (1984) *Gildas:New Approaches*, Boydell
Laycock, S. (2006) 'The Threat Within' in *British Archaeology, March/April*, 11–15
Laycock, S. (2008) *Britannia: The Failed State*, The History Press
Laycock, S. (2009) *Warlords: The Struggle for Power in Post-Roman Britan*, The History Press
Leahy, K. (2007) *The Anglo-Saxon Kingdom of Lindsey*, Tempus
Lewis, G. & Williams, R. Translated, *The Book of Taliesin*, Penguin
Liddle, P. (2000) *An Archaeological Resource Assessment of Anglo-Saxon Leicestershire and Rutland*, Leicestershire Museums
Liebeschetz, W. (1993) 'The end of the Roman Army in the Western Empire' in Rich, J. & Shipley, G. eds. (1993) *War and Society in the Roman World*, London
Lloyd, Scott (2017) *The Arthurian Place Names of Wales*, University of Wales Press
Lyne, M. 'Fourth Century Roman Belt Fittings from Richborough' in *Journal of Roman Equipment Studies 10*
MacDowall, S. (1994) *Late Roman Infantryman*, Osprey
MacDowall, S. (1995) *Late Roman Cavalryman*, Osprey
Maddicott, J.R. (2005) 'London and Droitwich, c. 650–750: trade, industry and the rise of Mercia' in *Anglo-Saxon England, Vol. 34*. Cambridge University Press
Martindale, J.R. (1980) *The Prosopography of the Later Roman Empire: Volume 2, A.D.395–52*, Cambridge University Press
Miller, M. (1996) 'Date-guessing and pedigrees' in *Studia Celtica* 10–11
Miller, M. (1975) 'Bede's use of Gildas' in *English Historical Review* 90
Miller, M. (1977) 'Starting to write history: Gildas, Bede and "Nennius", in *Welsh History Review* 8
Mattingly, D. (2006) *An Imperial Possession, Britain in the Roman Empire*, Penguin
Millett, M. (1990) *The Romanization of Britain*, Cambridge University Press
Mills, A.D. (1991) *A Dictionary of British Place-Names*, Oxford
Mills, A.D. (1999) *Dictionary of English Place-Names*, Oxford
Mills, N. (2000) *Celtic and Roman Artefacts*, Greenlight Publishing
Milner, N.P. trans (1993) *Vegetius: Epitome of Military Science*, Liverpool University Press
Morgan, R, (2016) 'Paths and Perambulations' in *Brycheiniog, Cyfnodolyn Cymdeithas Brycheiniog, The Journal of the Brecknock Society*, Cyfrol/Volume XLVII

Morris, C. with Batey, Brady, Harry, Johnson & Thomas (1990) 'Recent Work at Tintagel' in Medieval Archaeology 43, 206-215

Morris, J, (1980) *Nennius, The British History and the Welsh Annals*, Phillimore

Morris, J. (1995) *The Age of Arthur*, Phoenix

Niblett, R. (2001) *Verulamium, the Roman City of St. Albans*, Tempus

Nicolle, D. (1984) *Arthur and the Anglo-Saxon Wars*, Osprey

O'Brien, E. (1999) *Post-Roman Britain to Anglo-Saxon England: Burial Practices Reviewed*, British Archaeological Reports, British Series 289

Oppenheimer, S. (2006) *The Origins of the British, a Genetic Detective Story*, Constable

Ordnance Survey (1974) *Map of Britain in the Dark Ages*, Ordnance Survey

Ordnance Survey (1994) *Roman Britain, historical map and guide, 5th edition*, Ordnance Survey

Pearce, S.M. ed. (1982) *The Early Church in Western Britain and Ireland*, BAR

Pearson, A. (2002) *The Roman Shore Forts*, Tempus

Portable Antiquities Scheme, The, finds.org.uk

Pretty, K. (1989) 'Defining the Magonsæte' in *The Origins of Anglo-Saxon Kingdoms*, ed. Bassett, S., Leicester University Press

Prosopography of Anglo-Saxon England, pase.ac.uk

Pryor, F (2004) *AD*, Harper Collins

Rahtz, P. (1970) *Excavations on Glastonbury Tor, Somerset, 1964–6*

Rance, P. (2001) 'Attacotti, Déisi and Magnus Maximus: The Case for Irish Federates in Late Roman Britain' in *Britannia* 32, 243–70

Reece, R. (1997), *The Future of Roman Military Archaeology*, National Museums and Galleries of Wales

Rich, J. & Shipley, G. eds. (1993) *War and Society in the Roman World,* London

Richards, J.D. & Naylor, J. (2010) 'A 'Productive Site' at Bidford-on-Avon, Warwickshire: salt, communication and trade in Anglo-Saxon England' in *Portable Antiquities Scheme Conference 2007*, BAR 520

Ridley, R.T. trans (1982) *Zosimus: New History*, Australian Association for Byzantine Studies

Rivet, A. & Smith, C. (1981) *The Place-Names of Roman Britain*, Book Club Associates

Robertson, A.S. (2000) *An Inventory of British Coin Hoards*, Royal Numismatic Society Special Publication 20

Room, A. (2003) *The Penguin Dictionary of British Place Names*, Penguin

Russell, M. & Laycock, S. (2010) *UnRoman Britain*, The History Press

Russell, M. (2017) *Arthur and the Kings of Britain*, Amberley

Salway, P. (1993) *The Oxford Illustrated History of Roman Britain*, Oxford University Press

Salway, P. (2002) *The Roman Era, Short Oxford History of the British Isles*, Oxford University Press

Savory, H.N. (1964) 'The Tal-y-llyn Hoard' in *Antiquity*, Vol. 38
Schaffner, P. (1984) 'Britain's Iudices' in Lapidge, M. & Dumville, D.N. eds. (1984) *Gildas: New Approaches*, Boydell
Schrijver, P. (2007) 'What Britons Spoke around 400 AD' in *Britons in Anglo-Saxon England*, ed. N. J. Higham, The Boydell Press
Schulze-Dörrlamm, M. (2002) *Byzantinische Gürtelschnallen und Gürtelbeschlägeim Römisch-Germanischen Zentralmuseum,* Mainz
Sims-Williams, P. (1983a) 'The settlement of England in Bede and the Chronicle' in *Anglo-Saxon England 12*, 1–41
Sims-Williams, P. (1983b) 'Gildas and the Anglo-Saxons' in *Cambridge Medieval Celtic Studies 6*
Sims-Williams, P. (2003) *The Celtic Inscriptions of Britain*, Publications of the Philological Society
Snyder, C. (1998) *An Age of Tyrants: Britain and the Britons A.D. 400–600*, Sutton
Snyder, C. (2003) *The Britons*, Blackwell
Sommer, M. (1984) *Die Gürtel und Gürtelbeschläge des 4. und 5. Jahrhundertsim Römischen Reich*, Bonner, Hefte zurVorgeschichte 22, Bonn
Suzuki, S. (2000) *The Quoit Brooch Style and Anglo-Saxon Settlement*, The Boydell Press
Swanton, M.J. (1973) *The Spearheads of the Anglo-Saxon Settlements*, The Royal Archaeological Institute
Swift, E. (2000) *The End of the Western Roman Empire, An Archaeological Investigation*, Tempus
Swift, E. (2019) Re-evaluating the Quoit Brooch Style, in *Medieval Archaeology*
Sykes, B. (2006) *Blood of the Isles*, Bantam Press
Talbot, J. (2017) *Made for Trade: A New View of Icenian Coinage*, Oxbow
Thomas, C. (1994) *And Shall These Mute Stones Speak?* University of Wales Press
Thompson, E.A. (1979) 'Gildas and the history of Britain' in *Britannia* 10
Thompson, E.A (1984) *St. Germanus of Auxerre and the End of Roman Britain*, The Boydell Press
Thornton, D. E. (2007) 'Some Welshmen in Domesday Book' in *Britons in Anglo-Saxon England*, ed. N.J. Higham, The Boydell Press
Thorpe, L. ed. and trans. (1974) *Gregory of Tours: History of the Franks*, Penguin
Tyler, D. (2005) 'An Early Mercian Hegemony' in *Midland History* 30
Van Arsdell, R.D. (1989) *Celtic Coinage of Britain*, London
Vermaat, R., www.vortigernstudies.org.uk
Vinaver, E. (1971) *Malory: Works*, Oxford University Press
Wacher, J. (1995) *The Towns of Roman Britain*, Batsford
Wade-Evans A.W. & Lloyd, S. (2013) *Vitae Sanctorum Britanniae et Genealogiae: The Lives and Genealogies of the Welsh Saints*, Welsh Academic Press
Wallace-Hadrill, J.M. (1993) *Bede's Ecclesiastical History of the English People: A Historical Commentary*, Oxford University Press

Walton, P.J. (2011) *Rethinking Roman Britain: An Applied Numismatic Analysis of the Roman Coin Data Recorded by the Portable Antiquities Scheme*

Walton, P. & Moorhead, S. (2016) 'Coinage and Collapse? The contribution of numismatic data to understanding the end of Roman Britain' in *Internet Archaeology 41*

Ward-Perkins, B. (2005) *The Fall of Rome and the End of Civilisation*, Oxford University Press

White, R. (2007) *Britannia Prima*, Tempus

Williams, H. (1899) *Two Lives of Gildas by a Monk of Rys and Caradoc of Llancarfan*, Cymmrodorion Record Series

Wilmott, T. & Wilson, P. (2000) *The Late Roman Transition in the North, papers from the Roman archaeology conference, Durham 1999, BAR British series 299*, Archaeopress

Winterbottom, M. (1978) *Gildas: The Ruin of Britain and other documents*, Phillimore

Wright, N. (1985) 'Did Gildas read Orosius?' in *Cambridge Medieval Studies* 9

Yorke, B. (1989) 'The Jutes of Hampshire and Wight and the origins of Wessex' in *The Origins of Anglo-Saxon Kingdoms*, ed. Bassett, S., Leicester University Press

Yorke, B. (1990) *Kings and Kingdoms of Early Anglo-Saxon England*, Routledge

Yorke, B. (1993) 'Fact or Fiction? The written evidence for the fifth and sixth centuries AD' in *Anglo-Saxon Studies in Archaeology and History 6*, Oxford University Committee for Archaeology

Youngs, S. (2005) 'After Oldcroft: a British silver pin from Welton le Wold, Lincolnshire' in Crummy ed, *Image, Craft and the Classical World*, Monogr. Instrumentum 29, Montagnac

Index